WISE AS SERPENTS
HARMLESS AS DOVES
Christians in China Tell Their Story

Interviews by Jonathan Chao, Ph.D.
Edited by Richard Van Houten, Ph.D.

William Carey Library

• PASADENA, CALIFORNIA 91104

CHINESE CHURCH RESEARCH CENTER
P.O. Box 312, Shatin Central P.O., Shatin, N.T., Hong Kong.

Published by
William Carey Library
P. O. Box 40129
1705 N. Sierra Bonita Ave.
Pasadena, California 91104
and
Chinese Church Research Center
P. O. Box 312
Shatin Central P. O.
New Territories, Hong Kong

Cover art by Samson Au
Printed in the United States of America

Library of Congress Cataloging in Publication Data

Wise as Serpents, Harmless as Doves
Christians in China Tell Their Story

By Jonathan Chao, Ph.D., Interviewer
and Richard Van Houten, Ph.D., Editor

1. Christianity — China   2. Christians — China — Interviews.
I Chao, Jonathan   II Van Houten, Richard L.   III Fulton, Brent.
BR1288.W57 1988   275.1'082   87-10244
ISBN 0-87808-212-3

Contents

Contents

PREFACE

In the fall of 1974 I met a Chinese Christian family in Paris. This family came from Wenzhou, Zhejiang Province in east China, and they ran a family restaurant. During the course of the conversation I learned that the son and daughter of the restaurant owner had just come from China only a month ago. They told me that in Wenzhou the young people often held weekend retreats in nearby mountains, each time attended by sixty people or so. The house church leaders there also held periodic spiritual retreats. I was very excited over this discovery of house church activities in China; for in those days we heard very little of what was going on among the believers in China.

The following week I was invited to Upsala for some church business, and there I was asked to address a group of missionaries. I told them what I had learned about Wenzhou in Paris. The people there were so blessed by such good news that they urged me to write it up, which I did upon my return to my home in the States. Later I published this interview under the title: "A Glimpse of the Church in China," which received wide circulation in the 1970's.

In 1977 my wife and I came back of Hong Kong to teach at the China Graduate School of Theology, to which we had given ten years of our life during its founding stage. We have since left CGST, in 1980, for China ministries. In 1977 China began to open her doors to the outside world. I wanted to know what had happened to the believers in China since 1950. So I began to interview Christians who left China to stay in Hong Kong or who were passing through Hong Kong on their way to other countries.

In the fall of 1978 I started the Chinese Church Research Center. Our first project was an interview project entitled "State of Church in China." With the help of some Christian friends we were able to carry on this project for two years, producing one to two interviews in English translation every week. Even after the funding stopped, the Center continued to conduct these interviews both in Hong Kong and later in China. We eventually collected hundreds of these interviews with Chinese manuscripts transcribed from the tapes. Sister W.W. Chou did most of the transcription work. However, only a small portion of the many interviews were translated into English. In the beginning I did most of the translation and Chris Morris the editing. Some of them were published earlier in our magazine, *China and the Church Today* (CCT).

The idea of publishing a collection of these interviews in English was long entertained. Their selection and editing went through several stages and with much delay due to staff shortage. Naomi Morris produced the first draft for popular readers. The project began to grow. Brent Fulton, editor of *CCT*, worked on the manuscript as style editor. Richard Van Houten, Ph.D., Director of CCRC's Research Department (1982-1987), put many hours into the preparation of this book for publication. He has provided a brief overall historical introduction, arranged the interviews in a chronological manner, and supplied detailed introduction for each period and interview. Without his painstaking effort, this book could not have been completed. The secretarial staff of CCRC under Angel Yam and Jennifer Yau also put in many hours of typing.

I have here added another introduction under the title "Church and State in Socialist China, 1949-1988" so as to assist our readers to interpret these interviews within China's political and historical context.

On behalf of the Chinese Church Research Center, I would like to express my appreciation to William Carey Library for taking on this project for co-publication and distribution.

Finally, the real credit must be given to the hundreds of Chinese Christians who shared their testimonies with us. Listen to what they have said and ponder upon them prayerfully. I believe that you will be greatly blessed by the tender voices from their heart. In grateful response to their courage and testimony, let us continue to uphold those Christians in China who are bearing a faithful witness to Christ and who are serving as instruments of God's redemptive grace to the millions in China.

Jonathan Chao, Director
Chinese Church Research Center
January 1988, Hong Kong

INTRODUCTION 1

> Behold, I send you forth as sheep in the midst of wolves; be ye, therefore, wise as serpents and harmless as doves. Matthew 10:16 (KJV)

The survival and growth of the Chinese Church is one of the great stories of God's work in this century. A tiny minority in 1949 when the communists won the civil war, the Church experienced great pressure, first, to break off its contacts with Christian brothers and sisters abroad, and, secondly, to restrict its activities in its own land. Obstacles piled up until the churches were forced to cease almost all public activity. The survival of a remnant seemed to be the only hope that an anxious church abroad could hold out for the Chinese Church.

When Chinese Christians began communicating with the outside world again in 1979, one of the phrases that our staff at the Chinese Church Research Center heard again and again was that the attitude the Chinese adopted in order to survive was to be "wise as serpents and harmless as doves." They changed and bent with the times in order to preserve themselves as Christians. When pressure was strong, their meetings were small and secretive. When society relaxed, they became more open in their witness. The stories and testimonies that appear in this book are a witness to God's blessing on their attempts to remain faithful to Him in the midst of opression and rapid change.

The Church in the PRC — a Brief Overview

Plans for government and Communist Party supervision of religion in China were made early. Even before the victory of the Communist army in 1949, a Religious Affairs Bureau had been formed to oversee the activities of religion.

In April 1951, after some time of propaganda work among Christians, government leaders and some Christians already sympathetic to the Communist Party programs met to create an organization of Christian leaders that eventually became known as the Three-Self Patriotic Movement (TSPM). Although its expressed goals were primarily political in nature — to support the Communist

Party, to foster patriotism, and to support socialism — it nevertheless became an umbrella organization for the churches. No churches could communicate with the government except through the TSPM, and by 1958 there were no open churches whose leaders had not joined the TSPM committee.

Christians who opposed the TSPM were persecuted. The freedom of religion granted by China's constitutions could only be exercised through the government-recognized bodies such as the TSPM. Through various political campaigns and the use of arrest, the opposition was intimidated or forced to meet in secret. Such secret meetings were the beginnings of the "house church" phenomenon that was the main vehicle for Christian life in the dark years that followed.

Under increasingly radical political campaigns, the number of open churches began to decline rapidly in the late 1950s. When Chairman Mao launched his Cultural Revolution in 1966, nearly all remaining churches were forced to close down. The Religious Affairs Bureau and the TSPM stopped activity, and freedom of religion in any sense was practically dead in China. Individual Christians all over China were subject to questioning, beating, and imprisonment or exile by leftist bands of Red Guards. Many died at the hands of their interrogators.

However, this period of intense persecution was fairly brief. By 1969 the radical actions of the Red Guards had been quelled, although the radicals were not defeated enough to allow religion to have public existence again. Until 1979 there was virtually no public Christian activity.

Mao died in 1976. His followers lost out in the power struggle that followed. The so-called Gang of Four, who had assisted Mao in the Cultural Revolution and who had become a force in their own right in Mao's last years, were themselves arrested and given showcase trials. After two more years of maneuvering for power within China's leadership, Deng Xiaoping established some control and reinstated the policy of freedom of religion, more or less as it had been understood in the early 1950s.

After many delays, a few churches were opened in the second

half of 1979 under the leadership of the TSPM. To the great surprise of nearly everyone concerned, Chinese Christians filled these churches to overflowing. Tears flowed down the cheeks of people who had not been able to worship publicly for more than a decade. The number of young people attending was also surprising to the leadership of the churches and of the Communist Party.

As the Chinese press proclaimed freedom of religion, Christians who had been meeting secretly in house groups began to meet more openly. The meetings were enlarged, evangelism was carried out, and itinerant pastors began traveling from village to village to meet the needs of rapidly growing Christian groups.

The TSPM leadership attempted to win over all the Christians and have them accept the TSPM. They initially gave approval to house meetings, because nearly every Christian had participated in some house meetings before the churches were reopened. However, sometime in 1981, the Party began anew to enforce the policy that religion would have to be confined to the legitimate public organizations such as the TSPM and the newly created China Christian Council (CCC). Then local officials began telling house churches they could not meet so often, and the Religious Affairs Bureau worked with the TSPM and CCC to see that all Christians met only in approved places with approved leadership.

From 1981 to 1984 there was fairly strong pressure for Christians to work within government-approved organizations. On the one hand, the Christians in these organizations argued that it was best for the Church to lead an orderly public life and that it was detrimental for Christians to be seen as an antisocial, anti-government element in society. On the other hand, the police arrested those leaders who failed to cooperate with the TSPM after due warnings. Also arrested were those who had contact with foreign Christians or those who traveled to preach the gospel outside of their home districts.

After 1984, pressure on the churches to conform to the pattern set by the national leadership seemed to lessen. As social freedom for the Chinese people increased, the number of Christians willing to participate in public life also increased. Although we believe that the number of Christians in house meetings is still greater than those in open churches, there were over 4000 churches open in 1986 and over 30,000 meeting points registered with the Religious Affairs Bureau.

The picture of church life in China is not a simple one of open churches and house churches. There are several shades of acceptance of the TSPM, ranging over a spectrum of complete acceptance, grudging acknowledgement, studied indifference, and unequivocal rejection. These shades are reflected in the interviews and testimonies contained in this book.

The testimonies in this book end in 1984. There is no reflection on the changes that have taken place in the last few years. The varying attitudes reflected in these interviews and testimonies still reflect the range of opinion in China among what may loosely be called house church leaders. As for the leaders of the TSPM and the CCC, their opinions have already been published widely elsewhere, and, of course, must also be read in order to get a complete picture of Christian life in China.

We present these documents to the Christian world for its edification. The few voices that speak in these pages do so, I believe, for millions of others. In their halting and fragmented manner, the speakers tell the story of one of the greatest movements for Christ in this century. May His name be glorified through them.

Richard L. van Houten, editor
Director of Research
(1982-87)

INTRODUCTION 2

Church and State in Socialist China, 1949-1988

By Jonathan Chao

To understand these interviews properly it is necessary to read them from an historical perspective and in relation to their political context. That historical context is essentially that of church and state in Socialist China.. Church-state relations may seem to be a settled question in Western, Christianized countries. But in socialist countries like Mainland China and in other third world countries where revolutions are still going on, the relationship between church and state is usually the most important issue affecting the life and witness of the church. In Hong Kong, it is a live issue today, especially in view of the transfer of power to China in 1997.[1]

This matter is now being debated in relation to the drafting of the Basic Law, the future constitution for Hong Kong.What Christians fear most is that they too might come under a similar religious policy to what which has been practiced in China.[2]

To deal with this subject of church-state relations in Mainland China, we must first understand Chinese Communist religious policy. Secondly, we must analyze the main ideological sources contributing to the development of that policy. Thirdly, we have to trace the historical development of the church-state relationship since 1949. We shall confine ourselves to the Protestant experience.

The Nature of Chinese Communist Religious Policy

In socialist China, the Communist Party's religious policy forms the framework within which church-state relations take place. The policy is that "citizens of the People's Republic of China (PRC) enjoy freedom of religious belief," as stated in article 36 of the 1982 Constitution.[3] This policy is more fully expounded in Document No. 19 of the Chinese Communist Party (CCP) Central Committe issued on March 31, 1982. However, "freedom of religious belief" is defined essentially in terms of freedom of inward faith: the right to believe or not to believe in one's heart.[4]It does not include freedom of propagation or freedom to conduct church life as prescribed in the Scriptures, or according to the wishes of religious bodies. Nor does freedom of religious belief include the social expressions of one's faith: religion must not interfere with politics, education, marriage and family life, etc.[5] Religion is to be kept as a private matter and is not allowed to exert any influence on society. Religious activities may be conducted so long as they are done under the control of the state and are carried out under the supervision of the patriotic religious organizations. These are called "normal religious activities," which are to be conducted in "designated places," by designated religious personnel (clergy approved by the patriotic organizatons such as the Three-Self Patriotic Movement), and even approved clergy must work only in designated areas.[6] This is called the "three-designates" policy.[7]

All religious activities conducted by believers themselves outside the control of the state and its patriotic religious organizations are considered "abnormal religious activities," and hence are regarded as illegal and anti-revolutionary. Such activities, like independent home meetings and itinerant preaching, are not considered as religious activities, but as political violations of state policy, and violators are dealt with as political criminals.[8]

With this kind of definition of normal and abnormal religious activities, there is no legal provision for a direct relationship between mainland Chinese believers and believers or churches in foreign countries as religious people. Foreign religious bodies are forbidden to develop a direct working relationship with churches in mainland China.[9] The independence of the mainland Chinese church is stressed by the state and its patriotic organizations in the name of the former Protestant missionary goals of the "three self": self-support, self-government, and self-propagation.[10]

However, the united front theory dictates that religion be used as an avenue for winning international goodwill in order that mainland China's national program might be advanced. For this purpose, patriotic organizations, such as the Three-Self Patriotic Movement (TSPM) and the Chinese Catholic Patriotic Association are encouraged to receive foreign religious groups as well as to send delegations to other countries.[11] Domestically, united front thinking also directs government officials and patriotic church leaders to win the support of the religious masses to contribute toward the national program of modernization.

These religious policies are formulated by the United Front Work Department of the CCP Central Committee in consultation with the Institute of Research on World Religions under the Academy of Social Sciences, the State Council Religious Affairs Bureau (RAB), and the national leaders of the patriotic religious organizations.[12]

Religious *policies are implemented by the Religious Affairs Bureau,* which has a national office that directs the provincial and municipal bureaus, which in turn direct the numerous county level bureaus.[13] According to the directives of the RAB, policies are carried out by the major patriotic religious organizations, namely, (1) the Buddhist Association of China, (2) the China Taoist Association, (3) the China Islamic Association, (4) the Three-Self Patriotic Movement Committee of Protestant Churches of China (1954), which established the Christian Council of China (1980), and (5) the China Catholic Patriotic Association (1957), which in turn formed the Chinese Catholic Bishops College and the National Administrative Commission of the Chinese Catholic Church.[14]

These patriotic associations report to the RAB, which is usually a part of the local United Front office under the Party branch, and which works closely with the local Public Security Bureau (PSB). Religious policies are enforced by the Public Security Bureau. Without this enforcement, the policies and the patriotic organizations are powerless. Suspected violators of the policy are warned and interrogated by officials of the RAB. Sometimes, they are arrested by the Public Security Bureau and kept at its "detention centers." Often, officials of the TSPM act as informants.[15] Arrested suspects are further interrogated by the Public Security Bureau, and then the case is investigated by the Bureau of Investigation which turns the case over to the court. The district court would then either sentence the accused or release him.[16] This process from arrest to sentencing could take anywhere from six months to two years or even longer. Those sentenced are then transferred from the Public Security Bureau's detention center to prison.

There is an interlocking relationship between the United Front Work Department, the Religious Affairs Bureau, the patriotic religious organizations (such as the TSPM), and the Public Security Bureau at national, provincial, and county levels.

How, then, did these religious policies and practices develop?

Historical Sources of Chinese Communist Religious Policy and Practice

There are four major sources contributing to the formation of Chinese Communist religious policy. These interact with each other producing a blend of traditional and modern Chinese totalitarian state control, the essential nature of church-state relations in socialist China.

First, there is the tradition of state control of religions in traditional China. In imperial China the state assumed a right of sovereignty over all aspects of its subjects' lives. There was no separation of church and state as understood in the West, neither in theory nor in practice, and the Chinese people have never established their right to question such overall sovereighty of the state. Since the late Han Dynasty and definitely after the mid-Tang Dynasty, Confucianism enjoyed the status of "official orthodoxy," not only as a system of political philosophy, but also as a way of life.[17] With this affirmation of Confucian orthodoxy, all other systems of belief were considered "heterodox." However, major institutional religions were tolerated so long as they were brought under the control of the state. Through law codes and government control, the state reduced the influence of religious groups to a level of socio-political insignificance. At the same time, the state developed a system of control whereby religious expansion was contained, and the activities of religious groups were strictly controlled by the government, which used religious leaders who worked for the Board of Rites.[18] All other sectarian groups were not only considered heterodox, but also viewed as potential rebels, and hence were outlawed and often suppressed by force. Catholic Christianity suffered nearly 150 years of suppression as a foreign heterodox sect before it was tolerated in 1844.[19] Protestant and Catholic Christianity enjoyed freedom of propagation primarily on account of the toleration clause included in the Treaty of Tientsin (1858).

This tradition of state control, official orthodoxy, state toleration, and the suppression of heterodox sects, is illustrated by the following diagram:

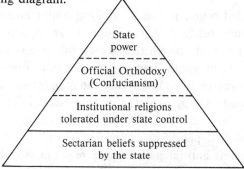

The second source is the anti-religious thinking which arose from the New Culture Movement of 1920-21. As a result of the debate on religion, Chinese intellectuals of the May Fourth era adopted the position that all realities must be tested by science and in the process rejected all religions as having no value for the building of a modern China. Religious beliefs were considered a hindrance to the development of a young and modern China.[20] This anti-religious sentiment influenced many of the intellectuals and students from whom the Chinese Communist Party drew its first recruits.

Some intellectuals tried to make room for religion by relegating it to the realm of subjectivity while acknowledging that science is the test for objective realities. This is why even today, Chinese Communist theoreticians still relegate religion to the private sphere, denying it any objective social value.[21]

The evolutionary view of religion that prevailed in the nineteenth-century West greatly influenced Chinese intellectuals of the May Fourth era. Religion was seen as a historical phenomenon in the evolution of human society, which had its own process of rise, development, and disappearance. Religion, it was claimed, arose as a result of primitive man not understanding the natural forces around him. Religions began to develop when man entered into class society and could not free himself from its system of exploitation; and they will disappear when man enters into a socialist society, when the social basis for their existence has been removed.[22]

The third source is Lenin's anti-imperialist attitude towards religion. Lenin believed that religion is an opium which the imperialists give to the people to dull their will to resist exploitation. Therefore, to fight against imperialism, one must oppose religion. Lenin's view was imported into China and propagated widely by the Socialist Youth Corps under the leadership of the Chinese Communist Party during 1922-23.[23] Later, during the Chinese Communists' first period of collaboration with the Kuomintang (1924-27), Lenin's anti-religious views were popularized by the anti-Christian movements which the CCP and the KMT sponsored as part of their anti-imperialist campaign. Since then Christianity has been regarded by the Chinese Communists as the vanguard of foreign imperialism, and missionaries and Chinese pastors have been seen as the agents of cultural aggression.[24] This view was so widely propagated for so long that even today many Chinese people are still influenced by it.

The fourth source is Mao Tse-tung's theory of contradictions and the united front policy. Mao asserted that there are antagonistic contradictions, such as political and ideological contradictions, and nonantagonistic contradictions, such as religious differences among the people. Mao also differentiated primary contradictions from secondary contradictions, and he stressed the mobility of these contradictions according to changing historical situations. Under this system, religion was considered a nonantagonistic and secondary contradiction.[25]

When this system of contradictions is applied to the united front policy, the task of the Party is to unite with, or befriend, secondary contradictons in order to oppose primary contradictions. For example, since 1969, mainland China has been befriending the United States in order to oppose the Soviet threat, which has become Peking's primary contradiction. Similarly, the religious masses must be won over to fight against backwardness in the pursuit of modernization. While uniting or befriending secondary contradictions, religious people must also be educated so that they will gradually abandon their subjective worldview, and take on an "objective" materialistic worldview, thus abandoning their religious superstitions. They will then be won over to the Party's side. These are the positive dimensions of the united front policy.

But the united front policy also has its negative dimension, namely, those who refuse to accept the Party's lenient, educational persuasion and persist in their own views must be dealt with in a more aggressive manner, by criticism, threats and, if necessary, force, so that in the end the recalcitrant person will be isolated and his influence minimized. But who is to determine what is a primary contradiction (which should be attacked) and what is a secondary contradiction (to which a policy of friendly persuasion should be applied)? Historically, this has been determined by whoever holds power in the Party in relation to what kind of national program he desires to implement. The historical context, therefore, determines how the united front policy is to be implemented in the realm of religion and in other areas.

The Development of Church and State Relations as Seen from the Protestant Experience, 1949-1988

How has the Chinese Communist Party dealt with the Protestant church which it all along regarded as an instrument of cultural imperialism? What procedure did the Party take to bring the pluralistic Protestant church in mainland China under its control? How did church leaders respond to government pressures? What kind of changes in the relationships have occured during the long historical process since 1949? We shall now examine these questions in a historical manner.[26]

1. During the initial stage (1949-50), the state sought to establish a patriotic agency to give direction to the Protestant church: the rise of the Three-Self Movement.

During the initial months after the Communist takeover of China (October 1949 to July 1950), the new government was too busy establishing economic and political order to bother with religious affairs; the churches were left alone to "do their own thing" without much interference. Church activities, such as revival meetings, were carried on as usual. Many missonaries stayed with their Chinese colleagues. However, a small nucleus of pro-government church leaders was already being formed. These churchmen were invited to attend the Chinese People's Political Consultative Conference held in Peking from September 23-30, 1949.[27] At that Conference the new government was born, and on October 1, Mao Zedong declared the formal beginning of the People's Republic of China. After the Conference, the Protestant participants, headed by Y. T. Wu (the former Y.M.C.A. publications secretary), formed a "Christian Visitation Team" to visit the Protestant leaders in a few major cities, and to explain to them the new government's "Common Program" and its policy of freedom of religious belief.[28]

During May 2, 6, 13-21, 1950, when this group of leaders was visiting the churches in Beijing, Premier Zhou Enlai summoned its members to discuss the future course of Christianity in mainland China. The end result of three nocturnal visits was the publicaton of a document called "The Path of Endeavor for the Chinese Protestant Church during the Course of China's Construction," known in the West as the "Christian Manifesto."[29] Published on July 28, 1950, this document was immediately circulated among church leaders throughout mainland China for signature. The document basically called for Christians to oppose imperialism and to accept the leadership of the Chinese Communist Party. It also called upon Protestant churches to become self-supporting, self-governing, and self-propagating, and hence it became the founding charter of the "Three-Self Movement." The signature movement differentiated the "patriotic" church leaders who signed it from those who refused to sign it.

Prior to Zhou Enlai's summons, the National Christian Council (NCC) of China (formed in 1922) and already made plans on January 26, 1950, to hold a National Christian Conference from August 19-27 to study an appropriate Christian response to the new situation, but this plan was aborted soon after the May meeting between Zhou and Y. T. Wu and his associates.[30] The new body, which took on the name "Three-Self Reform Movement," soon replaced the NCC as the national coordinating body representing Protestant Christianity in mainland China.

The church-state relationship at this initial stage may be illustrated by the following chart:

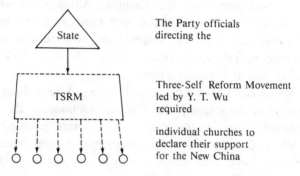

State	The Party officials directing the
TSRM	Three-Self Reform Movement led by Y. T. Wu required
	individual churches to declare their support for the New China

During this stage individual churches still retained their autonomy. They could continue to conduct their regular religious activities. The state did not exercise its control directly over the churches, nor did it use existing Protestant channels, such as the NCC, to influence them but created a new informal body made up of pro-government clergy and assisted by Party secretaries. Through this body the state made its postion known to the churches, and required their loyalty. This informal body, known as the "Three-Self Reform Movement," was not an ecclesiastical organization, but a "political movement" which published the "Christian Manifesto" mentioned above, and which was signed by forty prominent church leaders.[31] This movement, headed by Y. T. Wu, began to give political direction to the Chinese Protestant church on behalf of the new government, and church leaders had to deal with it accordingly.

2. During the 1951-54 period, the state controlled the churches through the formation of the Chinese Protestant Anti-America and Aid Korea Three-Self Reform Movement.

After the outbreak of the Korean War, especially after the PLA crossed the Yalu River, the United States became an antagonistic contradiction in relation to Communist China. On December 29, 1950, the United States froze Chinese assets in America, and Beijing froze American assets in mainland China. This change in Sino-American relations seriously affected the Chinese Communist government's attitude toward the Christian church, both Protestant and Catholic. All churches which had received, or were receiving, financial subsidies from the United States immediately became suspect, and were required to register themselves with the appropriate local authorities, to which they had to make regular financial reports.

From April 16-20, 1951, the Religious Affairs Bureau of the Ministry of Education and Culture summoned 151 Chinese Protestant leaders from churches which were receiving foreign subsidies to come to Beijing. At this conference these church leaders were told to sever their relations with U.S. imperialism. They were also taught how to conduct accusation meetings against "reactionary" missionaries and Chinese pastors who had at one time or another collaborated with Chiang Kai-shek or who had failed to pledge their support for the new government. Furthermore, at this meeting the "Preparatory Committee of the Chinese Protestant Anti-America and Aid-Korea Three-Self Reform Movement Committee" was formally organized.[32]

After the Peking conference, the 151 delegates were told to carry out anti-imperialist accusation meetings in their own churches.[33] Those who had successfully conducted such meetings were urged to join the Three-Self Reform Movement. Simultaneously, this movement also began to organize provincial and local committees. These committees were made up of church leaders who had declared their allegiance to the government. Meanwhile, the movement for signing the "Christian Manifesto" continued. By 1953 nearly 400,000 out of a total of 840,000 Chinese Protestants had signed this document.

Church-state relations during this stage may be illustrated as follows:

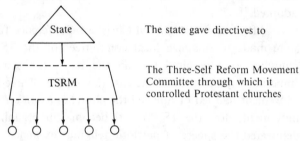

The state gave directives to

The Three-Self Reform Movement Committee through which it controlled Protestant churches

Some of the ways in which the state exercised control over Protestant churches included the following: (1) Churches were required to fly the five-star flag and/or display Mao's picture, with failure to comply being used as evidence of reaction, and reactionary churches were prosecuted; (2) Churches were required to sign the "Christian Manifesto," and to conduct anti-imperialist accusation meetings; (3) Christian educational and medical institutions founded by foreign missions were taken over by the state, and church boards disbanded by 1952; (4) Theological schools in the north were amalgamated into the Yenching School of Theology, and those in the south into the Nanking Theological Seminary; (5) Christian publishers were told to comply with the policies of the new regime and most of them were closed down before 1954.

By 1953, all Protestant churches founded by foreign missions were brought under the control of the state through the agency of the Three-Self Reform Movement.

3. During 1954-58 the state reformed the church through political educaton

In July 1954, China promulgated its first constitution, and

the churches were called upon to support it. The Korean War was over by 1953, and a new name was needed for the anti-America Aid-Korean Three-Self Reform Movement. This movement, therefore, held the first "National Christian Conference" in July 1954 in Beijing. At that conference, the name of the body was changed to the "Three-Self Patriotic Movement" and a TSPM constitution was adopted.[34]

After the first National Christian Conference further efforts were made to organize local committees of the TSPM, and all churches were required to join the body, the symbol of anti-imperialist patriotism. Whereas the earlier Three-Self Reform Movement had led or directed the churches as an *ad hoc* patriotic movement, now the TSPM had become an organization which delineated the sphere of patriotic religious existence.

Churches which refused to join the TSPM *ipso facto* declared themselves "non-patriotic." Furthermore, whereas in the earlier period mainline churches founded by foreign missions were the main targets of attack, after 1954 indigenous Chinese churches came under pressure. In 1955, those church leaders who resisted the TSPM, such as Wang Mingdao in Beijing and Lin Xiangao in Canton, were arrested.[35] Similarly, Chinese Catholic clergy who refused to cooperate also came under scrutiny. Bishop Gong (Kung) Pinmei was also arrested in 1955.

The relationship between church and state during this period may be illustrated in the following manner:

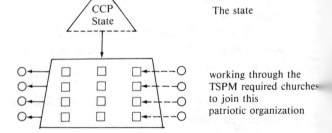

The TSPM attacked those which refused to join it.

CCP State

The state

working through the TSPM required churches to join this patriotic organization

However, even at this stage, individual churches remained intact in that each church could still make its own ecclesiastical decisions, including whether to join the TSPM or not. Within the framework of the TSPM, the state conducted political education classes for pastors, hoping that they would come to the viewpoint of the Party on the place of Christianity in socialist China.

4. During 1958-66, a union of church and state took place in the formation of three-self (state) churches

Starting in the summer of 1957, the CCP began to conduct a "Socialist Education Movement," which was further intensified after the beginning of the Great Leap Forward Movement in 1958. In the fall of 1958 in Shanghai, pastors who had already joined the TSPM were told to attend political study sessions away from home. These sessions lasted for six months. a second series of sessions was conducted during the first half of 1959.[36] During the course of study, the question of the class nature of preachers came up. Are preachers exploiters or exploited? Those who realized that they were exploiters "volunteered" to join the proletarian class by becoming factory workers.[37] Those who were less "enlightened" were sent to do manual labour anyway.

The prolonged absence of these pastors from their churches and their subsequent departure from the ministry left most churches half empty and without pastors. The TSPM then called for a "church union" movement. Some of the congregations "offered" their church buildings to the state; others united themselves with neighboring congregations. The result was a remarkable reduction in the number of churches. For example, the 200-plus churches in Shanghai were reduced to eight, and the sixty-six churches in Peking to four.

The few churches that remained after the amalgamation movement were led by men appointed by the TSPM and they were called "three-self churches." A team of pastors from several denominations who did well in their political studies or whose respected names were still useful to the TSPM, worked in these three-self churches.

The relationship between the church and the state during this period may be illustrated as a union of church and state:

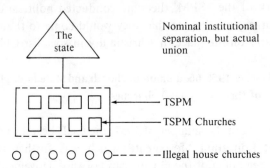

Individual congregations in the TSPM no longer had autonomy. The congregations could no longer make decisions on the election of church officers or the appointment of pastors. After 1958, country churches were closed down by the government, and independent church meetings were considered illegal. Their leaders were subject to arrest. House churches had to meet in secret.[38]

5. During the Cultural Revolution (1966-76), the state sought to destroy the church

When the Cultural Revolution broke out in August 1966, the Red Guards stormed party headquarters, closed down the United Front and the Religious Affairs offices, and closed all existing three-self churches. In their attempt to destroy the "four olds," they sought to do away with all organized religion along with Chinese folk religion, all of which they considered to be superstition. Their attacks represented a drastic shift from the soft-line, united front-oriented religious policy that was operative during 1958-66, to a hard-line policy which left no room for religion in the new revolutionary society.[39] Although no documents on religious policy were published during the latter part of the Cultural Revolution (1969-76), the actual practice of the state as carried out by its local revolutionary committees may be described as a policy of relegating religion to a position of illegality and suppressing its reemergence. The state no longer tolerated some religious practices. It simply outlawed them all. The state had become a monolithic institution.[40]

However, Chinese Christians continued to meet secretly in their homes, especially in the countryside. Such meetings were illegal and were subject to closure. Their leaders were subject to arrest. Nevertheless, because of the people's need for comfort, community, and hope, needs which house church Christianity fulfilled, these house churches began to grow in size and in number.[41] They sustained no formal relations with the state, but existed as illegal groups and were often suppressed by the local authorities. The church-state relationship may be illustrated as follows:

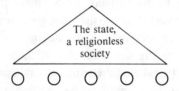

Even after the death of Mao Zedong and the arrest of the Gang of Four in 1976, the above state of affairs continued to exist. It was a totalitarian state which left no room for religion. The more open policy adopted by Deng Xiaoping after his return to power in 1977 necessitated a reduction in the degree of religious suppression, but there was no change in the hard-line policy until April 1979.

6. During 1979-82 the state began to restore its soft-line religious policy and revive the patriotic organizations

With Deng Xiaoping's return to power, as evidenced by the reform policies of the Third Plenum of the CCP's Eleventh Party Congress (December 1978), the Central Committee's United Front Work Department was reestablished in March 1979.[42] This was followed by reestablishment of the Religious Affairs Bureau in April the same year. Simultaneously, the Chinese Communists began to restore their pre-Cultural Revolution soft-line policy of "freedom of religious belief."[43] The Protestant church in Peking has allowed Chinese worshippers from April 1979.

In August 1979 the Shanghai Committee of the Three-Self Patriotic Movement was reorganized. Former TSPM churches in larger cities, which had been closed down since 1966, started to reopen in September 1979. In February 1980, the Executive Committee of the TSPM National Committee held an "extended meeting" in Shanghai — the first since 1961. In October 1980, the TSPM held its third National Christian Conference in Nanking, thereby formally reconstituted the defunct Protestant patriotic organization, the Three-Self Patriotic Movement.[44]

However, at the Nanking conference another organization called the Christian Council of China (CCC) was formed. The TSPM has been described by its officials as a "mass political organization" whose function is to assist the government in implementing its religious policy and to educate the church to become patriotic. The role of the new council is to take care of ecclesiastical matters in the TSPM churches, such as Bible printing, theological education, Christian publications, and conducting fraternal visits with churches in other lands. In reality, however, the staffs of these two organizations are almost identical, and they almost always meet jointly.

To the Peking government, the TSPM is a patriotic religious organization, but to church councils abroad, the CCC is a church body representing the church in China, and so the name Christian Council of China is used when TSPM leaders go abroad on goodwill trips.

The situation of church-state relations during this period may be illustrated as follows:

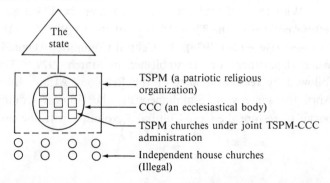

As the TSPM and the CCC began organizing themselves at the provincial level in 1981 and at county level during 1982, they ran into conflicts with the numerous house churches that had been flourishing since 1970.[45] But in the countryside house churches continued to grow in strength and number. They had to operate as illegal entities, their leaders were subject to arrest. Yet they maintained their autonomy as Christian groups independent of state control.

7. During 1982-88, the state consolidated its control over all churches

As stated earlier, the Party has worked out a comprehensive religious policy for the current transitional stage of socialism, namely, the policy of "freedom of religious belief" as contained in Central Committee Document No. 19 of 1982 which was circulated to county level Party secretaries. To study this policy the TSPM held an extended Executive Committee meeting in Peking in September 1982. Thereafter, the TSPM and the CCC, in concert with the local RAB offices, began to implement the "three-designates" by urging existing house churches to join the TSPM/CCC.[46] A few of them joined, but the remaining majority refused to do so, preferring to preserve their own ecclesiastical autonomy in order to conduct their ministries according to the teachings of Scripture. Those who refused to comply came under pressure beginning from August 1982, and they experienced severe persecution from the latter part of 1983 until the end of 1984.[47] On the other hand, in those areas where there were no open churches, the local authorities complied with the believers' requests to restore their former churches.

In October 1984, the Party passed a "Decision on Reform of the Economic Structure."[48] This became the basis of a national program for economic reform, which included toleration of the urban market economy. As a result of this general relaxation of controls, the suppression of house churches was eased off somewhat during 1985-86, and quite a few house church leaders who had been arrested during 1982-84 were released or had their sentences reduced. During this period, a number of independent house churches in the countryside joined the TSPM county committees and paid their annual dues, but continued to conduct their religious activities as before, keeping their ecclesiastical autonomy while submitting themselves to TSPM policies. Still, the majority of house churches remained outside the TSPM. Hence, the church-state relationship during this period may be illustrated as follows :

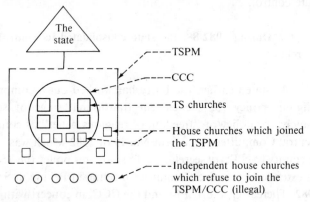

Concluding Observations

Church-state relations in socialist China since the founding of the PRC have been determined by the Chinese Communist Party. The Party took the initiative and dictated the terms for the existence of religions. Religious bodies, such as the Protestant church, were never given an opportunity to negotiate the development of a mutually satisfactory church-state relationship. From the very beginning, independent Christian bodies representing the Protestant church, such as the National Christian Council of China, were gently pushed aside and later forced to dissolve themselves. The control of the state over Protestant Christianty was supreme and unquestioned.

From the very beginning, the Party set up its own body, the Three-Self Reform (later Patriotic) Movement, to lead and direct Chinese Protestant churches, and called it the spokesman for the Protestant churches. This control has never been relaxed. The TSPM may be seen both as the arm of the state controlling the church and the limit of state toleration for church affairs. The realm of the TSPM is the realm of legality, and that realm also defines the limits of religious freedom. Within that realm there is also socialist education for the clergy. The TSPM is more of a representative of the socialist state to the church than a representative of the church to the state. But in their propaganda the TSPM and CCC claim to represent the Protestant church in mainland China. Even if they truly represented the 4,000 churches and the three million members under their administration, they certainly would not be representing the more than fifty million believers who meet in at least 200,000 locations outside their control.

The relation of church and state in socialist China basically follows the pattern of state control of religions in traditional China. The parallel between the two is very obvious:

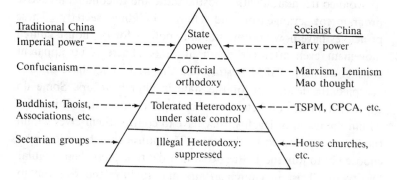

Traditional China		Socialist China
Imperial power — — — — — — — — →	State power ← — — — — —	Party power
Confucianism — — — — — — — →	Official orthodoxy ← — — — — —	Marxism, Leninism Mao thought
Buddhist, Taoist, — — — — → Associations, etc.	Tolerated Heterodoxy under state control ← — — —	TSPM, CPCA, etc.
Sectarian groups — — — →	Illegal Heterodoxy: suppressed ← —	House churches, etc.

In the matter of state control of religion, the present totalitarian socialist state inherited the position of the former feudalistic, imperial state. Hence, it may be said that current Chinese Communist religious policy is both totalitarian and feudalistic. If mainland China is to make any significant progress toward modernization and to develop any kind of authentic "spiritual civilization," its leaders will have to reexamine their current theories and practice regarding religion and make changes appropriate to a modern, developing and democratic society.

The response of the Chinese Protestant church to state initiatives may generally be described as passive. During the 1950-58 period, the majority of the nearly ten thousand Christian workers gave in under pressure. They signed the "Manifesto," accused their former co-workers, and joined the TSPM. Only a few chose the prophetic role of demonstrating their loyalty to Christ — and they suffered for this. After 1958, those who remained in the three-self churches accepted the leadership of the government in church affairs, but a number of faithful lay leaders began to develop underground meetings, accepting the consequences of civil disobedience for conscience's sake.

During the Cultural Revolution, Christians were forced to confess Christ, and such pressure and concomitant suffering trained many believers for faithful witness in subsequent years. They learned from experience to be "gentle as doves and shrewd as serpents." They sought to witness Christ by living exemplary lives, to avoid confrontaton with a hostile state, and to conduct an active program of evangelism and church building secretly. These principles have now become standing polices for the house church movement even after the death of Mao. (There is no apparent conflict between TSPM pastors and the state. They have already accepted the leadership of the state in church affairs. Some do experience inner conflicts, but in order to conduct their ministries within the realm of legality, they have to confine themselves within the limits determined by the state.) The house church leaders who choose not to join the TSPM do so in order to express their singular loyalty to Christ in church affairs and to have the freedom to conduct evangelistic work.[49]

From the Christians' viewpoint, the basic issues in church-state relations in a socialist country like China are essentially three: (1) the question of leadership over the church: who leads the church, Christ or the state? (2) the question of evangelism: to evangelize or not to evangelize? (3) the universal character of the church: should a national church cut off its fellowship with the international body of Christ or not?

For mainland China, the above conflicts cannot be resolved until Beijing abandons the view that its own ideology is orthodox while that of its competitors is heterodox. Secondly, until there is a genuine separation between the Party and the state according to law, the pattern of state control of religion can hardly be changed. Finally, until mainland China adopts a policy of ideological pluralism, Christianity cannot enjoy genuine freedom under law. These, therefore, are future challenges for those who pray for China and who wish China well.

NOTES

1. "Zongjiao ziyou yu jibenfa" (Religious Freedom and the Basic Law), *Mingbao,* Dec. 5, 1986; Feb. 3, 4, 1987.

2. See Chao Tien-en, "Cong Zhonggong zongjiao zhengce kan jibenfa yu zongjiao ziyou" (The Basic Law and Religious Freedom as seen from the Perspective of Chinese Communist Religious Policy), *Jiushi niandai* (The Nineties), No. 206 (March 1987), pp. 46-48.

3. The full text of Article 36 reads: "Citizens of the People's Republic of China enjoy freedom of religious belief. No state organ, public organization, or individual may compel citizens to believe in, or not to believe in, any religions: nor may they discriminate against any citizens who believe in, or do not believe in, any religion. The state protects normal religious activities. No one may make use of religion to engage in activities that disrupt public order, impair the health of citizens, or interfere with the educational system of the state. Religious bodies and religious affairs are not subject to any foreign domination." For the Chinese text of the 1982 constitution, see *Zhongguo shouce 1984* (Hong Kong: *Dagong bao,* Oct. 1, 1984), p. 4.

4. For the full text of Document no. 19 in Chinese, see *San zhongquanhui yilai zhongyao wenjian xuanbian* (Selected Important Documents Since the Third Plenum) (Tianjin: Renmin ribao chuban she, 1982), pp. 1218-1240.

5. Ibid., p. 1226.

6. Ibid., p. 1230.

7. This term, *"san ding,"* is used in the various local Three-self Patriotic Covenants *("Aiguo gongyue").* See, for example, "Guanyu weihu zhengchang zongjiao huodong de jueding" (Resolutions on

Maintaining Normal Religious Activities), published by the Yunnan Three-Self Patriotic Movement Committee and the Yunnan Christian Council, March 29, 1982 (circulated locally).

8. Section 10 of Document 19 reads: "While we resolutely protect all normal religious activities, we must resolutely attack illegal criminal activities and anti-revolutionary destructive activities under the cloak of religion, as well as various superstitious activities which do not fall into the realm of religion, but which are harmful to the national interest and to the lives and property of the people." Ibid., p. 1235. Section 11 reads: "We must intensify our awareness, paying close attention to hostile foreign religious forces attempting to establish underground churches and other illegal organizations. Institutions where espionage activities are carried out under the cloak of religion must be resolutely attacked." Ibid., p. 1237.

9. Part of Section 11 of Document 19 reads: "International reactionary forces, especially imperialist religious forces, including the Vatican and Protestant missions, will attempt to use all kinds of opportunities to conduct infiltration activities, seeking to return to mainland China. Our policy is to positively expand friendly international religious relations and, at the same time, resolutely resist the infiltration of all hostile foreign religious forces." Ibid., p. 1236.

10. See Ding Guangxun, "Sanzi zai renshi" (Re-understanding of Three-self), *Tianfeng*, new series, No. 14 (Feb. 1983), pp. 2-9.

11. The TSPM sent delegations to Hong Kong (March 1981), Canada and the U.S. (October 1981), Scandinavia (1982), Australia and New Zealand (March 1984); Japan (Sept., 1984), W. Germany, Hungary and Switzerland (November 1983), and India (February 1985).

12. This process can be observed in the consolidation of religious policy between December 1981, when consultation with TSPM leaders began, and December 1982, when the constitution was promulgated.

13. For a description of the inner workings of the RAB, see

Chapter I of George Patterson's book, *Christianity in Communist China* (Waco, 1970) and Holmes Welche's *Buddhism Under Mao* (Cambridge, 1971), Chapter I. The source for both appears to be the same person.

14. For the Chinese original, see Section 7 of Document 19, Ibid., p. 1231: "The task of these patriotic organizations is to assist the party and the government in carrying out the policy of freedom of religious belief, to help the broad mass of believers and religious personages to continuously raise their patriotic and socialist consciousness, to represent the legal rights and interests of the religions, to organize normal religious activities and deal with religious affairs. All patriotic religious organizations should accept the leadership of the Party and the government, and Party and government cadres should become adept at supporting and assisting religious organizations in solving their own problems, and should not try to take over themselves."

15. This working relationship between the TSPM, the RAB and the Public Security Bureau is commonly known by Christians in mainland China who have gone through the experience of interrogation, but it is little known outside the mainland.

16. In a recent case, a woman evangelist was arrested by the Public Security Bureau on December 14, 1984 and charged with conducting anti-revolutionary activities. Her criminal activities were described as joining an illegal Christian organization (house church), participating in an evangelistic team to Sichuan, engaging in itinerant preaching, and developing churches, etc., activities which "deceived the masses and seriously disturbed social order." On December 14, 1985, the Bureau of Investigation moved her case to the district court. In the Letter of Prosecution, the investigator stated that the accused "by conducting illegal missionary activities and seriously influencing social order, and production order, has violated Article 158 of the Criminal Code of the PRC and so is guilty of the crime of disturbing social order." On January 28, 1986, the district court released her, citing sections 1 and 2 of Article 158 of the Criminal Code. These facts are taken from the certificate of court decisions given to the accused.

17. For studies on official Confucian orthodoxy, see Paul A. Cohen, *China and Christianity, The Missonary Movement and the Growth of Chinese Anti-Foreignism, 1860-1870* (Cambridge, 1961), pp. 3-60. See also Arthur Wright, *Buddhism in Chinese History* (Stanford, 1959), especially his section on the Sui period, pp. 65-85.

18. For a description of the history of this control, see C. K. Yang, *Religion in Chinese Society* (Berkeley, 1961), pp. 180-217.

19. See Searle M. Bates' unpublished paper on "Church and State in Traditional China," seminar on Modern China, Columbia University, November 1967, p. 13.

20. For a fuller analysis of this debate on religion and anti-religious sentiment in the May Fourth era, see chapter III of my thesis, "The Chinese Indigenous Church Movement: Protestant Response to Anti-Christian Movements in Modern China, 1919-1927," Ph.D. thesis in Oriental Studies, University of Pennsylvania, 1986. See also Yu-ming Shaw, "Reaction of Chinese Intellectuals towards Religion and Christianity in Early Twentieth Century," in *China and Christianity* (Notre Dame Conference book 1979), pp. 154-183.

21. See the various responses of religious leaders to the article on religion in the Constitution , "Guojia baohu zhengchang de zongjiao huodong," *People's Daily,* July 3, 1982, p. 4.

22. See Xiao Xianfa (former director of RAB), "Zhengque lijie he guanche dang de zongjiao xinyang ziyou zhengce" (Correctly Understanding and Implementing the Party's Policy of Freedom of Religious Belief) *People's Daily,* June 14, 1980. This interpretation was repeated in a similar article in *Guangming Daily,* February 18, 1985, the latest document on religious policy, which simply repeated what Xiao said in 1980 and what was published in Document No. 19 of 1982.

23. For an account of the anti-imperialist propaganda in China by the CCP and the Socialist Youth League, see Jonathan Chao, op. cit., pp. 169-195. For original sources, see *Zhongguo Qingnian* (1924-1927 period); *Xuesheng zazhi* (1923-1926); *Juewu* (1924-1926); *Zhongguo guomindang zhoukan* (1924-25). For studies on the anti-Christian movement during this period, see Ka-

che Yip, "The Anti-Christian Movement in China, 1922-1927, with Special Reference to the Experience of the Protestant Missions," Ph.D. dissertation, Columbia University, 1970 (later published as a book).

24. See Chen Duxiu's denunciation of missions in *Xiangdao,* No. 22 (April 1923), p. 160, and the Socialist Youth League instructions to the students to struggle against the church in *Zhongguo Qingnian* No. 34 (June 7, 1924), p.12.

25. See Mao Zedong, "Maodun lun" (On Contradiction) (1937), Collected Works of Mao (Chinese text), I, 279–283. For a recent application of the united front theory, see Li Weihan, "Mao zedong sixiang zhidao xia de Zhongguo tongyi zhanxian" (Chinese United Front under the Direction of the Thought of Mao Tse-tung), *People's Daily,* December 17, 1983, pp. 4-5.

26. For a fuller historical study on how the Chinese Communists sought to control the Protestant church, see George Patterson, *Christianity in Communist China* (Waco, 1970), Richard Bush, *Religion in Communist China* (Nashville, 1969), and Jonathan Chao, ed., *Zhonggong yu Jidujiao de Zhengce* (Chinese Communist Policy towards Christianity) (Hong Kong: Chinese Church Research Center, 1983).

27. Protestant participants in the first CPPCC were: Wu Yaozong (Y.T. Wu), Deng Yuzi, Zhao Zichen, Zhang Xueyan, Liu Liangmo. See "Women canjia renmin zhengxie huiyi de jingguo" (The process by which we joined the People's Political Consultative Conference), *Tianfeng* No. 128 (Oct. 1, 1949), pp. 1-4.

28. For a brief study of this initial period, the beginnings of the Three-self Movement, see Yang Yang, "Sanzi yundong weiyuanhui chansheng de jingguo" (The Process by which the 'Three-self' Movement Committee was Born), *Zhongguo yu jiaohui,* No. 28 (May-June 1983), pp. 2-10. Original sources from *Tianfeng* are listed in the notes.

29. For the original text, see "Zhongguo Jidujiao zai xin Zhongguo jianshe zhong nuli de tujing," *Tianfeng,* Nos. 233-234 (September 30, 1950), p. 2. For a recent reprint of the document, see Jonathan Chao, op. cit., pp. 271-272. For the English translation of

this document, see Wallace Merwin and Francis P. Jones, eds., *Documents of the Three-self Movement* (New York, 1963), pp. 19-20.

30. On April 15, 1950, *Tianfeng* reported that the National Conference was postponed, and on August 5, it was reported that the conference was cancelled.

31. For a list of the original forty signatories, see *Tianfeng*, Nos. 233-234, p. 3.

32. On the formation of the Preparation Committee of the anti-America, Aid-Korea Three-self Reform Movement, see *Tianfeng*, Nos. 262-263 (May 8, 1951), pp. 30-31. For an analysis of the events of this period, see Yang Yang, "Zhengfu daoyan xia chansheng de kongsu yundong" (The Accusation Movement Produced under the Directorship of the Government), *Zhongguo yu jiaohui* No. 30 (Sept.-Oct., 1983), pp. 1-10.

33. For articles and reports on local accusation meetings conducted in Shanghai, see *Tianfeng*, No. 264 (May, 19, 1951), pp. 1-5.

34. Yang Yang, "Sanzihui de fazhan he gonggu" (The Development and Consolidation of the Three-self Movement), *Zhongguo yu jiaohui*, No. 31 (Nov.-Dec., 1983), pp. 11-20.

35. On the accusation of Wang Mingdao, see *Tianfeng*, Nos. 471-495 (July-Dec. 1955); also Richard Bush, *Religion in Communist China* (Nashville, 1970), pp. 214-215.

36. See Yang Yang, "Dalu jiaohui lianhe dingxing" (Mainland Churches Unite and Consolidate the Form), *Zhongguo yu jiaohui*, No. 32 (Jan.-Feb. 1984), pp. 7-14. Original sources are cited from *Tianfeng*.

37. On the discussion of the class nature of preachers, see *Tianfeng*, No. 559 (Aug. 2, 1958), pp. 27-30. See also Shen Yifan, "Gaizao ziji, zuo laodong renmin de yiyuan" (Reforming Myself and Becoming One of the Laboring People) *Tianfeng*, No. 556 (July 14, 1958), p.10. In Shanghai, for example, after the first political study session, the TSPM had church leaders write a "Self-Reform Covenant." See *Tianfeng*, No. 557 (July 28, 1958), p.15.

38. See "Jiangsu sheng Jidujiao sanzi aiguo daibiao guanyu

xiaomie hunluan xianxiang he yiqie feifa Luodong de chuangyi shu" (A proposal by the conference of the Three-self Patriotic Movement of Jiangsu Province concerning eliminating the phenomenon of confusion and illegal activities),*Tianfeng*, No. 553 (June 2, 1958), p. 12.

39. For an analysis of religion during the Cultural Revolution period, see Wan Waiyao, "Wenge shinian" (Ten Years of the Cultural Revolution), *Zhongguo yu jiaohui*, No. 12 (Sept.-Oct. 1980), pp. 13-14. For a Protestant believer's description of what Christians went through in those days, see ibid., pp. 2-4.

40. See Fr. L. Ladany "Religion," *China News Analysis*, No. 935 (Oct 5, 1972), pp. 1-3.

41. See Jonathan Chao, "The Witness of a Suffering Church," *China and the Church Today* 5:55 (Sept.-Oct. 1983) pp. 8-11. See also David Adeney, *China: the Church's Long March* (Ventura, 1985).

42. The CCP Central announced the restoration of the United Front Work Department, Ethnic Work and Religious Affairs Bureau on March 16, 1979. See *People's Daily,* March 19, 1979.

43. The initial announcement was made in an editorial "response to questions from readers" which appeared in the *People's Daily*, March 15, 1979.

44. See J. Chao, "An Analysis: Christian Conference Meets," *China and the Church Today*, 2:6-3:1 (1981), 1-2.

45. See "TSPM Wants You, But Do You Want Them? Apparently Dongyang House Churches Say No," *China and the Church Today* 4:4-5 (1982), 3-4.

46. On the decisions made at the Beijing Conference, see the report of the Second Meeting of the Third Conference of the Three-self Patriotic Movement Committee in *Tianfeng*, New series, No. 13 (Jan. 30, 1983), p. 1. See also the speech by Qiao Liansheng, Director of the Religious Affairs Bureau, given at the September Beijing TSPM conference. There he urged the implementation of the "three-designates" policy. Ibid., p. 13.

47. See the "Chart on Political and Church Developments in 1983," in *Zhongguo yu jiaohui*, No. 32 (Jan.-Feb. 1980), pp. 21-22.

48. See "Zhonggong zhongyang guanyu jingji tizhi gaige de

jueding" (Decision on the Reform of the Economic Structure by the Central Committee of the Chinese Communist Party), *People's Daily*, Oct. 21, 1984.

49. See Jonathan Chao, "Christianity in the Totalitarian State," *China and the Church Today*, 5:1 (Jan.Feb., 1983), pp. 7-11.

I   The Road to "Liberation" (1949-1965)

INTRODUCTION

In a normal history of the People's Republic of China, the years 1949 to 1965 would have to be divided into several periods. Since the persons whose interviews are recorded in this chapter all told their stories a decade or more after the events, their memories of those years tended to run together. Rather than to try to disentangle these accounts, we decided to arrange this chapter to cover several phases of history.

This period begins with the founding of the People's Republic of China in 1949. The early years were spent settling and formulating policy. They were also years of terror as the army and the Party continued to eliminate their most visible enemies. Their policy towards Christians was not well-articulated in the first few years, but they were clear about two objectives: they wanted to break the foreign connections of the Chinese Christians, both institutional and personal, and they wanted to establish a front organization through which they could manage and control Christian activities.

The first objective was largely accomplished by the end of 1951. The vast majority of foreign missionaries had left; those who remained were neutralized either by severe restrictions in movement or by imprisonment. Institutions that had foreign connections were regulated and taxed until they broke such connections or ceased to exist. In many schools and hospitals, the government took over management.

The second objective was realized with the formation of the Three-Self Reform Movement Committee [later to be re-named the

Three-Self Patriotic Movement Committee (TSPM)] in April 1951 at a meeting between government and sympathetic Christian leaders. The TSPM committee immediately began calling on churches to join it, and by the middle of 1952 it was virtually the only legitimate organization of Christians that could deal with the governemnt.

There was resistance to the TSPM, primarily from leaders of China's indigenous churches, such as Wang Mingdao and Watchman Nee. In 1955 and 1956, as part of a general campaign against counter-revolutionaries, these church leaders were attacked in meetings called by the TSPM and the Religious Affairs Bureau of the government, as well as in the press, both Christian and secular. Eventually these resistors were arrested and sentenced to prison terms of 15-20 years.

With the major, vocal opposition eliminated, Mao Zedong and the Party launched at the end of 1956 a campaign known as the Hundred Flowers campaign. They called on intellectuals to voice their true opinions and criticize the Party if they wished. They apparently hoped to diffuse and deflate the intellectuals' discontent by letting them voice minor criticisms. Some Christians took this opportunity to speak out against the government's policy on religion and against those communist cadres who showed no respect for Christians. However, the time of free speech quickly ended as the Party found themselves faced with serious criticisms that questioned the foundations of socialism itself. An anti-rightist campaign followed in 1957 to punish those whose criticisms were too sharp. Many Christian pastors found themselves the object of investigation during this time, and many were imprisoned. Most of these remained there until 1978, when Deng Xiaoping declared a general amnesty for rightists convicted in this campaign.

In 1958 the Great Leap Forward was launched, and communes were formed. Everyone was expected to be engaged in productive labor, and church work was not considered productive. Except for important persons in the TSPM committees, all pastors were expected to do some productive labor.

With virtually all visible opposition gone, the TSPM launched a campaign to eliminate denominational differences and consolidate the churches. As a result, fewer and fewer people attended the public services, and the churches declined rapidly. In Beijing the number of churches was reduced from sixty-four to four. *Tian Feng*, the TSPM's magazine, appeared for the last time outside China in 1964, and with the launching of the Cultural Revolution in mid-1966, the few remaining churches were closed down.

Nevertheless, as some of our documents indicate, starting about 1958, a number of Christians began meeting privately in their homes. Christianity in China was by no means dead.

1.1 Beijing, 1956 to 1965

This is the first of two interviews concerning Beijing and portrays the start of the persecution of Christianity there.

Q: We know that from 1956 on, the Communist government increased its control and pressure on the church. We would like to know what the actual situation of Christians in Beijing was at that time.

A: The year 1956 was the period of the "Anti-Counter-revolutionary Movement," which included a severe attack on the church. There were only a dozen or so churches left in Beijing, and the brothers and sisters who went to church were very few. The sermons had a strong political content. I went only to Wang Mingdao's church and the Little Flock Church (the church led by Watchman Nee). About that time, Wang Mingdao was arrested, along with a lot of Christian laymen. Because of this, only a few people went to the church. Wang Mindgao was then released for a period, but he didn't preach. I heard he suffered from psychological problems.

Q: You said you attended the Little Flock Church. Was the situation there as bad as it was for Wang Mingdao?

A: The "Responsible Brother" for the Little Flock Church was Yan Jiale. He was one who participated in the "Three-Self Movement," and because of this he didn't receive any pressure. He even had a position in the Chinese People's Political Consultative Conference. After the 1958 consolidation of churches, his church was one of the last four to survive until the Cultural Revolution (in 1966).

Q: In the next few years, did government control become tighter?

A: In 1957 there was a relaxed stage. Several church leaders and
members who had been arrested were released. But in the 1958 "Anti-
Rightist Movement" things again tightened up. Many influential
people in the church — pastors, members, etc. — were labelled
"rightists." At that time, the Three-Self Movement had a national
conference, in accordance with the government's directives. It criticized
these "Rightists" and did a lot of damage to the church. Public
struggles were held in the churches; everyone had to take part in them.
If you didn't have the correct attitude, then you would be struggled
against. [In a "struggle meeting," several persons would gather around
one, arguing with him, yelling at him, and occasionally beating him
in order to get that person to admit errors or crimes.]

     Where I worked, there was a brother from Wang Mingdao's
church. He was arrested at the end of 1957 and not released until
1973 or 1974. His "crime" was having sold books for Wang Mingdao.
He was arrested for refusing to acknowledge having participated in
the "Wang Mingdao counter-revolutionary movement." He had
graduated from the economics department of Xiamen University in
1953 and afterwards worked for the Beijing Import-Export
Corporation. So he lost a very promising career and future. After
he was released, he was sent to a rural village in Fujian to do labor.
He has a great testimony.

Q: Many overseas Chinese are concerned about Wang Mingdao's
story. Do you have any detailed news about him?
A: After Wang Mingdao was arrested [1955], his church was closed.
Because he admitted "anti-revolutionary activities," many others were
also arrested. After Wang Mingdao was released the first time [1956],
he was criticized by many brothers and sisters. Everyone was unhappy
about his confession in prison that he was "anti-revolutionary."
Because of this, after he was released, he went to the Religious Affairs
Bureau to renounce that confession. At that time many people
admired Wang Mingdao. His second arrest impressed many
Christians.
     We Christians have this attitude: we will obey the government,
but when the government pressures us to deny the existence of God

we are not afraid to sacrifice our jobs, our families, and even our lives for the truth. In fact, when the conduct of Christians is good in any situation, the masses can see this very clearly. But when a movement comes and we are under strong pressure, what can we do? Who would dare defend Christians?

Wang Mingdao was the editor of the *Living Bread Quarterly* until it ceased publication in 1956. But letters still came to the magazine after that time, because outsiders didn't know he was arrested. Many university students had subscribed to this magazine.

I have not heard about his writing a testimony of his prison life. He is still in prison in Shanxi province. His wife was arrested at the same time, but they were not together in prison. I've heard she has been released, probably with eye trouble. She lives in Shanghai with her son. I've also heard that Wang Mingdao is a janitor in the prison, but I'm not sure about that.

Q: You said that Yan Jiale was a church leader and cooperated with the government. Can you give us some information about this group of clergymen who cooperated with the Three-Self Movement?

A: Yan Jiale was one of the administrators of the Three-Self Movement in Peking. Yan Jiale started cooperating with the government very early. In 1956 when there were nationwide arrests of religious leaders, the "responsible people" of the Little Flock were all arrested, except for Yan Jiale. At that time, if you supported the government, agreed with its policies, and participated in the Three-Self Movement, then not only would you not be arrested, but you could even be given a good position. He became a Beijing City Council member and Standing Committee member. Afterwards he was a representative to the Fourth National People's Conference.

People like Yan Jiale were everywhere. They only said they believed in God, but in fact they betrayed God and didn't realize how many people they harmed. They couldn't rise unless they trampled on brothers and sisters. Afterward, their work was to find out the situation of the groups of believers and report it to the Public Security Bureau. Now the work of spreading the Gospel on the mainland is being done by those brothers and sisters who have come out of the prisons. Their work and testimonies have greatly moved people.

Q: We know that in the 60's most believers started having private, small-group meetings. Was this the case in Beijing?

A: In Beijing, after 1958, only four churches survived. Although I can't remember them too clearly, I think that in northern Beijing, on Broad Street, there was Christ Church. On Pig Market Street in Southern Beijing was another church whose name I can't remember. In West Beijing there was one at the Vat and Tile Market, and in East Beijing there was one on Rice Market Street. The names of these two I cannot remember. My time in Beijing was short since I was in Tianjin most of the time. After 1958 the church had no public activities. The brothers and sisters adopted the "house meeting" form to preserve their private gatherings. They could contact each other, but often, when the political pressure became great, political movements would tighten control in Beijing. This would make the people dare not to make contacts or have public activities.

The constitution says there is "religious freedom," but in fact there is no true freedom. Because of this, every true believer must be prepared to follow the times. He must also be prepared to sacrifice himself for God. Cadres in any small place can arrest and sentence you without regard for truth. Although you can appeal to those above for a reversal of the decision, it is very rarely given. Only if you have a friend higher up, someone with whom you have personal relations or who feels he owes you something, can you be helped, but this is very rare. He probably will not be moved by your problems; he has to protect himself.

Q: After believers are arrested and put in prison, what is their situation like, and what witness do they bear?

A: There are no Bibles in prison. So Christians outside tear pages out of Bibles to wrap things up to send in to the prisoners. Sometimes they receive these, but of course it is not very complete. And keeping this kind of "Bible" is very dangerous too. If a prison guard discovers it, the prisoner can be punished. There are some brothers and sisters in the prisons who die for God. They have beautiful testimonies for God because, during all their time in prison, all they had to do was deny God and they could have been freed. But they didn't do this.

1.2 Beijing and Shanghai, 1950-1961

The interviewee went to China to "see the world," and became a Christian there. This interview covers the eleven years until he was able to leave China again. His wife followed four years later.

Q: Why did you go to China?

A: I went with a group of some 100 students who had graduated from Chinese high schools in Malaysia. They showed a great sense of patriotism in going, but then the Chinese embassy had done a lot of propaganda work in the high schools, too. I wanted to study Mandarin, since we had so little Chinese language in my school.

Q: What did you do in Beijing?

A: I asked if there was a special language school there in which I could study Mandarin, but they did not have any such school. But then they asked me to teach Malayan at Beijing University and said I could teach part-time and take Chinese courses at the university part-time. So I did this for three years. In the fall of 1952, Beijing University was combined with Yanjing University, and everyone moved out to the Yanjing campus. There had been a Christian student group at Yanjing, and now some of the Beijing University students started participating.

Q: What was this group like? How many students attended?

A: It was called the Beijing University Christian Young People's Group. About 30 young people would meet together for 30 minutes of Bible reading and 30 minutes of prayer. They were openly tolerated by the other students at the university, since there was still a measure of freedom at that time. Most of the Christians attended Wang Mingdao's church, Watchman Nee's church, or Wang Chen's church.

Q: How many people were attending services at those churches at that time? We have not heard much about Wang Chen's church.

A: On Sundays, Wang Mingdao's church would be filled, with maybe 400 to 500 people. Watchman Nee was arrested in 1952 (April), but his congregation continued to meet, with 250 to 300 people attending. Wang Chen was an independent evangelist who had started his church around 1948. It was non-denominational, and had always been self-supporting and self-governing. I didn't attend there, so I dont't know how many people went.

Q: When did you go to Shanghai?

A: I went to Shanghai in 1953 and stayed for two years. I went to the Shanghai Spiritual Training Seminary there. The president was Rev. Jia Yuming, who was in his eighties then. He had started this school around 1927, after having graduated from Jinling Theological Seminary in Nanjing. There were 40 to 45 students. To enter, they had to write their testimonies down and have a personal interview with Rev. Jia. He would personally decide whether to admit the applicants. This way he could make sure all the students were evangelical. The courses were on the Bible, rather than on the practical subjects of how to be a pastor or evangelist.

Q: What did he do about joining the Three-Self Movement?

A: Oh, Rev. Jia was very clever. He avoided joining. I think he probably used his old age as the excuse. Also, at that time there were other seminaries still operating in Shanghai. But Beijing, Jinling, and Nanjing seminaries were all pro-government. Rev. Jia never said much, and when he did, he would talk very mildly. The school stayed open until 1958, and then he retired.

In 1955 I went back to Beijing, where I entered the Evangelism Training Center. This was a practical training school. In the mornings we would study two chapters from the Bible, for 3 hours every morning. Then in the afternoon we did practical work. There were about 50 students there, but 30 of them were older people. They came from all over China and would usually stay 3 to 6 months.

Q: Who was in charge of this school?

A: Dr. Chen, who herself was a pupil of John Song.

Q: What about the Beijing University Christian group at this time and the other churches in Beijing?

A: The student group was no longer meeting. Wang Mingdao's church was closed after his arrest. Few churches were open. Those that were open were pro-government and supported the communist policies. Most Christians just stayed home, read their Bibles, and prayed alone.

Q: Did they have contact with other Christians?

A: No, very few contacts; they just stayed at home, alone.

Q: How long did you stay there?

A: The center was closed in 1956. So then I went back to Shanghai, where the Spiritual Training Seminary was still open.

Q: How could that be open?

A: Well, Rev. Jia was very clever. He never disagreed with the government outright. The school stayed open until 1958, and then he retired.

Q: So he was never accused or struggled against?

A: No. He just retired and stayed in his home. After the school closed, I applied to leave China, but I was not given an exit visa.

Q: What did you do?

A: I just stayed in Shanghai. I could have worked, but if I worked, I could not get out. People who worked didn't get exit permits. I just stayed in my room, and waited, and read books, and so on. People who didn't work were regarded as a nuisance, as troublemakers. I came from Malaysia, so they couldn't arrest me. If I was from China and refused to work, I would have been sent to a labor camp. People had to work.

Q: Were Christians meeting in groups? Did you meet with Christians at that time?

A: With individuals. They didn't go to church.

Q: How did you live when you weren't working? Did your parents send you money?

A: Yes, a little. And so did Christian brothers and sisters. There was one Christian sister, a granddaughter of a very good Christian woman in Beijing, who always helped me. The older woman regarded me as her godson when I was in Beijing. And her granddaughter in Shanghai gave me $10 every month. For $10, I could eat for 3 weeks, but only very poor food.

Q: What about other Christians at that time?

A: They were suffering. They didn't go to church. They stayed in their rooms and had almost no contacts; they didn't want to get into trouble.

Q: Where there ways that they could witness about their Christianity to other people?

A: Very few and very seldom. Already there was almost no

freedom.

Q: Did they have to participate in political discussion groups where they worked?

A: Yes, mostly self-criticism and criticizing others, telling what their opinion was about certain policies of the government. When they [the government] made a new policy, they had to say what they thought about it.

Q: So it could be rather dangerous if you said the wrong thing?

A: Of course! People just said what the government wanted to hear.

Q: Who would lead those meetings?

A: Communist cadres, government officials. Such meetings were like a nightmare. But the Christians were very careful. They were very clever, very careful, and used as few words as possible.

Q: Where did you meet your wife?

A: In the training center, the evangelist training center in Beijing. She was a student. We were married before I left. But people advised me to go first, because her exit permit was more difficult than mine. We were separated for four years.

Q: Do you think that the Christians in China were prepared to live under a communist government?

A: Christians? No. Christians in the churches started by evangelical pastors, without financial backing from the West, usually were more spiritual and more earnest. But some churches were like clubs. It was too easy for the Christians in them. They depended on people, on Western Christians, so their churches became like business firms.

Q: Did you expect that in the future your freedom would become so limited?

A: At that time people didn't know for certain. It was unpredictable. Policies changed suddenly. The seminary teachers tried to avoid political subjects. They tried not to get involved.

Q: So it was hard for the teachers to know what to teach the students to prepare for the future.

A: They taught how to preach, how to take care of the congregation, spiritual things, not about politics because then the government had very sharp ears. They knew what was happening in the churches and in the seminaries. When Wang Mingdao was preaching, the government people sat there as if they were Christians. You didn't know if the man in the pew was a Christian or if he was a government official.

Q: Do you think some of the students in the seminaries were sent by the government?

A: In a small seminary, probably not. In a big seminary, it's difficult to know. If students didn't know each other quite well, there was some concern.

Q: Recently some churches have been opened by the government. Do you feel that's a good thing?

A: If the policy of the government becomes relaxed a little, maybe it's a good thing. It depends what the policy is later. If more churches open, then it would be good. If it's only a showcase, then....

1.3 Amoy in 1958

This is a summary of a portion of a long interview with Dr. Tan, covering the period 1958-1973. Dr. Tan was born in Amoy. He left China but returned at the invitation of Zhou Enlai in 1958 to Beijing where he worked at the Science Research Center of the Academia Sinica.

During his Amoy visit in 1958, Dr. Tan attended church services in his home church. The pastor preached, and there were communist cadres listening in the pews. The pastor said that he could not preach against the Party; if he did so, he would be called a "reactionary." At that time the attendance ranged from ten to twenty, and those who went were mostly in the 40-60 age group. None below 20 years of age were found. He heard of no baptisms, but he learned that the older believers still retained their faith.

1.4 A Housegroup in Shanghai

Many emigrants from China are reluctant to talk about their Christian activities there. This woman came to the CCRC and gave only a short interview. A few weeks later she wrote us a long letter, most of which is translated here.

In the past, I believed in Jesus Christ but didn't really know the meaning of salvation. When I was young, I studied in a Methodist school but never heard the Gospel. During World War II God gave me a great deal of grace in Hong Kong. Unfortunately, at that time I was too young to understand that all those things given by God were testimonies.

Then I went to Kunming, in Southwestern China. I used to attend the Little Flock church, but the people there did not testify of the Gospel either. Soon after, I went to Chongqing and met a Seventh Day Adventist missionary lady. She came to my house and helped me study the Bible. But she emphasized the writings of some teacher, and it didn't enlighten me at all.

After World War II was over, I went back to Shanghai and worshiped in a small independent church, where I heard many testimonies which warmed my heart. Two years later, my husband suddenly died of apoplexy. But instead of despairing, I offered myself to God, even though I didn't know where it would lead. My husband's death left me with five children from two to 15 years old. We had a large Christian funeral, which again spread the name of God.

Because my husband died from working so hard, we depended on the government for our livelihood afterwards. At that time the [Nationalist] government wanted to give me some compensation and a job or to support all my children until they graduated from university. So every month the government continued to give me my husband's salary. What I did with it was to start a kindergarten. I also started a home worship meeting every Saturday evening. I invited all my friends and the parents of the children in my kindergarten. I asked the teachers and students of the China Theological Seminary to come preach to them.

In the second semester, our ten kindergarten students increased to eighty. We worked hard to run the kindergarten well, and more people wanted to send their children. But before the end of the second semester, Shanghai was liberated [by the Communists]. Although most of my friends fled, I only wanted to keep on with my work, so I didn't move. After the second semester was over the Chinese Communist government wanted to take over our building, and the kindergarten stopped. After we were forced to move, some of the furniture was taken by the government. Our situation was very miserable, so we moved to another place.

A missionary encouraged me to continue the house fellowship meetings, and so I again started family worship meetings on Saturday. At Christmas and Easter we always had special meetings at our house, and the crowd would be much larger than that of the regular worship meetings. I always invited the most spiritual pastor to preach. I organized the sisters for fasting and praying. Everybody took responsibility for our fellowship. Later I became acquainted with the teachers and students of the Spiritual Training Institute and invited them to come to preach. At that time, the Religious Affairs Bureau wanted every house worship group to belong to a church, so our house group joined the Spiritual Training Institute.

In 1956 Mr. Wang Mingdao was arrested. Many Christians were frightened and most of the house worship meetings stopped. I often cried before the Lord and prayed for increased strength. As long as the government didn't force the meetings to stop, I wanted to continue to the end. In 1958, the Anti-Rightist Campaign reached its peak. My family was again forced to move. I had no house and was accused in the courts. Those were truly hard days. I thank the Lord that when I cried before Him, I read Isaiah 54:4-5 and had great peace. ["Fear not; you shall not be put to shame, you shall suffer no insult, have no cause to blush. It is time to forget the shame of your widowhood; for your husband is your Maker, whose name is the Lord of Hosts; your ransomer is the Holy One of Israel who is called God of all the earth."]

In the second half of 1958 the Religious Affairs Bureau started a struggle movement in all the churches. A lot of lay leaders were arrested. Some had no family in Shanghai and didn't have anything to take with them to prison. People had to send them what they needed. All the letters they wrote were inspected first. They would be sent to Qinghai, Anhui, or other such places to do labor reform. From 1959 to 1962 there were food shortages in mainland China. A great many of the prisoners died of hunger. We often mailed them food and goods which kept some of them alive.

Because my class background was bad, and because I had participated in religious activities, I was watched by the government. My relatives worried about me very much. Because of this, I frequently traveled to Guangzhou, Wuhan, and Beijing. Everywhere I knew many brothers and sisters, and of course in the Shanghai area I had a great number of friends. Because of this, I myself never thought I would be permitted to leave China. But thanks to the grace of God I finally received permission to come to Hong Kong.

Since coming to Hong Kong, the thing I enjoy most is going to church and listening to the preaching, which I haven't been able to do for more than 20 years. Besides this, there are so many fine books I can read here.

1.5 Thirty Years in China (I)

This interview is continued in 2.5 and 3.9. The interviewee is a late middle-aged overseas Chinese man, who lived in China from 1946 to 1977.

Q: What was the state of the church in Fujian after 1958?

A: After 1958 most churches in China were closed. Only a few remained. In Beijing there were four. But still there were small-group meetings.

Q: Did Christians suffer much in those years before the Cultural Revolution?

A: Oh yes. I remember that many brothers and sisters suffered. They were usually sent to labor-reform camps. Some of them were there for as long as twelve to fifteen years. After their time there, they would be released but usually sent to remote villages. Yet the amazing thing is that, even there, many would still find other believers and would resume preaching.

Q: Who were the victims? Did the authorities concentrate on certain age groups, for example?

A: No. Even the very old and the very young would be arrested and sent off like that. Even people who were sick.

Last year I visited the family of a friend of mine. Their father had been arrested in 1955. He was sent to do hard labor far away in Northeast China. At that time his wife and children were very young, and they were left with no way to support themselves. They were classified as a "reactionary family." They couldn't get enough food. The children were taunted in school and their prospects of ever getting a higher education were lost. But the brothers and sisters rallied together and supported the whole family. They supported the family of their brother who had been sent away because of his faith and testimony. Last year I visited them. The children are grown up now, and they are wonderful, living testimonies.

1.6 Living in Amoy

This account is given by the son of Professor Shi (pseudonym), who escaped to Hong Kong in 1978.

Professor Shi was from Gulangyu, an island section of greater Amoy, where two to three million people live. He and his wife recall that Gulangyu was probably the most Christianized land in China. Before the Liberation practically everyone went to church on Sundays, holding Bibles in their hands. There used to be the *Sanyitang* [Trinity Church], the *Fuyintang* [Gospel Church], the *Jiangdaotang* [Word Proclamation Church], the *Anxiretang* [Watchman Nee Local Church], the *Tianzhutang* [Catholic church], etc. The first three churches were Presbyterian in background.

In the early 1950's there was not much control by the Religious Affairs Bureau (RAB). But the Three-Self Movement under the RAB required each church to send delegates to its office to study the government's policies. By 1958 all Christian churches came under the control of the Three-Self Movement, which forced the churches to unite. Church attendance was reduced because of the members' staggered work schedules and because the young were reluctant to go. Different church groups used to worship in one of the rooms at the Trinity Church. The Little Flock people under Watchman Nee's influence didn't use that church building; neither did they conduct any organized house worship, because as soon as a group was organized it had to send delegates to the RAB office for political studies.

The Trinity Church was still operating until the eve of the Cultural Revolution [CR] in 1966. When the CR broke out, all organized churches came to a complete stop. Individuals still held private meetings, especially in the villages. Professor Shi himself did not attend any house church meetings but stayed at home and read his Bible. One of the liberal YMCA secretaries, who betrayed other Christians before the CR, was himself severely beaten by the Red Guards during the CR. Later he got cancer. He wanted to be burned to death with his books. He was a graduate of Changzhou Theological College and later studied theology in a liberal seminary in the U.S. After the CR he would not talk about the Christian faith whatsoever. After a while he died of cancer.

In Amoy there used to be seven to ten Christian workers belonging to the Little Flock group. During the mid-1950's, at least six brothers were known to be arrested and imprisoned. One was released without being charged, a second one suffered a mental breakdown, and a third one was released two years ago. The rest of them are probably still in prison. Watchman Nee's followers — his "responsible brothers" in different places — were practically all captured during the 1956-1957 period. In 1948 Nee bought a training camp near Fuzhou, a place called Kuling, and he was then giving discipleship training to his followers. After the Chinese communist takeover, the government began a program of Land Reform in the Fuzhou area in 1951. Nee had his followers sign a petition urging the Communists not to implement the Land Reform. This infuriated the Chinese Communist Party. For these reasons, plus the fact that the Little Flock was well organized, the Communists captured nearly all of their local leaders and sentenced them to fifteen to twenty years of imprisonment.

1.7 Early Days in Beijing

This university graduate was an active Christian in Beijing even after the Revolution, so he was in a good position to describe the church there.

Q: When did you come from Beijing to Hong Kong?

A: At the end of August, 1978.

Q: On what basis were you allowed to leave?

A: I was allowed to leave China as a "relative-visitor." I hold a Chinese passport with a five-year duration.

Q: Can you tell us something about the church situation in Beijing since Liberation?

A: Sure. In the beginning there was not much pressure or persecution; at least it appeared that way on the surface. However, there was some occasional persecution. During 1949 and 1950, there were still some missionaries in Beijing. The last missionary left around 1952.

In Beijing we used to have a Christian Student Association, made up of high school and university students. Every year we used to hold joint summer and winter conferences, or revival meetings. Many came to Christ during those conferences. We first felt [political] pressure in 1954. In March of that year, the government arrested a large number of Catholic priests and nuns who refused to join the Catholic Three-Self Movement. In other cities such as Qingdao, arrests took place even earlier. No action, however, was taken against Protestants, except the arrest of pastor Li Yuanting of the Assembly of God Church in Beijing.

In the summer of 1954, a National Christian Patriotic Conference was held in Beijing. Christian ministers from all over China were summoned to it. At that time Pastor Wang Mingdao refused to attend this conference. Another pastor, Wang Chen, and the Watchman Nee group in Beijing also refused to join.

Q: What were Wang Mingdao's reasons for refusing to attend the 1954 conference?

A: At that time Mr. Wang's position was that believers must not mix with unbelievers, that one must not mix with the world. It was primarily a matter of faith. There was no intention of opposing the government. Mr. Wang felt that if one joined the Three-Self Movement and walked according to the will of the government, the final result would be the betrayal of the church, the betrayal of Christ. Thus by the summer of 1955 we began to feel heavy pressure from the government.

In August 1955, a large number of church leaders in Beijing were arrested. It began on August 7th and continued to the end of the year. All the rest had to join the Three-Self Movement. At the time there was a clear distinction between the fundamentalists and the liberals. Those fundamentalists who were not arrested were all forced to join the Three-Self Movement.

Mr. Wang Mingdao was criticized as an anti-revolutionary, an intelligence agent of the United States, one who worked for the enemy. They even accused him of cooperating with the Japanese during the Sino-Japanese war, when actually Mr. Wang had refused to join the Christian Union organized by the Japanese. He was accused of all sorts of offences. Furthermore, all the members of his church were criticized and struggled against in their work units. [A work unit is the place where one is employed, such as a commune, factory, school, party department, etc. It is at this level that a person's political sentiments are tested, and a personal dossier compiled.] Thus, criticizing Wang became a part of the campaign against counter-revolutionaries.

In the early months of 1956, arrests and struggles became somewhat relaxed. By the summer of 1956 Wang Mingdao was released. His church meetings were resumed. The Gospel was faithfully preached there. A certain pastor Li, who had joined the Three-Self Movement but who was also arrested, said, "So long as I am allowed to preach the Gospel, anything is alright with me — whether I have to join the Three-Self or not does not matter. What I care about is preaching the Gospel." This period of relative relaxation lasted until the summer of 1957, the eve of the "Anti-Rightist" campaign.

First there was the "Let a Hundred Flowers Blossom; Let a Hundred Schools Contend" movement, through which the government encouraged the people to speak out. Then came the "Anti-Rightist" campaign, in which the government struggled against those who had spoken out. These movements were also carried out within the church. Many pastors were castigated as "rightist" and were forbidden to preach and to visit their flocks. Until then the Chinese government had propagated the slogan of separating church and state, yet this labelling of pastors as rightists was a clear example of the state's intruding into the internal affairs of the church.

In April 1958, the majority of the so-called "rightist" pastors were arrested. Although Wang Mingdao was not a rightist, he was still arrested a second time. By then only eight churches were left [in Beijing]. Of these, four were Catholic and four were Protestant. The four Protestant churches were: (1) the Little Flock (Nee) group on Broad Street, (2) the Chinese Christian Church in the Vat and Tile Market, (3) the Methodist church in the Poultry Market, and (4) the church above the Bible Society. The rest were all closed down. Some were used as schools, others as storage houses, and still others as factories. Of the pastors who held a Biblical faith, some were arrested, and others labelled Rightists and arrested or forbidden to preach. Those who continued to serve as pastors were those who cooperated with the government. What they said and what they did was all according to government instructions. They had to give the government a list of persons who went to worship.

Those who held orthodox Christian faith no longer attended the organized churches. This was true from 1958 to 1966. The average age of those who attended these churches was between fifty and sixty. There were practically no young people. The few that went did so during Christmas. The majority of Christians avoided going to these official churches, because, when they did, what they said and with whom they talked would all be reported. Afterwards they would be called up for talks and "education" in the units where they worked.

The "pastor" in charge of these official churches would occasionally visit some believers in their homes. They did so with the pretense of urging them to attend church, but in reality they wanted to learn with whom the believers still kept up contact, which of them still talked about their faith, and whether they still read their Bibles and prayed every day. This was part of their intelligence work. What I am reporting here is not my personal conjecture, but facts verified by the experiences of many believers.

After 1958, all true believers were criticized in their schools or work units. Many Christians were arrested when the government discovered they met secretly for Bible reading and prayer — the so-

called "secret meetings." Other times they were plainly notified by
the government not to conduct such activities any more. It may be
said that during 1958-1966, though the pressure was quite strong, it
was not so obvious. Many who truly loved the Lord devised all sorts
of ways to communicate the Gospel. They taught English, which in
reality was none other than Bible study in English. When they
gathered together, they prayed and sang hymns, even though in a
muffled way, and received much comfort. Under such conditions,
they comprehended more deeply the meaning of hymns and their
implications for themselves. For many years young people joined these
kinds of meetings.

From 1958 to 1966, many Christians spent days and years in
prison. Some were imprisoned when their children were still very
young. The financial burden on their families was heavy. Often
finding means of support became quite difficult. Yet somehow they
got through. For example, there was a brother in Beijing who had
children. When he was arrested in 1958, his wife and children were
left without any income. His wife went through much hardship. Many
who wanted to help him couldn't do it; they did not dare to. In spite
of all these hardships, his children grew to manhood and are working
now. When one of his sons, who is now in his twenties, went to see
him in one of the labor reform camps, the brother did not recognize
him.

"Who are you?" he asked.

"I am your son. I have come to see you," his son replied.

"Why have you spent so much money to travel so far to see
me? There is actually no such need. Remember, if we meet in this
life, it will only be briefly. You should take heed to yourself so that
we can meet again in our eternal home in heaven. It would be the
most fearful thing if we fail to meet each other before the Lord. That
would be most tragic."

So he encouraged his son, and the son reported all this to his
mother. I heard this just a few weeks before I left China this year.
Thus, though the situation was not good, our brother was still filled
with joy. Like Paul, though living in prison, he worked for the Lord.

Another sister, who was born in Guangdong, was arrested in

1958. She continued to preach the Gospel in prison. I have personally met her. She was imprisoned along with all kinds of prisoners: corrupt officials, robbers, immoral persons, political prisoners, etc. There was one prisoner who gave everyone a hard time. Not even the prison warden could do anything about her. She would not wash her face, brush her teeth, or comb her hair. Whenever she got a chance she would open her mouth to scold others. No matter what the warden did to her — and he applied all sorts of punishments to her — still it was useless. The Communist prison keepers then asked this Christian sister to talk to this hopeless prisoner. "Alright, I'll try," replied our sister. Sister Chen then lived together with the other woman prisoner. She prayed for her. Gradually the woman changed. She bathed herself, changed her clothes, and even combed her hair. The prison warden was greatly surprised and asked, "How did you change her?"

"I had no strength to change her. I prayed for her, and I believed that God could change her."

The transformed prisoner expressed her desire to receive Christ as her Saviour and Lord of her life. Many other prisoners in the same prison also came to believe in the Lord. They all said to the sister, "In the past we did not understand you. Now that we have lived together with you, we have discovered that you are different from others. Through you we have come to understand what it means to believe in the Lord."

After Sister Chen was released from prison, she told me that formerly the Lord has used her in public meetings to preach the Gospel to others or to lead revival meetings. She was glad when she saw so many people attend her meetings. Now the Lord is using her to do personal work, on a one-to-one basis, and she also sees great significance in this.

Another example comes from an older sister in the Lord who was imprisoned for many years. She gets up to pray every morning at three. Not too long ago she prayed for me. She told me that she had clearly heard the Lord tell her that I could leave China and would be able to see my mother. The next day when I was going to work, she waited for me by a particular street. I seldom took that street to work, but on that day somehow I went on that road and so met her on the way. She then told me what she had received from the Lord. A week later I received notice from where I worked that I was given permission to leave. I could not help but believe that it was God's will for me to leave and that He had arranged the early notice.

My circle of friends is not large, but we all love the Lord. Many believers pray for the Church in China. They pray for each other and care for one another. So many problems have been remarkably solved. For example, some who did not have residence registration in Beijing were granted permission to stay. Others arrested during the Cultural Revolution were released. Still others were sent down to the countryside, living under most difficult conditions, and yet did not neglect witnessing for Christ.

II   The Tiger Roars:
The Cultural Revolution
(1966-1969)

INTRODUCTION

The Cultural Revolution is one of the pivotal events in modern Chinese history. It is one of those events by which people mark their lives — "before and after" the Cultural Revolution. For the participants, the events had an intensity probably unmatched by any other part of their lives. No aspect of the psychology of Chinese youth today, nor even the politics and programs of the Communist Party leadership, can be explained without reference to the Cultural Revolution. Like World War II for the Europeans and the Japanese, the Cultural Revolution was an epoch-making event, with profound implications for today's China and probably for the China of decades to come as well.

The present regime in China views the Cultural Revolution with distaste, as indeed do most of its citizens. Commonly they date the Cultural Revolution as lasting from 1966 to 1976, and refer to it obliquely as the ten years of chaos, or the ten lost years. They speak about the continuation of policies from 1949 and their brief "interruption" in the Cultural Revolution. In their minds, the whole affair was simply an unfortunate aberration. In fact, however, the Cultural Revolution was the result of Mao's pursuit of policies begun in the mid-1950's. Some of the "old guard" in the Party opposed some of these steps, but there were also many who agreed with Mao at various stages in the development of the social climate of the Cultural Revolution. These agreements are now quietly ignored.

Mao was always concerned about the "people." He had an idea that this "people" was somehow an organic unity that would support socialism. He knew that some incorrigible elements existed that would always be "enemies" of the people, but the masses could always be roused to eliminate the enemies. After the basic economic changes of the first five to seven years of the new regime, Mao thought that the "people" could soon become of one mind. Ideological unity under his leadership was apparently an over-riding concern of Mao in the last decades of his life. In the Great Leap Forward of 1958-59 and the Socialist Education Movement of 1962-1966, one of Mao's goals was to bring the people's thoughts in line with the new social order that they were supposed to be experiencing. The trouble was that most of the Party did not believe this would happen as fast as Mao thought it would. Moreover, they felt their positions of power were threatened by these populist moves. So Mao turned against them. In his view, most of the Party workers had become bureaucrats who prevented the people from really benefiting from the new social order and thus prevented them from realizing the spiritual unity that he envisioned.

For Mao, religion had no place in this spiritual unity. Part of Mao's program was the atheistic education campaign, and he undoubtedly stimulated the great debate on religion in the press from 1963 to 1965. The basic issue of the debate was whether to get rid of religion by force or to let it die out gradually through control and education. The latter was the basic policy of the Party up to 1966 and from 1979 to the present. Mao, however, seemed to push the former; he was impatient with slow processes and wanted the people to realize sooner the happiness he thought they could have if they were all truly communists in their thinking. As a result, religious believers, along with intellectuals (of any and all sorts) and conservative Party members, became major targets in the campaigns of the Cultural Revolution.

The first rumbles of the Cultural Revolution were heard in late 1965 when criticism of a play was published. The play itself obliquely condemned Mao for dismissing Peng Dehuai as head of the Army in 1959. At the same time, Lin Biao was working with new political directives in the Army, and Mao was apparently stirring up the students at Beijing University to protest against the University's Chancellor. In May 1966, this stirring erupted into demonstrations at Beijing University, and Mao threw his weight behind the protestors by ordering the publication of "big character posters," a kind of wall poster that was the major way to express public criticism. Unrest spread to other universities and high schools, and youth all around the country began forming Red Guard units. Mao stayed in the background until August, when he put up his own poster attacking "capitalist-roaders" and appeared at a mass rally of a million Red Guards in Beijing's central Tiananmen square. He appeared dramatically on a balcony just as the sun was setting and donned a red arm band, the symbol of the Red Guards, to indicate his approval of their activities.

For the next half-year Red Guard activities dominated China. Mao gave them the mandate to "carry out and finish the Cultural Revolution, and oppose the capitalist-roaders who are the ruling power." Young groups of students first attacked their teachers but soon looked for other elements in the society. They moved systematically through neighborhoods, searching for anyone who represented the "four olds" — old thoughts, old ideas, old habits, and old customs. Under that broad mandate, they felt free to oppose almost anything they wished. They destroyed books, fine art, and anything else they felt belonged to the old culture. They attacked with words and fists anyone who appeared to think thoughts other than those thought by the Great Helmsman, as Mao was known in those days. The movement was active in schools, in the Army, and in factories. Red Guards were given free train travel so they could travel around the country, making revolution and learning from the peasants.

As factories and schools closed, the chaos of the mass action provoked by Mao began to make its effects known. Revolutionary groups began fighting with each other and with party cardres for power. One group of rebels in Shanghai declared the municipal government unauthoritative and began to set up a commune for the city of Shanghai. They took over the factories and began production again. Near the end of January, 1967, however, Mao became alarmed at this turn of events, and declared that the Shanghai commune was inappropriate. Instead he called for "Revolutionary Committees" made up of Army, veteran Party members, and Red Guard groups. In these committees, the Army and Party were clearly dominant.

However, the forces unleashed were not so easily brought back under control. After a relatively quiet February, mass demonstrations began again in March and continued through the summer. Mao called on the Army to "support the left," but it was not clear who "the left" were, and local commanders could not be relied on to carry out Mao's orders. In July, the commander of the forces in Wuhan actually staged an armed rebellion that took two weeks for other military units to put down. The hot summer of 1967 climaxed with the burning of the British Embassy in August.

In late 1967 and 1968, Mao called repeatedly for Revolutionary Committees and also urged that Red Guards be sent down to the countryside for labor. This removed them from the feverish activities of the urban centers and broke up the factions that had developed. "Going down to the countryside" was a new kind of experience for most Red Guards. For the first time they experienced the poverty of the countryside and the difficulty of labor. They also saw in part how much damage and harm they had done with their childish revolution. Finally, they saw it as a slap in the face from Mao, who told them that they were much too immature to govern anything. There was still sporadic violence — bloody riots took place in the south in mid-1968 — but the mass activity of 1966 and 1967 wound down.

This phase of the Cultural Revolution ended when the Party convened the Ninth Party Congress in April 1969. Much of the rhetoric of the Cultural Revolution remained. The Congress called for a "Flying Leap" forward, similar to the Great Leap Forward a decade earlier, but it also called for activist and reformed cadres to work together. No longer was the authority of the Party to be flouted. Reconstruction of the shambles of Party organization began, a process that in some respects is only being completed now.

There are many terms, movements, and countermovements peculiar to the time of the Cultural Revolution. We shall try to explain them as they appear in the following interviews.

2.1 Cultural Revolution in Amoy and Beijing

This completes the story of Dr. Tan which began in 1.3.
During the Cultural Revolution (1966-1969) Dr. Tan was in Beijing together with his immediate family. However, he learned about the fate of the Christians in Amoy from those who went through the ordeal. During the early phase of the Cultural Revolution, all church windows were smashed, the pews burned, and the crosses taken down. Every pastor had to "walk the street," [Wearing a placard around the neck detailing one or more "crimes," and often wearing a tall hat similar to a dunce's cap, people were paraded as a means of revealing their offences against the Revolution]. Many Christians were humiliated, and one woman was beaten to death. Communist cadres and Red Guards searched every house for Bibles, hymnals, and other Christian literature. They gathered over twenty YMCA and YWCA secretaries and forced them to kneel in front of a pile of burning Bibles, surrounded by the watching crowd. A large crowd stood around the great spectacle. As the flames intensified and radiated their heat towards them, they cried out because of the excruciating pain. It was a pitiful sight. Tormented by their extensive burns, most of them, including the general secretary of the YMCA, committed suicide by jumping from high buildings. These were the same progressive secretaries and pastors who had supported government policies in the 1950s and who praised the Party for having attained what Christianity had failed to do in a hundred years. Strangely enough, a few of the older faithful pastors who were "struggled against" previously were exempt from the torture, and the younger men of faith survived the ordeal. After the Cultural Revolution there were no more open church meetings.

In Beijing the Red Guards humiliated and searched the houses of most of the intellectuals and scientists in the Academia Sinica. During the early winter days of 1967, when house searches began, Dr. Tan began to burn all of his documents in his home stove. When it came to Christian literature and Bibles, he burned them in the following order over a period of several days: first he burned his hymnals; then he burned all his English Bibles except the Old

Testament portion without the cover; and finally he burned all his Chinese Bibles except the New Testament portion. He figured that the Red Guards could not tell the difference between the English Bible and scientific journals anyway, and as for the Chinese New Testament, he was willing to bear the consequences if he were caught. In those days, some Christians were sent to labor camps for possession of Bibles. Other Christians hid their Bibles in mountain caves.

2.2. Cultural Revolution in the Country

This piece and the one that follows are testimonies shared with Brother Paul, an itinerant preacher in Eastern China, who then recounted them to us.

In one place, the brothers and sisters who took care of me told me that, when they met during the Cultural Revolution, the commune police chief and a women's group leader would come and chase them away so they couldn't meet. But they would only chase them away. Why didn't they arrest them? Because there was nothing incriminating in any of their backgrounds. They were all poor and lower-middle class peasants, so they couldn't be arrested. But their meetings were stopped.

Afterwards, these brothers and sisters prayed to God, "God you delight in people worshiping you. But these people prevent us from meeting and worshiping you. What should we do? How about keeping them from coming?" Their prayer was very naive, but God heard their prayer.

The legs of the woman officer became paralyzed, and she couldn't walk, so she couldn't come to disturb them. The police chief had a pig at home which suddenly died, and he couldn't find the reason. Then within a week another pig died. Now when rural people raise a pig, it is worth more than RMB$100 which is equivalent to several years' total cash savings. The death of two pigs meant a loss of over $300. Nobody dared reprove the chief for his actions against the Chritians because he was such a ruthless man. But God used the mouth of his wife to do this. She said to him, "Look what you have done. What does people's worshiping have to do with you? You are ignoring your own affairs, and always interfering with others. Look at this. Two pigs have died. You really did it well!'

The chief couldn't say a thing. From then on he never came again.

2.3 Building for God

At another place, I was warmly welcomed at the home of a Christian couple who told me their testimony. They said, "Brother Paul, we built this house ourselves out of earth carried basket by basket.

During the Cultural Revolution, they said, the husband was "struggled against" and sentenced to six years' imprisonment.

The wife added, "Then people laughed at me and said: 'Well, what's the use of your believing in Jesus? Your husband was arrested and now you are left with four children and an old mother-in-law, six people! How can you feed them all?'"

But she ignored them and began to carry earth, basket by basket, to build her house. She said, "Brother Paul, I built this house by carrying the earth for it. but they continued struggling against me. They made me go to six communes to 'walk the streets', and then mocked me, saying, "After this, who would dare marry your children? Nobody wants you!'"

Then she said, "Brother Paul, this is my first daughter-in-law. This is my second daughter-in-law. My youngest daughter-in-law is not here at the moment. These are my grandsons and granddaughters. Nobody wanted me, but God had prepared things for me. Not even one member of my family died. Not only have my sons gotten wives, but I even have grandsons and granddaughters. All this is by the grace of God."

She continued by saying that three of the cadres who had struggled against her had not only cursed her but also God: "One of them said, 'Is there a God? If you have a God, why don't you tell him to make me mad?' Later I was told that someone whose hair was very long was that man. He has been insane for many years now, so deranged that he doesn't know anything."

Another cadre who cursed God later had an ulcer on his mouth and died. The tongue of another cadre hung out of his mouth down to his chest. He went to various big hospitals in Hangzhou, but the doctors told him, "This sickness is incurable. We have never seen such a problem before." It was really painful for him. He couldn't eat or speak.

"Later, somebody told him, 'You have cursed God. You had better beg Mrs. Zhou to pray for you. If she doesn't pray for you, I'm afraid you will die.' He didn't dare come himself, but he asked his wife to come to me and ask me to pray."

So this sister asked her, "Is he really willing to repent?"

"Then if he is willing to repent, tell him to come here."

So the cadre came to her house and the sister preached the Gospel to him. When she finished, she asked him, "How about it? Do you want to repent? Are you willing to accept the Lord Jesus?" He then nodded his head. So she prayed for him. While she was praying, his tongue contracted back into his mouth.

News of this incident spread far and wide. There was no need to preach the Gospel there. While I was there, those people all came and wanted to listen to the word of the Lord. Thank the Lord that this was the Lord himself coming to save and to work. Although their house was big, it was filled with people who had come of their own accord when they heard that someone from Shanghai [i.e., Brother Paul] was there. They hurried to come, and were thirsty for the Way of the Lord. They wanted to understand the saving grace of the Lord and what the Way of the Lord Jesus is. All this was God's own work.

2.4 Two Faithful Sisters

This longer piece gives a vivid picture of the suffering Christians underwent during this period. These two women were living in Southeast China at the time.

In going through great changes, each family has different experiences. Many people have good testimonies. Rev. Li Changxin's [pseudonym] two sisters are notable, especially his second sister, who is now over 60 years old. She has gone through a long imprisonment, but externally doesn't show the blows she has suffered, and she is full of happiness. My family was close to her, and her oldest sister was one of my teachers. Because of this, we had a close relationship with them and understood their situation rather well. Her husband also has a good testimony.

When the two sisters were young, they weren't believers, and their lives were not too upright. But after they were saved they changed completely. For more than forty years they have followed the Lord and done His work. They encourage those who received the Gospel, as well as brothers and sisters in the Lord, to lead pure lives. They are filled with love.

The second sister taught at the Ying Wa High School in Amoy where her husband was the principal. Both were highly respected by the students. In 1948, they left Amoy and went to a mountain area of interior Fujian Province to preach and establish a school. The people there had pitiful living conditions, yet they weren't put off by this. Afterwards they were invited to direct a school in the Philippines. Their passports were all arranged, but they were forced to stay behind in the mainland.

After Liberation, all church schools were turned over to the government. Principals and pastors went through criticism. In order to influence them, in 1951 there was a period of "persuasion." During this time the daughter of this couple rose up and accused her father and mother of making a profit from the school, of lulling the students into obedience, and carrying out teachings of enslavement, etc. Afterwards they were criticized and arrested. After a year, they were freed, but now had no liberty in their activities. The husband worked on the staff of a labor-reform camp.

Later, in 1958 or 1959 they were arrested a second time mainly for "preaching the Gospel." It was called a "crime" because the Gospel includes references to "the judgment of all people," and in the government's view these represented reactionary teachings, vain perversity, and "the hope that imperialism would come again." Such political crimes are serious ones. After a time they were released.

In 1965 they were arrested again. At that time their son was dating an unbeliever. Since the parents didn't approve of this, their son and daughter-in-law accused them, and they were again arrested. The father had forseen that this might happen and had prepared himself for it. He had made arrangements for his youngest daughter and had put his own things in order, because he knew that this time he would have a five-year sentence. Afterwards, he gave this testimony [about his imprisonment]: "This was God's protection, which brought me safely through the Cultural Revolution. If I had been outside, I probably would have been beaten to death by the Red Guards."

Many of his former students and brothers and sisters in Christ were criticized during the Cultural Revolution, and some were beaten half to death. He himself was branded a "secret agent," and those outside were falsely labelled "lackeys." Confessions were extorted in the hope of collecting enough materials to make a final case, but they [his accusors] never attained this goal.

While he was in prison, he continued to preach the Gospel, most successfully to a leader of the All-pervading Unity sect of Taoism. That person had been sentenced to death and was soon to be executed. Two days before the execution, the brother preached the Gospel to him, and he was clearly saved.

Because he was so old, at that time over seventy, he was put in the prison kitchen to work. He had never done this kind of work before and didn't know how to do it right. So he prayed, and God gave him the ability to do it well.

While her husband was in jail, his wife [in her prison] sensed that he was about to be taken home by the Lord. When she realized this, she got up early, sang songs, and had a happy face. Others felt this was strange, saying, "Why is this old lady so happy?" Afterwards, the prison authorities informed her that her husband had died, and she could come to get his body. She went, singing all the way, and got her husband's body, still singing and laughing. The people who saw her thought she was crazy, or that she must have had a terrible relationship with her husband.

But she answered them, "When a hen gathers her newly hatched chicks, she certainly won't cry over the broken eggshells; she can only be happy for the chicks. Now my husband has left the shell of his body and has gone to the most beautiful place there is. Why shouldn't

I be happy?" The others silently acknowledged that she was right. Later some brothers from outside the prison came in to bury her husband's body since her own children were all afraid to go near.

After her own sentence was finished, she was released. The authorities told her son to go and get her, but he wasn't willing. The Public Security Bureau told him, "Don't be afraid. We have already investigated this case politically, and there are no major problems. And going there cannot give you any added burdens; during her imprisonment outsiders sent her 9,000 dollars, and it is all here." This money had been sent by her former students and brothers and sisters in Christ from foreign countries — the Philippines, Malaysia, America, and Canada — in both the East and West. It was obvious that this money would not have been collected by the government if there had not been some political problems about her final sentence!

After she left prison, she continued giving her testimony and preaching the Gospel. Brothers and sisters in many places who were both saddened and moved to undertake heavy burdens wrote to her and received much encouragement and uplifting. All felt she was filled with the strength of the Holy Spirit. It was truly the grace of God.

Her arrest and imprisonment were God's testing of her. She called her manacles a pair of God-given "golden bracelets." She had no resentment, and very seldom talked of the injuries she received while in prison but rather used happiness to overcome all her painful experiences. In fact she testified that, after going through this refining, life was more and more abundant! She is not alone in this testimony. There are many brothers and sisters in China like her. This attitude is the source of the strength of the Chinese Church.

Last year, one of her students was arrested. His crime was mainly that he had ten copies of *Streams in the Desert* [a collection of devotional readings by Lettie Cowman that is very popular among Chinese Christians]. She wrote a letter about this situation, and in it expressed loving concern for her brothers and sisters in the Lord.

This sister never stops working for the Lord, courageously preaching the Gospel. The Public Security Bureau has no way of stopping her. They sometimes ask her, "Why do so many foreigners send you money?" She answers, "Before, when I was a teacher, some of my students were poverty-stricken. So I took care of them as if they were my own children. Now the children are sending money to the parents — what's so strange about that?" Her life is an extraordinary testimony.

Then there is her oldest sister. The change in this person's life especially shows the grace of God. She also was a school principal, and was arrested at about the same time as her sister and brother-in-law. But because there were some political complications [her husband was accused at that time of having been a regional member of the Nationalist Party], she was arrested as an anti-revolutionary and was made to wear a "hat." [Her being anti-revolutionary would bar her from many social activities.]

Her husband had been the principal of a primary and secondary school. Because he flattered the Communists, he was allowed to take off his "anti-revolutionary hat." But because her class background was not acceptable, she had to study the *Works of Mao* every morning when she got up, and report to the Public Security Bureau at certain times to take part in a political thought re-education group. They would always give her trouble.

Today her husband is over eighty years old, but he has changed. Every day now at a certain time he copies Christian books, especially *Streams in the Desert* and *Word of Peace*. He then gives these copies to other people. Because of this, the Public Security Bureau gave him some trouble, but, by the grace of God, they returned to their offices without arresting him. He continues to work for the Lord, helped by his wife since she retired.

Before he changed, he used to report to the Public Security Bureau the things that people who visited him said. This made the brothers and sisters afraid to visit him. Now, however, it is different. After repenting, he sought fellowship with the brothers and sisters received encouragement from them, and now testifies for the Lord. Their oldest daughter originally gave offerings to the church and preached, but later she turned away from her faith and backslid quite far. During the blows of the Cultural Revolution, she went through a lot of suffering because she had done interpreting for two foreign teachers and had participated in the "Little Flock" movement, which became labelled an "anti-revolutionary" group. So she was investigated, made to boil water for the whole school, and beaten.

Their second daughter was a doctor in a rural village. She cured people of their diseases and preached the Gospel to them at the same time. She has a fine testimony. She copied *Streams in the Desert* three times and gave the copies to others to encourage them in their faith. When I left, she was copying it for the fourth time, from a pre-1950 edition.

Pastor Li came from a large family of five girls and five boys. A third sister is still in Amoy. God also worked in her, producing a great change so that she is able to help many people now. Although she was an invalid because of her heart, she never neglected to testify to her visitors and have fellowship with them. In recent years her health has much improved with no serious setback.

2.5 Fujian, 1966-1969

Continuing the description of the church in Fujian, from 1.5.

Things were bad enough, before 1966, but then things got worse and all church institutions were closed. Church buildings were converted into warehouses, factories, or movie theaters. In Gulangyu, in the Amoy City area, one church which had survived after 1958 was also closed down. It was turned into the conference center for that district, since it was a big, strong building.

During that time, the Christian brothers and sisters met secretly for fellowship. Some of them were able to meet in a semi-open way, in family gatherings or private home visits. Sometimes in Gulangyu, meetings were held with as many as twenty or thirty Christians. But these had to be pre-planned. Ways of escaping were thought out ahead of time, in case of an emergency.

Excuses for holding house meetings included social occasions such as weddings and funerals, thereby avoiding attracting undue attention. For example, when the mother of one Christian sister died, visitors came for two or three days afterwards. While there, they would pray, have fellowship, and give thanksgiving to the Lord. But in

In this way, the "churches" became very family oriented, because this was the way that meeting and sharing was most convenient in those days.

Besides the suppression of public worship during the Cultural Revolution, there was also widespread suffering. One sister, a teacher, went through years of deprivation. After her husband died during the Cultural Revolution, she was dismissed by her school. But she had four children to support. In a letter which I recently received from her, she said that she has now been able to resume her job. Her four children are now grown, and two of them have done well in their higher exams.

Q: What is the general situation in Fujian now?

A;   Let me give you an example. A truck driver accepted Jesus in Amoy after hearing the witness of a Christian brother there. When the truck driver went back to his home in Xinmin, he told his whole family and brought them to the Lord. So the Gospel is spreading in ways like this.

Some Christians there believe that the number of full-time and part-time preachers in Fujian now is probably more than the number of pastors that were there before 1949.

2.6 Faith of My Father

A young man who swam to Hong Kong describes life "back home," during the Cultural Revolution.

Q: Does your family have a Bible, and do your parents read the Bible?

A: No, we didn't have any Bible at the time I left home. But recently, when one of my uncles living in Hong Kong went to Canton, he took a couple of Bibles with him, and gave them to my father who went down to meet him there.

Q: Did they have a Bible before the Cultural Revolution?

A: Yes, they did, but it was discovered by the Red Guards. Others had burned their Bibles long before the Cultural Revolution, but my father was not willing to part with his. So he hid it, but it was discovered. Because of that, he was imprisoned for nine months.

Q: Was he "struggled against?"

A: Yes, he was taken to the public square, made to wear a "high hat," and tried at a public "struggle meeting." He used to be a high school teacher in our village, and was highly respected. Everybody knew him. But during the Cultural Revolution he was publicly humiliated because he possessed "poisonous literature," the Bible. For many days he was tied to a pole every day in the open street, wearing this high hat, and everyone could spit on him. In the evening he was allowed to return home to sleep.

Q: How did he respond to such humiliation ?

A: He became very depressed. He felt that he was stripped of his dignity as a teacher and as a man. He felt that he could not face his students any more. After repeated humiliations, he became very depressed. During his nine months of imprisonment, he was frequently taken out to be struggled against. Finally, he felt that he could not go on living, and wanted to commit suicide. My mother realized this, and told my sister to watch him closely. One time my sister found a pack of poisonous pills and asked father what they were. Moved by her inquisitive eyes and lovely character, he refrained from taking his life. Another time he was going to take poison and then jump into a river, but he was caught by my uncle, who persuaded him to remember grandfather's charge to take care of his younger brothers and to think of his own children.

Q: How many uncles do you have?

A: I have nine uncles. They were all younger than my father, who really brought them up on behalf of my grandfather. I still remember how during the early days of the Cultural Revolution, my sister and I used to carry food to father and my nine uncles in prison. Twice a day we did that. It was an hour's walk each way, and it was a lot of food that we had to carry. I was only nine at that time.

Q: Why were all your uncles in prison? Were they all Christians too?

A: No, they were imprisoned because our family used to be a landlord family. All my uncles were baptized, but only my parents and two of my uncles were born-again Christians. Because of our former landlord status, none of us children were allowed to go to school. That is why to this day I have never studied in any school.

Q: How did you learn to read and write?

A: My father taught me at home. After he was released from prison, he was no longer allowed to teach; he had to farm. But after a long day's work, he would still try to teach me how to read and write.

Q: How is your father now?

A: He has recently been rehabilitated. The government recalled him to teach in our village primary school. They said that what the Gang of Four had done during the Cultural Revolution was wrong, that intellectuals today must be rehabilitated to use their ability for the good of society.

Q: Does this mean that in spite of the fact he is a Christian and was labelled a landlord, he is now allowed to teach?

A: Yes, my father said that today one can openly declare his Christian faith. It is no longer a crime to be a Christian.

2.7 "To live is Christ"

Some more episodes from the Cultural Revolution in the country-side.

There was a brother who was a school teacher. During the Cultural Revolution, his school struggled against him. There were two cadres, one of whom hung him up, while the other tied his bicycle around his neck. After those cadres did this, they made him sweep the floor.

But then he told me, "God cannot be violated." During the Four Clean-ups period [1970], the one who had hung him up committed suicide by hanging himself. The one who had hung the bicycle on him killed himself by jumping into a lake. Why? They had committed all four crimes that were being "cleaned up" and were afraid, so they committed suicide.

One place where I went there was a sister who was struggled against during the Cultural Revolution. This made her feel depressed, so she said to herself, "I am a good Christian and have never done anything wrong. You struggle against me but not against those who have done bad things." Yet she remained despondent and prayed to

God, "Lord, protect me."

At that time, several cadres asked her "Do you still believe in Jesus?"

She answered, "Yes, I do." Since she still believed, they continued to struggle against her.

They made a board for her and a tall hat for her to wear. They gave her a gong and told her to walk and beat the gong. On the hat they had written four characters: "God blesses." At the time, she was thinking in her heart, "God, why don't you bless me?" But when she put on the hat and saw the characters, he said, "Oh, 'God blesses!' What do I have to fear?"

So she put on the tall hat, beat the gong, walked down the street, and truly thanked the Lord. Afterwards, all the people in the area where she walked knew that she believed in Jesus. So later, all who believed in Jesus came to her house looking for her. Thus, when the brothers and sisters were struggled against, it was really an opportunity given to them by God to give a testimony to bring about the repentance of many and lead them to a belief in God.

One place where I went I met two Christians who were older and younger sisters. Someone told me, "Brother Paul, the older one was invited to join a Yue opera troupe. They said, 'You have a very pretty face. Doing Yue opera is very good. Will you come and join our opera?'

"The older sister shook her head and said, 'I would rather stay in the village my whole life. I won't come join your Yue opera troupe.' They said, 'But being in the opera troupe is very good. It's very enjoyable. You can travel everywhere.' She said, 'I would rather spend my whole life in my village. I don't want to join the opera troupe.'"

What about the little sister? When work places were being assigned by her school, she was told, "If you believe in Jesus, we will send you to a rural village. But if you drop Jesus and stop this belief, we will send you to a factory or a mine. It's up to you; choose for yourself."

But the little sister said, "I would rather have Jesus, so I would rather go to a rural village. Not going to a factory or a mine doesn't matter."

How old do you think they were? One was 18, and the other 16. Yet even at this young age, they loved the Lord so much that they would go to the worst place and endure the worst kind of suffering. They were not interested in enjoying the pleasure of this world.

When I was in Dongchun, there was an older brother who had been struggled against during the Cultural Revolution. He was arrested and the people questioned him about many things, but he remained silent. Finally they asked him, "Do you still believe in Jesus?"

He answered, "The Lord Jesus died for me. I live for the Lord Jesus."

The people got angry and hit him and struggled against him. But he remained silent. He neither wept nor cried out. The people again asked him, "Do you still believe now?"

He answered, "The Lord Jesus died for me. I live for the Lord Jesus." He only said these few words. They decided that there was nothing they could do.

After I heard this, I felt that this old brother was truly fine. These people love the Lord so much that they suffer much pain without faltering. Like Peter, they followed the Lord very closely, and the Lord loves them very much.

While one sister was in her village during the Cultural Revolution, the village cadres obtained the name list of the known Christians in the village. At a mass meeting, they made all those on the list stand up and carry placards around their necks. As each name was read, that person stood up and the placard was hung on him or her. Almost all the brothers and sisters stood up. When the last name was read, they were told to start walking.

But then this sister stood up and said, "Wait a minute! What about me? Why did you forget me?"

The cadres were surprised and said, "Alright, you wear a placard too and come with us!"

The main brother there said to me, "Brother Paul, she could have avoided the suffering of walking the streets with us, but she was willing to take up the cross and follow the Lord. You younger brothers and sisters, think about how much she loved the Lord and regarded suffering as joy. Thank the Lord, the grace of the Lord was leading her."

When I was there, this sister always sat in the front. Everywhere I went, she followed. She also contacted younger brothers and sisters to sing hymns together and memorize scripture. I don't know who gave her a Bible, but she loved it. She was not educated, but she jotted down all the important points in the sermons. She was thirsty for the Lord, loved the Lord. Their having suffered for the Lord never became a point of pride for them.

2.8 Song of Remembrance, by Yu Yang

Soon after the founding of the People's Republic of China, the government initiated programs to take control of religion. With the "Christian Manifesto" in 1950, and with the preparations for the Three-Self Patriotic Movement begun publicly in 1951, the government sought to break any loyalties to organizations outside of China and to establish new loyalties to itself. Churches were required to break off contacts with foreign missionaries and to purge their own ranks of leaders who were too sympathetic to foreigners or who had shown so-called bourgeois tendencies in their leadership style or preaching.

A group of young people, particularly those that moved in student groups such as Intervarsity Fellowship, saw these actions as a threat. They thought that life for the Christian in the cities, where most of them had grown up, would become increasingly restricted. There would be limited opportunities for preaching the Gospel. However, they were committed to lives of service and ministry. Gradually, under the leading of the Lord in their hearts, they came to the common conviction that they should move to rural areas in the western part of China, where the Gospel was still largely unknown. They formed themselves into a group called "The Northwest Spiritual Workers' League." Then these committed young men, most of them in their early twenties, moved out to the provinces of Xinjiang, Guizhou, Sichuan, and Yunnan for a lifetime commitment. For many, that lifetime was shorter than they expected.

For several years these young evangelists enjoyed relative peace. As the churches were being controlled and re-organized in the cities and in the populous areas in the east, they worked, planting churches and spreading the Gospel in the west. In 1957, however, anti-Christian action in the "Anti-Rightist" campaign affected this group. Their work was hampered; some were arrested, some restricted in movement. In this campaign and in the "Great Leap Forward" of 1958, young men like themselves were assigned to do "productive" work in factories or in the fields. Like pastors in the east, they were no longer allowed to do "unproductive" church work. Those who were not jailed in the late fifties were subject to further persecution in the Cultural Revolution beginning in 1966. They were struggled against, and some died in the mob violence that accompanied such struggle sessions. Others died amidst the harsh conditions of the labor camps.

The remnant of the original Northwest Spiritual Workers' League accepted this as part of the cost of discipleship. They remained faithful and bore witness to God's lovingkindness in the face of persecution. Some managed to survive through it all. The author of the free verse poem that we present here is one of the survivors. He calls himself Yu Yang, "the remnant sheep." Of his group of about ten that went together to a western province, four survived.

In the new political climate after the death of Mao and the arrest of the Gang of Four in 1976, Yu Yang was moved to commemorate a fallen brother. This poem is addressed to one of them, but in fact it is a eulogy for all. It is a testimony and tribute to the sacrificial work of a whole generation who were given a vision and acted upon it. In 1980 it was shared with a traveler from Hong Kong and permission was given to publish it for the edification of Christians outside of China.

Why does your anger smolder against the sheep of your pasture?
Remember the people you purchased of old,
the tribe you redeemed as your inheritance-
Mount Zion, where you dwelt.
Pick your way through these everlasting ruins,

all this destruction the enemy has brought on the sanctuary.
Your foes roared in the place where you met with us;
they set up their standards as signs.
They behaved like men wielding axes
to cut through a thicket of trees.
They smashed all the carved paneling
with their axes and hatchets.
They burned your sanctuary to the ground;
they defiled the dwelling place of your Name.
They said in their hearts, "We will crush them completely!"
They burned every place where God was worshiped in the land.
We are given no miraculous signs;
no prophets are left, and none of us knows how long this will be.
How long will the enemy mock you, O God?
Will the foe revile your name forever?
Why do you hold back your hand, your right hand?
Take it from the folds of your garment and destroy them!
(Psalm 74:1-11)

Brother, you have been gone for years.
Nevertheless,
In our hearts you are forever around us.

Like a branch of beautiful, fresh plum,
you scattered wafts of heavenly fragrance
in the midst of a severe winter,
where every creature has fallen
and all grass has withered.
In the depth of a spacious, lonesome, solitary, and dark night,
you radiated a beam of the Truth,
like a bright morning star.

Although it is years since you left us,
we still remember and reflect on you constantly.
We will never forget those difficult and distressing years.
The image of your brilliance and determination

is engraved on our hearts forever and ever.

It was the age of Mao and the Gang of Four,
where black and white became interchangeable,
and right and wrong became mixed up.
It was the days when the sun was concealed by the dark clouds,
the sky was gloomy, and the earth was dark.
Light was dark,
and dark was light.

In that time,
cudgel and knife, coming like destructive, strong gales
attacked the Church's light.
In that time,
crafty, dark night spread out its nets,
trapping the believers tightly.

In no time at all,
from the plain to the highland,
from the coast to the borderland,
no church was found that still worshiped Jesus Christ.
In no time at all,
from the city to the countryside,
from the level land to the mountain village,
the sign of salvation — the brilliant symbol of the cross —
could not be seen.

The altar was gone;
the sanctuary was closed;
the gospel of Truth was blocked.
Shepherds great and small were arrested and killed,
imprisoned and exiled.
Their sheep, by thousands, underwent persecution,
surveillance, and forced labor.

Oh, magnificent and democratic China,

with freedom of religion!
But the Church of the Lord was cold and cheerless.
Everywhere bleakness and desolation met the eye.

Brother,
you walked across the familiar street
to stare at the beloved church,
to look with grief and sorrow
at the place where you received salvation.

There,
you tasted the joy and peace of sin being forgiven;
the burden of your transgression was removed by Him.
There,
you received the enrichment and caress of love,
you were led back to the sheepfold by Him
and ended your drifting and wandering.
There,
you were baptised into the name of Jesus Christ
and received eternal life and the hope of glory.
There,
you brought a holy and excellent sacrifice
to offer before the Lord's altar,
with a heart constantly filled with devotion and thanksgiving.
There,
all of us bowed down to worship with sincere hearts
and with joyful voices offered our thanksgiving,
praise and songs to Him — our merciful savior Jesus.

But now,
your beloved church,
the place you desired day and night,
is only a courtyard as before.
The people are gone.
What was left for you was tears,
a broken heart, and great sorrow.

Brother,
you knelt and silently bowed,
poured out your heartfelt tears before the Lord.
Oh, Lord!
Why?
Why was Your name abused, blasphemed, and cursed?
Why?
Why were Your children for no reason intimidated and threatened?
Why?
Why were Your disciples everywhere sneered at and injured?
Why?
Why were Your servants,
law-abiding and devoted to others,
beaten and tortured?
Why?
Why were Your apostles,
broadcasting the Truth and saving others' souls,
persecuted and killed?
Oh, Lord!
Why?
Why did these things happen? What was this for?

The world could not tolerate Christ;
wickedness sent righteousness to the execution ground;
deceit looked with enmity at the truth;
darkness engulfed and crushed the light;

At that moment,
you suddenly awakened.
Indeed,
"The servant could not be greater than the master,
and the disciple could not be higher than the teacher.
Since they rejected Me,
would they leave you in peace?"

"Blessed are those who have been persecuted

for righteousness sake.
Blessed are you when men revile you, persecute you,
and say all manner of evil against you falsely
for My sake."

In order to enter the holy, glorious, and eternal kingdom,
one has to go through blazing fire,
fierce flames, frightening waves, and terrifying billows.
Then,
you stopped your tears of pain,
bound up the wound in your heart,
looked up to Jesus who hung on the cross.
Facing your brilliant home in Jerusalem,
you continued on this tortuous road.

Brother,
you picked up the lost war robe of God's servants
and lifted up their laid-down rod.
You learned to serve the delicate, newborn lambs,
whose shepherds were beaten and exiled.
You looked after the tender sprouts
in the midst of frost and snow,
for they needed to be watered and nourished.
You helped those grieving and weeping sisters
and brought them heavenly comfort and strength.
You were concerned with those frightened and wandering brothers
and encouraged them to guard the Truth firmly
and to find strength in the Lord.
You sympathized with those destroyed families
and relied on God's grace to bring fruit from your labor.
You provided them with their needs
and supported them with food and money.
You were concerned with those widows left behind;
with the loving and devoted heart of Christ
you relieved them of their poverty and wrapped up their wounds.

You stirred up the fire of love in the hearts of the sisters.
In the cruel winter's swirling snows,
they learned to care for each other,
embrace one another, and, as one body, to keep a faithful watch.
You strengthened the Christian faith of the brothers.
In midnight's gloomy darkness,
they learned to hold fast to the Truth,
persist to the end, and, as one body, to sing songs in gratitude.

Oh, dear brother!
It was you who followed the steps of our good Shepherd
and bravely protected the sheep of God.
It was you who willingly poured out the alabaster jar
to express your true love to the Lord, Jesus Christ.

Who knows!
Judas' disciples whispered reports;
Galilean descendants secretly followed you.
They said that your visits to brothers and sisters
were illegal activities,
that giving attention to suffering people
was inciting the masses to oppose the Party.
They said that your preaching of the Bible
was spreading feudal superstition to poison people,
that spreading the Gospel of Christ
was using religion as a cover for anti-revolutionary activities.
You did not expect those who feasted with you
to kick you,
nor those who kissed you
to betray you for a price.

Suddenly,
there they came!
They came riding fearlessly on the constitution.
They came like a beast,
trampling on the white snow, leaving their black footprints;

like a cruel wolf killing the sheep with one blow.
Then, our dear brother,
you were handcuffed and thrown into a dark jail.

Trials,
one after another,
failed to prove that you violated any law of the country.
Tortures,
day after day,
to try to make you revolt against Christ,
betray your brothers,
and forsake your belief.
Struggles,
one round after another,
to destroy your reputation, dishonor your person,
and distort your honest, upright, and innocent image.
They used all kinds of inhuman torture
to force you to admit
that proper religious life —
Bible study, prayers, and fellowship —
were against communism and opposed the Party.

Your honest and frank answers
were interpreted as stubborn and rebellious.
Your endurance of suffering
and resistance to pressure
brought forth more insult, affliction, and flogging.
Your silence provoked more oppression and injury,
branded upon your spirit and body
layer after layer of bloodstains and scars.

Oh, brother!
When did you ever fail to treasure freedom and a peaceful life?
But you treasured more
the belief that granted light to your life.
When did your fleshly body not fear

the merciless binding and caning?
But you feared more the blame from your conscience
and the ruin of your morality.
Thus,
you chose to suffer
and not yield to sin.

You refused to betray Christ
in exchange for "merciful forgiveness" and an ignoble release.
You earnestly prayed to the Lord, saying,
"Oh, Lord!
Let me not disgrace Your name,
and grant me the faith and strength
to overcome this suffering with head held high.
Oh, Lord!
Grant me this glorious blessing;
let me drink with You the bitter cup of the cross,
for the sake of Your holy name and the Truth."

How could a typhoon blow away the moon,
darkness block out a star,
or knives cut a stream of water ?
Calamity of calamities,
you could not snap away Christ —
the sun of love in my heart.

Staring at the shining stars and moon,
how you longed to meet your mother
who taught you uprightness,
to tell her,
"Mother, take care of yourself.
I have not turned my back on your nurture and hopes for me."
How you longed for a glimpse of the one
who was of one heart and mind with you,
your warm and gentle wife,
to tell her,
"Be strong!

No one can isolate us from the love of Christ."
How you longed to kiss your children,
who were innocent and knew no evil,
to tell them,
"Your Daddy is innocent.
Your Heavenly Father will protect you
and grant you peace and health."

But,
cruel reality ebbed away your most basic human right — life.
You lifted up your eyes to heaven,
then bowed down your head to pray silently
and presented to Jesus your deepest wish,
"Oh, Lord!
Remember Your gracious covenant,
rescue the remnant of Your people,
and revive the long-deserted churches.
Oh, Lord!
Please accept Your redeemed soul.
Grant me peace,
the everlasting peace within You."

Torrential rain,
Chilly wind,
Misty mountains,
Plaintive streams.
Dear Brother,
You,
who have done nothing to injure the fatherland
or its people
or any living creature,
were snatched from the world.
You,
who left your earthly home with grief and suffering,
departed from streams that listened attentively to you,
departed from mountain peaks that bore witness to you,

departed from your brothers and sisters in hardship,
departed from your wife, children, and mother,
who remember you;
You,
who laid down the suffering of this life
to climb "Mt. Moriah" with conviction,
to fly to your true home,
where sorrow and tears are no more.

Brother,
you are gone!
And gone forever!
Although you endured injustice and insult,
you have become the sheep on the right hand of Christ.
The righteous God will wipe away your tears,
and the risen Lord will grant you a precious, everlasting reward.

Brother,
you are gone!
And gone peacefully!
Your respect to our Father,
your attachment to the Truth,
was like a flag of victory,
encouraging us to march forward for the sake of the Gospel.

Brother,
You are gone!
And gone bravely!
For the churches of China,
for the spreading of the Truth,
you were like a seed that contained life,
dropped in the ground for the sake of Christ
and buried because of the Truth.

Dear Brother,
rest peacefully!
Your elderly, white-haired mother

is constantly being visited
and served by the brothers and sisters.
The orphans and widows are living peacefully
and in good health under the care of God.

Dear Brother,
rest peacefully!
We preserved the faith from the beginning
and have not gone with the current.
On this road to eternity,
we obeyed Jesus our Lord's teaching
to be prudent but blameless,
to be alert and keep watch for the revival of the churches.

Dear Brother,
rest peacefully!
We have endured the severe winter.
When our mighty God lifts up His own Church,
we shall surely be there to welcome it,
to welcome the beautiful spring light.

Dear Brother,
rest peacefully!
When that day the spring breeze of the Gospel
blows the earth green again,
and when the righteous sun shines brightly on China,
may you and we, in heaven above and on earth below,
play music on the harp,
beat the drum and merrily dance!

Give thanks!
Praise!
Sing!
Sing that God's lovingkindness lasts forever!
Sing that God's grace passes on to all generations!
Sing that Christ's dignity extends eternally!
Sing that God's holy name shines perpetually!

III Confusion and Resolve
(1970-1978)

INTRODUCTION

The years 1970-78 were years of political struggle in the aftermath of the Cultural Revolution. Although there were campaigns in these years, no startling new initiatives were taken. The old guard of the Party worked to reassert its control, while the leftist [or even ultra-leftist] elements, who were a minority, pushed to regain the momentum of the Cultural Revolution in which they had wielded so much power. This struggle took the punch out of the social campaigns as the various sides used Party documents and the press to pull the campaigns in their direction.

The first victim of the struggle was Lin Biao, defense minister and heir designate to Mao. As moves arose to get Lin pushed out of his position, he apparently began plotting to get his men in key positions in every Army unit. Mao apparently got wind of this plot, and in September, 1971, it was reported that Lin Biao and some of his followers had died while enroute to the Soviet Union. For the next four years, Lin became the focus of the struggle between the two lines — those who continued to support policies of the Cultural Revolution and those who very carefully began to dismantle those policies. Deng Xiaoping was restored to public office and became the first Vice-Premier. From that position he advocated economic restoration and foreign contacts, and discouraged excessive attention to ideology as the key to all problems.

On the international front, China adopted the policy of talking with her enemies, even while trying to exploit their weaknesses. In 1971 China entered the United Nations, displacing Taiwan, and in

1972 invited President Nixon to visit.

At the grassroots level of society, there was some easing of tension in the early years of this period, but local cadres still dominated life. There were no fundamental changes in the way work was carried out, in the constant attempts to raise production by unrealistic demands and quotas, nor in policies governing social and religious life. No churches were open except for two in Beijing open for foreign diplomats, and religion in China was dead as far as the outside world could determine. Some of the youth who had been sent down to the countryside in the years 1967-69 were allowed to return to the cities in the early 1970's. There were a few classes opened in the universities, but the onus on intellectuals (or "stinking intellectuals," as they were commonly called) was still so great that teaching and research were severely cramped or were performed by people utterly unqualified for anything but parroting the latest Party line. By 1976 there was still only one-third the number of university students that there had been in 1965.

The only flurry of excitement came in 1974 when three young men put up a poster in Guangzhou [Canton]. This "big-character poster" was 100 meters long and amounted to a little book. It called for a "socialist legality," for democracy and law, so that the people would be spared the arbitrariness of political changes, especially those experienced in the Cultural Revolution. "We are the 'fearless youth,'" the young men cried. "Though gobbled up by that animal [the Cultural Revolution], we were spit out; it could not swallow us. But we did not go unscathed. Today we are not a pretty lot, all mangled with scars."

Then in 1976 both Zhou Enlai and Mao Zedong died. The two men who had been leading China almost continually since 1950 were gone. Both deaths touched off some major events. Zhou had somehow been seen as a protector of the youth. When he died in January, former Red Guards laid wreaths in Tiananmen square in Beijing for several months. Finally the police were ordered to remove them, and on April 5, 1976 a full-scale riot was touched off in Tiananmen square. Although exact figures are not known, several thousand died and many more were injured. The incident touched off demonstrations around the country. They protested the dictatorship of Mao and supported what they then thought was the more rational and free leadership of the "old guard."

When Mao died in September 1976, it took only one month for the "Gang of Four" to be arrested. These were four persons, including Mao's wife, who were prominent in the Cultural Revolution and who still struggled for power as a leftist faction within the Party. Hua Guofeng was named to replace Mao, but he was never able to muster a real base of support and proved in the end to have been an interim, caretaker chairman, while the various factions sorted out power relationships.

The years 1976-78 in this period were a time of growing freedom, not because of specific policy changes from the top, but rather because of the uncertainty at the top. With the figure of the "Great Helmsman" gone, people felt liberated, even though in fact local cadres could arrogate as much or as little power to themselves as they pleased. Many cadres, however, pursued more moderate policies by default. They did nothing to oppose slight increases in individual freedoms.

In these later years, a few Christians became more open about their activities. Although there was no public talk of religious freedom in China, these interviews show that many private meetings flourished in this time. Relatively fast growth was experienced in many areas.

The period ends just as Deng Xiaoping gains political prominence, a policy of the restoration of public church life is put forward, and the Democracy Wall Movement appears. The Democracy Wall Movement was the last mass movement to rise from the Cultural Revolution. Once again, youths were spontaneously agitating for greater freedom, for redress of the wrongs done in the Tiananmen incident, for greater democracy, and for a legal system. They were allowed to continue for a brief time, but then Deng Xiaoping ordered an end to "Autocracy Wall," and a new phase of clear leadership and direction from the top in Chinese society began.

3.1 Fujian after the Cultural Revolution

The report is given by a doctor, a fourth generation Christian, who left China in 1976.

As of late 1976 and early 1977, Christians in the South Fujian area continue to meet for worship and fellowship. They meet separately according to their former groupings or often simply as believers. The more commonly known groups are the Little Flock founded by Watchman Nee, the True Jesus Church, the Seventh Day Adventist Church, and believers who formerly belonged to the Church of Christ in China. They still hold doctrinal differences on issues such as the perseverance of the saints, doctrine of the soul, Sabbath observance, etc. But these doctrinal differences no longer alienate them as before. There is much mutual care among all believers.

Most worship services or prayer meetings are held in private homes, and meeting places change from week to week. The content of worship services does not differ too much from what it used to be, except that they are now less formal and are not held in church buildings. The number in attendance ranges from twenty to thirty, and varies from place to place. During the years 1974 and 1975, Christians in the Fuzhou area used to have 300-400 attending services openly. But this is no longer the case since government authorities cracked down on them.

A typical order of service would be as follows: prayer, hymn singing, Bible reading, sermon, prayer, and fellowship. As a rule only trusted friends and relatives are allowed to come to prayer meetings or worship services.

The content of sermons preached usually falls under three categories: affirming the existence and reality of God, proclaiming the basic salvation message, and reassurance of the Christian hope. There is a great spiritual hunger among the believers generally. One brother expressed it, "If I could only sing out loud once again the hymns I love so much and hear the Word of God preached, I would be satisfied to depart from this earth!"

The teaching ministry is continued by retired pastors in their seventies or eighties. There is no systematic training of younger ministers, but children of former pastors or elders and deacons from earlier days carry on preaching and pastoral ministry.

Bibles are still very scarce in Fujian. During the Cultural Revolution most Bibles were confiscated and burned by the Red Guards. Thus the lack of Bibles is a serious problem for Christians in China. Some believers use their meager income to buy paper and copy Bible portions or other Christian literature on mimeograph masters and print them for local use at a great risk to their lives.

Evangelism is conducted only among very close friends and trusted relatives; otherwise one may be betrayed. Christians also take the initiative to restore fellow believers who have fallen under difficult times or whose faith was weakened.

Every few months there are occasions for baptism. Usually a baptismal service is conducted in the countryside by a village or mountain stream. Some twenty to thirty candidates from several surrounding villages, especially youths, gather together for baptism. There is no formal baptismal training class, but the candidates are asked about the major articles of faith. "You can be sure," Dr. Qin emphasized, "that a considerable amount of time goes into the training of the new convert before he is allowed to be baptized. In China, for a person to accept baptism means that he is willing to die for Christ."

Dr. Qin was asked what he thinks of the future of Christians in Fujian. He replied, "The Church will continue as usual, whether openly or clandestinely. So long as there is God, there is going to be His Church."

Dr. Qin reminded us that Christian activites described above hold true primarily for Fujian and Zhejiang provinces; this is not true of places like Shanghai, Nanjing, Wuchang, Tianjin, or Beijing, where Christians are very isolated and often find themselves in difficult situations. In most major cities of South Fujian, such as Changzhou, Shima, Lengyan, Quanzhou, Shixi and Qinqing, Christians continue to meet. Likewise, in Northern Fujian, especially around the Fuzhou area, Christians are quite active.

In Qinqing Chrsitians are especially active because many of them are overseas Chinese from the Philippines. Likewise, Quanzhou has a large overseas Chinese community, and many of them are Christians. But in Wuping, which is a small town in southwest Fujian, a thriving Christian community has emerged as a result of the witness of Christian youths who were "sent down to the countryside" after the Cultural Revolution.

3.2 House Churches in Wenzhou, East China

The interviewee lived and worked in Wenzhou for 35 years. As an old man, he left China for Hong Kong in 1978.

Q: How long have you been a Christian?

A: I have been a Christian since my early twenties. However, after the Communist takeover, I stopped going to church, During the Cultural Revolution I was a backslider. I was a weak Christian for a long time.

Q: Did you experience spiritual renewal recently?

A: Yes, after I retired, I began to attend Christian meetings in Wenzhou, where I had lived all my life.

Q: How often did you attend those meetings?

A: At least once a week. In Wenzhou, if you want to attend house meetings for Bible study and fellowship, you can practically do it every day, that is, if you want to. There are many such informal groups in different parts of the city, some for older people like me, others for young people and still others for those in between.

Q: Who organizes these house meetings?

A: The people organize themselves. There are no leaders for any group. Christians simply take turns opening their homes for prayer meetings. The only arrangements are when and where. No one dares assume leadership, because the Communist cadres would arrest him as soon as they found out about him.

Q: How many people usually attend?

A: That differs from time to time. In our group it ranges anywhere from twenty to a hundred people. You would be surprised at how a small house can contain nearly a hundred people, though we enter and leave gradually, so as not to disturb our neighbors.

Q: What kind of program do you follow during your house

meetings?

A: Usually prayer and preaching, followed by a communion service and an offering. Occasionally, when the situation permits, we will sing hymns from Scripture or old hymns that we had memorized years before. Most groups do not collect offerings, though some do it once a month for the needy and for those engaged in the Lord's work.

Q: How much would such an offering come to each month?

A: About RMB ¥20 (US$10 in 1978).

Q: Who does the preaching?

A: Ordinary Christian brothers. We do have some who are engaged in full-time Christian service, but the number is very small. Those brothers who are mature in their faith and have deep understanding in the teachings of Scripture usually give the message. In a village south of Wenzhou there are some old pastors who are occasionally asked to come up to Wenzhou to preach to us.

Q: What kinds of churches did these old pastors formerly belong to?

A: Mostly independent churches; others were from the former China Inland Mission Church, the Seventh Day Adventist Church, the Assembly Hall (Watchman Nee group), and the Brethren.

Q: What are some of the typical sermon topics?

A: They are mostly sermons of an edifying nature, or on the grace of Jesus Christ; they are often taken from the Pauline epistles. At other times messages of salvation are preached. You see, we have many who used to be confessing Christians but who have fallen or backslidden like I had. Even some former pastors backslid, denying Christ on certain difficult occasions. The task of the stronger Christians is to restore them back to the grace of Jesus Christ and enable them to stand up again.

Q: Do you have enough Bibles for these Christians to read?

A: No, Bibles are seriously lacking. Many believers copy their own Bibles by hand. Others use mimeograph machines to produce portions of the Scripture for limited distribution.

Q: Are believers still holding their faith in secret?

A: Yes, we remain quite clandestine. Some of our neighbors know that we believe in Jesus, but most of them don't know much about our faith.

Q: How then do you communicate the Gospel to non-believers?

A: Many non-Christians believe in the Lord because they have experienced healing. When they are in a desperate situation, they often come to Christians for help. Through much prayer and concern, the Lord listens to our prayers and heals them miraculously. Some Communist Party members have come to believe in Christ because their wives have been healed or their relatives freed from demon disturbance. Once they believed in Christ, they would stop persecuting believers. So those who experience healing bear dynamic testimonies for Christ. Often there is just one such believer, but gradually the rest of his family come to know Christ.

Q: How are young people responding to the Gospel?

A: Many young people are coming to believe in Jesus. The young people organize their own meetings and retreats. They are more dynamic than we are. They are even more zealous than we are. They are very efficient in their organization, and they do things more daring than we would ever dream of.

Q: What daring things?

A: They hold retreats or conferences in far away high mountains. They do this twice a year. They have a way of communication regarding time and place of their retreats that not even their parents can discover. One family told me that their son disappeared after midnight through the window. Even the night before, everything appeared normal. A few days later the son would return home rejoicing and just say that he had a good time with a group of his friends. Just before I left Wenzhou, the young people had their semi-annual retreat.

Q: That means that even the young people had to conduct their Christian activites in secret.

A: Yes. If they were caught they would have to go through a long process of "education."

3.3 Earthquake and Revival

This 50 year-old sister's testimony of life in north China is based on a time when she was an unmarried woman doctor. She eventually left China in 1978.

I have hundreds of testimonies to share and thousands of things to thank God for. Of these I wish to share with you two miraculous events that impressed me deeply.

In 1966, I was sent by my work unit to a rural clinic in Hubei Province. Then on March 8th, very early in the morning, a severe earthquake woke me up. Immediately I realized that it was dangerous for me to stay in the shabby house; it could fall down at any moment. But I did not even have enough time to leave. Suddenly I felt God's Spirit working in me, and felt peace in my heart. So I knelt down and prayed, "My Lord, I give my soul to you." At nearly the same time the house caved in. I felt ashes fall on my head, but surprisingly I was not hit or injured. Then I found that the three walls of my house had completely fallen down, and that all the other four nurses in my room were injured.

The one sleeping beside me was hurt the most seriously. She had started sleeping in my place when I stayed overnight in another village to see a patient. When I returned, she told me that she was afraid of rats running around, and wanted to change her place with mine. I was not very happy at first, and said to myself, "You might be afraid of rats, but I am even more afraid of them." However, when I reminded myself that I was God's child, I did not argue with her. Then when she was injured in the earthquake, I felt that she had been wounded for me, and that it was God's special grace to me. This special experience strengthened my faith very much.

Ten years afterwards, there was another severe earthquake in the area of Tianjin, Beijing, and Tangshan. It was on the 28th of July, 1976. At that time I was in Tangshan itself, staying in an old, small Japanese-style house. Opposite my house was a patients' ward. That building was very unsafe, too. The walls had been badly cracked ever since the 1966 earthquake; from the inside you could see the sky through them. The earthquake came suddenly that night and it was a very serious one. The building opposite my house also remained as it was. All around us many other stronger buildings fell down completely. The patients in my hospital thought that there must be "spirits" dwelling in my small house. Some said to me humorously,

"God blessed you." I replied, "This is really what happened."

After the first earthquake shock many people were badly frightened because nobody could tell exactly when the aftershocks would occur. Meanwhile, the government advised all residents of the city to stay outside all buildings at night. The Public Health Unit advised our hospital to move all the patients into tents. Some of my colleagues wandered in the streets all night, and some sat together until daybreak. However, unlike them, I had peace in my heart. I prayed, and felt that I could stay safely in my house. So I remained in my room every night, singing hymns and reading the Bible.

A week later, there still had not been any major aftershocks and people returned to their buildings. Many of my colleagues were exhausted because of insufficient rest, while I gained weight in those days. Many of them admired the strong faith I held and became more interested in my belief in Jesus Christ.

For many years, Christians in northern China did not meet each other for fellowship and service. Recently, however, they have started to gather together for prayer and sharing. Among Christians, two questions have been discussed the most. The first is what form the Chinese Church would have in the future. The second is how the Gospel should be communicated to our children.

Concerning the first question, the basic problems are what is meant by "a church" and who should lead the church. Many older Christians said that they could not predict the future form of Chinese churches. So then they turned to the Bible for an answer. They found that it was clearly stated in the Bible that the house-church form was a legitimate church. Paul mentions a house church in I Cor. 16:19: "Aquilla and Priscilla greet you warmly in the Lord; and so does the church in their house." (NIV); also in Col. 4:15: "Give my greetings to the brothers at Laodicea, and to Mymphe and the church at her house." Later, we found a book by Wang Mingdao on the institution of the Church. He held the view that where there were Christians, there was a church. We were very happy about this. We assumed that although our group consisted of only a few people, we actually were a church, and our head was Jesus.

The second question concerned witnessing in Christian families.

For many years some Christians had hesitated to preach to their children because they didn't want their children to suffer for their faith as they had. But after sharing with each other, the faith of these Christians revived and they began telling their children about Jesus and starting family worship.

Christian groups in Tianjin have a special characteristic of mutual love. Others can easily identify them as Christians. Once, a group of Christians was found by the Public Security Bureau during their meeting for prayer and fellowship. Everyone in the group demanded to be arrested. One said, "I am the owner of the house, I should be arrested;" another said, "I am the leader of the group. Please arrest me."

Of course, we have had problems in our groups. Sometimes government agents slipped into our group by pretending to be new Christians. Sometimes some Christians whose faith was small prevented others from attending our prayer and fellowship meetings by making them afraid of getting into trouble with the government. Some even spread a rumour that I was implicated in an "overseas relationship" and was under government investigation. Yet despite all these problems, our groups are growing.

3.4 A Village in East China

The girl interviewed here emigrated to the United States in 1973. During the active phase of the Cultural Revolution (1966-69) she was a Red Guard, but subsequently she became a Christian.

Q: Are there Christians in your village?
A: There are Christians in a village three *li* away. There are more Christians there, but not very many. In another village about ten *li* away, there are many Christians. In fact, it has the largest number of Christians in our whole county. About 30% of the people are Christians. One of the production brigades is all Christian except for one family. [Usually a village constitutes one production battalion, which has several production brigades.]
Q: How many households lived in that particular village?
A: About 100 households.

Q: How did it happen that an entire production brigade turned Christian?

A: In that particular production brigade there were two or three families who were unusually zealous for the Lord. They were really willing to pour themselves into prayer for the salvation of the entire production brigade. They helped everyone who needed their help. Non-Christians in that village were exceedingly moved. They felt that it was great to be Christian. So they, too, believed in the Lord.

Another important reason is that, wherever Christians are active, the devil is also extremely active. At one time there were many in that village who were possessed by demons. Not a few were mentally sick, too. So all the Christians prayed for them, and they were healed, and the demons were expelled.

There is real power in the prayers of Christians. When they pray for the demon-possessed, demons flee away. But if a person does not confess his sins thoroughly, the demon returns to him, and he becomes re-possessed by the demon. But if his whole family prays sincerely and wholeheartedly, and the demon-possessed person himself confesses his sins thoroughly, and then Christians pray for him, the devil will flee away, never to return to him again.

Q: So, if a person gets sick and the Christians pray for him, will he be healed?

A: Yes, usually, except sometimes in cases of prolonged chronic illnesses. But demon-possessed persons are usually healed at once after prayer. Demons flee away as soon as Christians pray. This is really marvellous. You may not believe this, but I have seen demons expelled.

Q: Now that the sick are healed and demons exorcised by prayer, what kind of impact do these events have upon the non-Christian community?

A: Of course they feel that it is great to be Christian. But Christians have no status in China. When national movements are staged by the Communist Party, Christians have to eat "the bitter and the sour." They undergo persecution and suffering. So, many do not want to become Christians themselves, but they highly respect Christians. Only those who are utterly helpless, those who have "no way out," come to the Christians to ask for prayer.

Q: In addition to healing and demon exorcism by prayer what are some other factors which lead the people to believe in the Lord?

A: One other important factor is that [Christian] parents are usually able to, and eventually do, lead their children to Christ, or at least one or two of them. This personal approach extends to relatives and friends, too.

Q: Do Christians in your village and those in the other villages meet together for worship and fellowship?

A: Yes, they do.

Q: How and when do they meet?

A: They meet on the Lord's day. Until 1962 we had a church in our village. That was located about ten *li* away. Services were held every Sunday. But after the Cultural Revolution [1966-1969], all services were terminated.

During that period Christians could not have fellowship with each other. If they congregated for fellowship, they would be called in by the battalion headquarters for interrogation. Christian leaders or preachers would be put under "struggle." They would be placed on an accusation platform built in the center of the village, and everyone would come and "struggle" against them. But after the first high wave of the Cultural Revolution had passed, Christians resumed personal fellowship and restored the night meetings or met together during rainy days. That was so in our village.

Q: So rainy days are meeting days!

A: Yes, and so are evenings. Usually those of us who lived near each other got together. Someone would get the word around, and we all would gather together. Often there were no preachers available to us, and so we didn't have anyone to preach to us. Not many of us can preach. But many elders from the pre-Revolution days now assume the responsibility of preaching. Whenever an elder came to a village, word of his arrival would be spread around, and the Christians would get together for Bible reading, prayer, and fellowship.

Q: Did you have Bibles in your village?

A: Yes, we did. The Bibles that we used were almost entirely preserved in the homes of those who belong to the category of "lower-middle class farmers." For example, my family was designated as "non-desirables" because my father used to work with the former Nationalist Government. Therefore we could not keep Bibles. During the Cultural Revolution the Red Guards entered homes of our category and searched everywhere, so it was impossible to have a single Bible preserved.

Q: Who are the non-desirables?

A: They are seven classes of people known as the "seven black kinds;" (1) landlords, (2) capitalists, (3) rich farmers, (4) rightists, (5) anti-revolutionary elements, (6) capitalist-roaders in positions of power, and (7) "no-goods."

Q: Are they regarded as non-citizens?

A: Right. They cannot enjoy the privileges of citizens. Their children are called "children of the seven non-desirables."

Q: Tell us about the pastor's daughter who went about preaching.

A: Oh, yes, this person used to live in a town about 100 *li* away from us. She had a junior high education, which is considered pretty good by us villagers. Her father used to be a pastor, and she also has the gift of preaching. She really preaches very well. So we often asked her to come to preach to us. She was also frequently invited to preach in Shanghai, being escorted there secretly, of course. She has been invited to preach in most of the counties in our province. But she still has her own work. If one does not have a regular job, he or she is suspected by local authorities.

Q: Do communist cadres know about your Christian meetings?

A: Sometimes they do. In some instances it is quite marvelous. For example, in our neighboring village, the mother of the secretary of the production battalion became a Christian, and so there was nothing that he could do. His mother was once very sick. She sought help from doctors everywhere, but she could not get help. So as a final resort she asked friends to invite Christians to come to her home and pray for her. The Christians really prayed for her, time and again for two months, and finally she was healed. She became a very earnest believer. So then the Christians went to the cadre's home for meetings.

Q: During periods of national movements, were Christians

affected?

A: Yes, but it was perfectly all right for the lay people. Preachers sometimes got into trouble during those periods. But if you were a lower-middle class farmer and you went around preaching, nothing serious would be done to you even if you were caught. You would be lectured, of course. But if you were one of the seven non-desirables, then you could expect trouble.

3.5 Further Information on Wenzhou

This information was given by a young man who left China in 1976 and now lives in Europe. Like the woman in the previous interview, he was an active Red Guard, and he came to Christ in about 1973. His home was used as a house church for many years, but even as a Red Guard he and his brothers never denounced their parents.

Mr. Wen reported that in his home town of 400,000 there are about 50,000 Christians. They meet regularly in small house group fellowships, and among all of them there is only one ordained pastor from before the Liberation. This pastor is now over eighty, but still has an active ministry of Bible teaching and counselling to Christians who come to visit in his home. The house group fellowships meet almost every evening of the week, with varying numbers present. The meetings may take the following forms:

1) *Prayer meetings.* This is the most free type of meeting, as no accusation can be laid against the Christians for praying, and quite a large number will gather for prayer meetings.

2) *Bible Study.* Bibles are far too scarce and precious to be taken to the meetings, but the one leading the meeting copies out the chapter to be studied ahead of time using carbon paper so a number of copies can be made. Then each person is given a copy, which he later takes home. Thus, after completing a study of Matthew, for example, each Christian could have his own handwritten copy of the book. At the Bible study everyone is expected to take an active part in discussing the meaning of each verse.

3) *Witness meetings.* The Christians encourage each other with testimonies of what the Lord is doing among them. Miracles such

as relatives being released from prison are a special joy.

4) *Practice in Preaching.* Every Christian, man or woman, is expected to speak on some occasion, so training is given in evening meetings on how to preach the word.

The meetings are frequently moved around from one Christian home to another for the sake of safety.

Brother Wen stressed the fact that all Christians were able to cooperate, with the exception of Seventh Day Adventists and brethren of the Little Flock. There had been dialogue with these two groups, but they had not been able to reach an agreement. The mainline churches were especially unable to accept Saturday as the day of worship and the insistence on women wearing hats in the Brethren Group. This brother was also aware of the fact that there were Roman Catholic Christians in the area, but they had no contact with them.

The aspects of the ministry are as follows:

1) *Breaking of Bread* meetings are held on the first Sunday of every month for communion, and usually the Christians are divided into old, middle-aged and young, with meetings for the elderly in the morning, middle-aged in the afternoon, and young people at night.

2) *Baptisms* are by immersion, occasionally in very free times at the seaside or riverside, but usually in country areas in an improvised baptismal tank in a barn.

3) *Offerings* are given quite freely by Christians, and homes that are used for meetings are remunerated out of these offerings for use of electricity, water, etc. Almost all Christian workers support themselves by other work as well. Offerings are mostly given to Christians in other areas who are especially poor or suffering from famine.

4) *Women* have free and equal ministry with men in the church, taking part in prayer and also in preaching. The head covering is seen as a symbol of submission to the husband as head, but in the church both men and women uplift Christ as their head and submit to Him in all things. As a recognition of the man's responsibility to represent Christ, the Head, in the family, a woman preaching in church meetings will first ask a man to pray. This is a sign of submitting

to the authority of Christ.

5) *Gifts of the Spirit* are recognized and used, not regularly, but in special times set aside for prayer. Both the gift of tongues and the gift of interpretation are used on such occasions.

3.6 House Churches in Amoy

This interview is continued in 5.2. Fujian province was the area of China with probably the strongest Christian community before Liberation in 1949.

Conversion through house groups

At present, the fellowship of the brothers and sisters in China is not open. It is held in houses, and under other names, such as visiting the sick or celebrating weddings. There are also meetings of twenty-thirty people, with prayer and Bible reading. But they don't dare sing, for fear that the sound would be too loud, and cause others to notice. For example, one time a meeting was discovered, and the Public Security Bureau went and asked what they were doing. They traced the people who were at the meeting and questioned them individually, hoping to find some political activities. Later, because some people betrayed others by blindly telling false stories, Christians were reprimanded and given a lot of trouble.

In this group, there was one sister from a rural village who gave her testimony. She came from a poor, uncultured family. Suffering from an incurable internal disorder, she prayed to Buddha and sought out doctors, but all to no avail. Later, she ran into a meeting where she heard the Gospel preached. She received salvation. Believing in God, she depended on the prayers of the brothers and sisters in Christ, and God healed her sickness. So she had this testimony, and many people were moved to believe in God because of it. Her name is Laura; she is more than fifty years old, and has been saved over three years now.

A pastor's son who was a kind of vagabond and loafer was sent to a rural village to work. He heard the testimony of sister Laura and reformed, believing in God. The change in him was very great, and he testified about himself, influencing others to return to God.

His father, the pastor, had cooperated with the Three-Self Movement and had betrayed many brothers and sisters. But when he was about to die, he repented. There are many cases like this, such as Mr. Chen who taught at the Qiantao Theological Seminary. His faith should have been pure, but he was a spokesman for the Three-Self Movement. He had cancer and died a painful death. But before he died, he also repented.

3.7 Christianity in the North

Rosemary, the middle-aged lady who gave this account, now lives abroad. She first started applying to leave China in 1962 but was not allowed to leave until 1978. Even this she considers a miracle as she had been told she would not be allowed to emigrate due to her religious belief.

Since the fall of 1976, Christians in Tianjin have been feeling that there is going to be a revival among Christians in China. Until then Christians were only able to meet in two's or three's while they visited each other as friends. In the course of their conversations, they would share the fruits of their daily or occasional devotions. But after the death of Mao and the overthrow of the "Gang of Four" in 1976, Christians there began meeting more regularly in different homes, although the size of such gatherings was still small.

During the early days of these renewed Christian gatherings, the hosts spent much time and money on preparing food for entertaining the guests. One sister would devote two or three days preparing for a weekly occasion. On the day of the gathering she would become so occupied with entertaining that she sometimes lost her temper and scolded her children. The Christians came to feel that there should be much less entertaining in order to devote the time more to prayer and sharing. The situation was soon corrected in this way.

Bibles are still rare. As elsewhere in China, Christians in Tianjin divide a Bible into many parts to distribute or rotate portions among many families. Some copy the portions loaned to them for the week.

Most Bibles were taken from Christian homes during the Cultural Revolution [1966-1969]. Some were burned; others were kept in storage rooms by the local Public Security Bureau. In one case, the Bureau recently returned three Bibles to a Christian sister because one of the Bibles contained her name, "Gracious Light." But after receiving it, she realized that the Bible actually belonged to a Christian brother with the same personal name. It was a personal Bible with detailed comments in beautiful calligraphy written all through it.

Even after the fall of 1976, it was still illegal for Christians to meet together openly. Christians, therefore, are still divided into many local groups, to keep the size small and also to facilitate travel. Often Christians are called in by the Public Security Bureau and questioned about their participation in Bible studies and prayer. But the Christians have learned to be wise as serpents, while being gentle as doves. The Lord gives them wisdom in answering the officials without implicating others. Even today, Rosemary said, if the Public Security Bureau officials find a Christian group engaged in worship, arrests are made. Everyone knows that, while it is constitutional for an individual to hold religious faith in his heart, it is still a crime to share that faith with others or to gather for worship.

Believers in Tianjin are now very concerned about the Christian upbringing of their children. During the last two years, many parents have begun teaching their children the basics of salvation. When adult Christians gather for prayer, their children now also sit in and listen. Many of them gradually come to a knowledge of salvation and confess Christ as their Lord and Saviour. To encourage them to study Scriptures, memorization contests for the children have become part of their gatherings, which usually run two hours. Some children can memorize one to two chapters in one sitting; even preschool children can follow their older brothers and sisters in memorizing long passages.

A thirteen year old boy who used to live in Tianjin had moved with his father to Shanghai. He had some problems in his new school and wrote back to his Christian "aunties" to request them to pray for him, as well as to share with them his progress in Christian growth.

Christian children at home have learned to identify which

visitors are fellow believers and which are not, and to choose their words and response patterns accordingly.

The Cultural Revolution, the effects of which lasted ten years [1966-1976], instilled much fear in Christian believers throughout China. Unlike Zhejiang and Fujian Provinces, Christians in North China are fewer in number and more scattered. Until the overthrow of the "Gang of Four," Christians in most cities in north China did not dare meet in groups.

But now, as believers from Tianjin and Beijing visit Christian friends in cities such as Jinan, Qingdao, and Qifu, they share what the Lord has been doing in their home towns. On their return, believers in their home cities take new courage and revive their meetings. However, this openness of Christian interchange is true only of the last year or so.

3.8 A Southern Farmer

This man was allowed to leave China to join his parents in a Southeast Asian country. His wife and child were still in China at the time of this interview, in early 1979.

Q: What part of China did you come from?

A: I came from a village in eastern Guangdong Province.

Q: How large is the village?

A: They are over 10,000 inhabitants in our village.

Q: What do most of the villagers do for a living?

A: They are mostly farmers, and so was I.

Q: Have you been a Christian all your life?

A: I come from a Christian family, but I was not born again until 1970.

Q: Was there a church before Liberation?

A: Yes, there used to be a Baptist church, and our family belonged to that church. The church was confiscated by the government in 1953 during the land reform movement.

Q: Are there still Christians in your village?

A: In our village the formerly well-to-do and the poor used to live in separate sections. I belonged to the poor group, which were called "good elements" after Liberation. In our section there were over ten households, a group of more than seventy people, who were Christians. We met frequently.

Q: How frequently do Christians meet?

A: At least twice a month. But the frequency depends on when an itinerant preacher comes to us. Whenever one of the preachers came, we would spread the news to other Christian families and get together for worship.

Q: How many of these itinerant preachers were there in your area?

A: There were five to six of them. All of them were farmers like me who lived in nearby villages. One of them, who is now in his mid-sixties, at one time studied in a theological school in Swatow. The rest of them are in their fifties. They also travel to other villages to encourage Christians.

Q: When and where did you hold your meetings?

A: In our homes and usually at night after supper.

Q: How many would attend?

A: Usually sixty to seventy people. Nearly all the Christian families brought the entire family over for worship in one of our homes.

Q: Did the local authorities know about the meetings?

A: Yes, they did, but they did not bother us. In the formerly rich section, the local militia people oversee these meetings.

Q: What did you do during your meetings?

A: We prayed, read the Bible, sang hymns using the *Putian Songzan* [Hymns of Universal Praise] hymnal, and the itinerant preacher expounded the Scriptures.

Q: Did you invite non-Christian families to your meetings?

A: No, we didn't. Only Christian families met together. No strangers were invited. Neither did we proselytize or evangelize outsiders.

Q: How long have you been meeting?

A: Since 1970. Prior to that there were no meetings, not since the church was closed in 1953.

Q: How did you become a Christian?

A: It began with God's work in my life. Prior to 1970, I did not have much faith, even though I was born into a Christian family.

Through illness and hardship I came know God. Then my mother, who lives in Southeast Asia, sent us money to build a big house, and we were able to meet in my house.

Q: How were the meetings arranged?

A: When a visiting preacher arrived in the afternoon, word would be spread to other Christian families that a prayer meeting would be held that evening. The next morning the preacher would leave for his next meeting.

Q: Did each family have a Bible?

A: Yes, nearly every Christian family had a Bible.

Q: Weren't most of the Bibles discovered during the Cultural Revolution?

A: Yes, but some of our overseas relatives supplied us with new Bibles.

Q: Did you celebrate the Lord's supper?

A: No, we did not have holy communion after Liberation.

Q: Have there been any baptisms?

A: No, there have been none.

Q: What are some of the problems that Christian families faced?

A: We faced the same kind of problems in life as other non-Christian families. In daily life we were like others as well. Life in the Chinese village was hard, and our Christian faith was not strong. That is why we appreciated the visits of those itinerant preachers who came to strengthen our faith.

Q: How can we Christians outside help those in Swatow?

A: Gospel broadcasting is helpful. But it usually comes between 10:30 and 11 p.m. We go to bed before 10 p.m., because we have to get up before 6 a.m. We have breakfast at 7 a.m., and then will be in the fields by 7:30 a.m. After a short lunch break we work until dusk. Relatives who return for visits can take Bibles with them.

Q: Would the Chinese authorities give trouble to your family if they learned that you are talking about Christian activities in China?

A: It depends upon one's political status. For us, the poor, it's quite safe.

3.9 Fujian Revisited

This report is a continuation of 1.5 and 2.5, concerning the church in Fujian province.

Q: What about after the active phase of the Cultural Revolution, say after 1971?

A: There was a period of two to three years of much greater freedom. Large meetings of Christians once again were resumed. The leader was a brother with no particular theological training. He was a teacher after he finished university. But later he quit his job and did only preaching. He lived completely on faith.

Q: How big were these meetings?

A: Two or three hundred people would come. They met in country houses. There were no chairs or desks in their meeting rooms, just some long wooden planks. Their facilities were crude, but they were all strongly devoted to their faith. Many came to believe in Christ because of those meetings. Their influence extended to Fuqin and the Min River area. They also exorcized evil spirits by prayer and healed a number of people with incurable diseases.

     Then in the spring of 1973, some heresies began infiltrating the group. The large meetings stopped gathering. And once again, small family meetings began to be held by the faithful. The people who attended these groups were mostly young with some middle-aged people.

Q: Were there other groups like this?

A: Yes, there were similar groups in Amoy and Qinzhou, like that one in Fuzhou. The largest, in Qinzhou, had more than 100 people attending. But then the government noted who the leader was and arrested him. After that, this group also broke down into the smaller family groups.

Q: What was the content of these larger meetings?

A: It included the basic thing. Usually it started with some Bible readings, and then a sermon. The sermons consisted mainly of testimonies and sharing, and often included an evangelistic message for personal salvation. Although there was hymn singing, this was not too frequent. Sometimes there was also group Bible study.

3.10 Churches in Guangzhou

This extract is translated from a memoir of a man, now in his late forties, who has left China.

From 1971 or 1972 onwards, Guangzhou house churches revived once more. In 1972, I attended several family meetings [house churches]. I found the Christians all very dedicated and able to keep their faith despite the unfavorable government policy. These meetings, held once or twice a week, were usually led by elderly brothers. They called each group a "point." Each "point" consisted of eight to ten Christians. If the size of the "point" was too big, it might cause trouble. I knew someone who was arrested because he organized a house church. Similar cases continued to occur even after the downfall of the "Gang of Four" in late 1976.

When Christians came together, they usually shared their personal testimonies. If a Bible was available, they would read it together. They changed the meeting place from time to time. Sometimes they stayed inside a house, but more often they met in public gardens. I got to know eight of these Christian groups, actually only a small fraction of the total number. I found that some brothers who knew more about the Bible served in more than one group and worked especially among young people. These brothers usually taught them basic doctrines and explained what the Bible was all about. Young people were mostly close friends of the members of the groups, or members of the families of older Christians. They never invited people they knew little about.

Most older pastors were "struggled against" in the 1950s, or at least during the Cultural Revolution. Recently, more young people have begun to lead house churches. Some of them work as itinerant evangelists. Those who have a Bible [received mainly from Christian friends outside China] learn to preach from it. But most of them do not possess a Bible. Everything connected with "the four olds" was destroyed. As a result all Bibles and Christian literature were either burned or confiscated. This was done by Red Guards from Beijing. Recently the need for Bibles has become desperate in Guangzhou. Christians came to understand how important the Bible is to Christian life when they lost it. Some even lost their faith because they had forgotten the word of God.

IV The Taste of Freedom (1979-1980)

INTRODUCTION

For Christians in China, the years 1979-80 were probably their years of greatest freedom in the first thirty years of the People's Republic. Not only was it a time when limited freedom of religion was restored as an official policy and churches were opened for the first time in 13 years, but it was also a time when local leaders of house meetings spoke out boldly, moving to a semi-public status. How did this all come about?

Today's Chinese political leaders all mark the beginning of reform by the Third Plenum of the Eleventh Party Congress, held eighteenth to twenty-second December 1978. (A Plenum is a full meeting of the 200-member Party Central Committee, appointed at the full Party Congress.) Basic agricultural reforms were formally undertaken. The Plenum also resolved that there would be no mass political movements to disturb steady economic progress. This was in marked contrast to Mao, who had suggested that there would probably have to be a cultural revolution every decade in order to maintain revolutionary fervor. To achieve modernization, the Plenum emphasized individual initiative and responsibility. People should be paid according to their work. "There must be more hard work, and less empty talk," said Deng Xiaoping.

The economic revitalization of China was clearly premised on anti-Maoist principles. However, it was a problem to come right out and say so. Hua Guofeng continued as Premier and Chairman of the Party, and, as Mao's heir, he was interested in preserving Mao's stature. He supported the new programs, however, in concession to

Deng Xiaoping's growing power. Nevertheless, criticism of Mao began to come out. The *People's Daily* began to criticize anyone who took Marxism as an object of faith. The Red Guards were formally dissolved, and the little red books of Mao's quotations disappeared from the newsstands in late 1978. Deng himself articulated two principles for the new order: "Practice is the sole criterion of truth" and "Seek truth from facts." Both of these de-emphasized ideology, although they were quite consistent with Marxism. Appropriate quotations from Mao himself were dredged up to prove their truth. The model agricultural commune, Dazhai, which was a paragon of communism in Mao's day, was declared a hoax, and the Daqing oil field, an industrial model, was declared an economic failure. These changes gradually led to the formal assessment of Mao in mid-1980 as a good leader, but one who made many mistakes, especially in the last two decades of his life.

The moves toward a more open society, such as the lifting of many restrictions on intellectuals and artists, also resulted in increased freedom of religion. In early 1979, the Religious Affairs Bureau became active again. In March, the Beijing church that had been open for foreigners since 1972 allowed Chinese to come and worship. Former Three-Self Patriotic Movement Committee pastors around the country were being contacted, and finally in September 1979 the Moore Memorial Church of Shanghai was re-opened. By December, several churches in the large coastal cities were re-opened, and crowds surged to the churches. The churches were packed with both young and old; extra services had to be created.

The TSPM leaders slowly gathered themselves. In February 1980, a conference was held in Shanghai that restored the national executive committee, and the committee began planning for a national Christian conference. There were several issues facing the TSPM, discussed at both preparatory meetings and at the conference itself. The delegates wanted to know when Bibles could be published, how a new generation of leaders and pastors could be created, and whether there was really a need for the TSPM to continue to exist. They also had to face the problem of the relationship of the open churches to the house church meeting points around the country.

New Testaments were already reprinted before the national conference began. The need for the TSPM was affirmed. It had to exist, the conference declared, to promote patriotism and to protect the Chinese church from foreign, anti-Chinese elements. The conference also established the China Christian Council (CCC). The CCC was created to handle tasks that individual churches could not handle, namely, to train preachers, to publish Bibles and other literature, and to strengthen contacts among churches across China.

The conference implied that house church meetings in China were legal. It called for unity among Christians everywhere, without reference to where the Christians met. A month earlier, Ding Guangxun, head of both the TSPM and the CCC, gave a speech at the People's Political Consultative Conference at which he said, "We cannot interpret the constitution as saying that there is freedom of religious belief within church buildings, but no freedom of religious belief at home." The conference seemed to endorse this view, although it was not stated explicity. They appeared to reject the attitude expressed in Shanghai in the summer of 1980, in which park meetings were ordered to disperse.

House churches around China had become fairly open about their activities in the year prior to the conference. They appeared to receive the conference with cautious optimism. They continued pursuing their own programs and building up their churches. It was to be more than a year before they were faced with more organized attempts to control or take over their activites.

4.1 Home Visit

Lin, a Christian from Hong Kong, went home for family reasons but was unexpectedly able to meet with Christian brothers and sisters and so gain a picture of rural Christianity in southern China.

After twelve hours of travel, Lin and his mother finally reached their hometown, Zhouyang. The church that was situated behind his grandmother's house had been made into a warehouse. The church building reminded him that God must have His people within the vicinity. He asked his cousin if there were still Christians around the village. His cousin was not a Christian, but he brought him to a fifty-year-old Christian sister. This sister had suffered during the Cultural Revolution and was not willing to share much. Instead she introduced him to another brother named Wang. Wang's love for the Lord was so great that he opened his home for worship.

Wang had come to salvation at the age of sixteen, but he had backslid for a period. Yet God still kept him. In 1967 during the Cultural Revolution, when many Christians were falling, he returned to the Lord. His return was a result of some problems he had to face in life. Since then he has opened up his home for family worship. As a matter of fact he was jailed in 1968 because he opened his house for worship.

Our traveler would not have met brother Wang except for the introduction of the sister and also for the fact that he had brought some Bibles. A deep bond of trust quickly developed between them. Through Wang's arrangement Lin was able to meet with other Christian brothers and sisters and had an opportunity to preach.

There were some questions in Lin's mind: Have there been any changes in the underground churches in China? What is the present situation?

Lin and his cousin cycled from Zhouyang to Shangang. He did not realize that he would have to preach there. The worship services were normally held on Saturdays and Sundays. The leaders taking the service depended on a rotation of four or five evangelists; when there were any visitors they would ask the visitors to speak.

The meeting was arranged for 8 o'clock in the evening. At about 7 o'clock, each household, whether young or old, gathered together to prepare for worship. One could see families coming into the service together. At about quarter to seven, Wang led in singing. The hymns they sang were from 1951. The words were handwritten, and they were hung up for every one to sing.

Lin spoke on Paul's letter to the Ephesians, chapter one. He used the local dialect. The contents included greetings, words of comfort in suffering, encouragement, and some doctrine. He preached for an hour. Everyone was very attentive. Even the children there sat very still and were attentive.

When the service was over, some of the worshippers talked to Lin's cousin, who was not a Christian. Wang and another elderly sister, leaders of the group, spoke to him with others helping them.

The method employed by the elderly sister was very direct. She spoke of the fallen nature of man in Genesis and of the Final Judgement in the book of Revelation.

Through the power of God's Word and the enthusiasm of the members, this group has been steadily growing, with thirty to forty new converts annually.

Lin was to return home that evening, but, through the persuasion of the worshippers to share more the following day, he decided to stay overnight at Wang's home. Even the children pleaded with Lin, and they even said that they would miss school to hear him.

The service began at 8 o'clock the following morning. The number attending was smaller, as some had to work; nevertheless, thirty to forty people came. The worshippers kept asking him to preach, so he gave three sermons lasting for three hours! No worshippers were bored.

Lin made some observations on the nature of the house churches. The words in the Scriptures "that you and your household shall believe" were realised in the house church situation there. The worshippers were all Wang's neighbours. There was a family spirit. One brother brought some broth, syrup, and milk. Although it was an unfamiliar environment, he felt at home, with no feelings of uneasiness. It was in such a relaxed atmosphere that Lin brought the message of God's Word.

During prayers, Lin could sense that the worshippers were very close to God; their prayers sprang forth from their hearts. They were filled with the Spirit. Every word or phrase uttered was full of content and meaning. They committed themselves to God. Lin felt that the prayers of the Hong Kong believers could not be compared to the Chinese believers' prayers in honesty and sincerity. There were also testimonies of how demons were cast out and sicknesses healed. Lin felt that fellowship with the Chinese believers in China brought him back to the experience of first-century Christians in the Book of Acts.

4.2 Letter from Shanghai

A believer in Shanghai wrote a letter to the Chinese Church Research Center about the church during that time (1980). Part of it is reproduced here.

The "Park Church Meeting" is at the east side of Shanghai People's Park, facing Moore Memorial Church, Starting last year, it has gradually become one of the biggest public meetings of Christians in Shanghai.

Here, nobody preaches and nobody leads, but in everything we can see the Lord Himself working. Most believers here are old; only a few are young. Some teach others how to sing hymns of praise. They copy the words on big sheets of paper, hold them in their hand, explain them, and sing at the same time. Some give their testimonies and tell of God's abundant grace. Others explain a Bible passage, pray for healing, or cast out demons.

This is also the place for house churches to make contacts, have fellowship, and exchange addresses, because most of the believers here regularly attend house churches. Most of the house church meetings are public now. Quite a lot of people attend, and they are mostly new believers. It's a pity that there are not enough preachers. However, they come to the park to communicate with each other and to invite each other to preach.

Here we can hear how the house churches in each district of Shanghai are doing. More than half of the meetings are held where the working people live; "God is fair to everyone." Because the brothers and sisters thirst and seek after the Lord, the Lord inspires preachers to shepherd them. The Holy Spirit is also working in them. Now many meetings have gotten back on the right track. They have changed from noisy, public, church-style meetings to partly open or closed meetings, which are much better for the preachers. So the meeting in the park has become even more important.

But this is only temporary. It is not suitable for the situation in Shanghai. Concerning its direction for the future, we need the Lord to direct us.

There are many visitors in the park, so it's also an important place for spreading the Gospel. Many of them hear the Lord's name for the first time here. They believe in the Lord, receive grace, and whenever they have a day off they come to listen to the explanation of a passage, to give their testimony, and to pray. They are so thirsty for the Lord. Then gradually they start attending the house church meetings.

There are also people here with bad motives. They are dangerous for the house churches. They clothe themselves with sheepskin, but inside they are cruel like wolves. We can only put everything in the hands of the Lord and pray for his judgment and his giving of wisdom and revelation to the brothers and sisters. From the fruits people bear, we are able to recognize them.

Truly, "God's Word cannot be bound." The park church meeting is a reflection of the Church's revival in China. Not only is People's Park like this, but other parks are like this too, or even better than People's Park. Their methods, times, and places are all wise, because the Lord is working there Himself.

4.3 Later News from Shanghai

About three months after we received the previous letter, letters and articles were published in Shanghai newspapers criticising the People's Park meetings. The articles accused the meetings of being noisy, intrusive, and disturbing to the park's atmosphere. Perhaps most tellingly, they asked, since official churches were now open, one being right by the park itself, why shouldn't Christian believers go to church were they wouldn't be disturbing anyone else? The following is an account of the ensuing developments, the steps taken by city, Party, and government authorities to control the park meetings.

The "New Wind Propaganda Team" was set up by a committee of men from the Shanghai Religious Affairs Bureau, the Shanghai local government's Religion Department, the Shanghai Public Security Bureau (police department), and the park administration. From May thirtieth to June first, these teams were sent to every park to control meetings being held in them, in the name of restoring order in the parks.

The teams held anti-Christian propaganda demonstrations at the places where Christians usually met. They exclaimed that, "Such open propagation of superstition in the public parks has never been seen in the 30 years since liberation!" They also said that there were many false testimonies being given to promote superstition: "Some people said that they had been cured of tumors by prayer, when actually they were cured by the free medical care provided by the Communist Party."

They also said that the message that unbelievers would go to hell was damaging the Communist Party's policy of religious freedom, because the Party not only permits freedom for people to hold beliefs, but also protects their freedom not to believe in religion. They said that evangelists hate and revile the broad masses of working people, praying for specific people, whose faces become grey and whose bodies shake. They claimed that, generally speaking, there are some who take advantage of this religious superstition, Christianity, to destroy the order and rule of socialism and to oppose the leadership of the Communist Party. Because of this, they said, these park meetings must be controlled.

According to the propaganda teams, they would be lenient in educating the deluded crowds (meaning the believers), but would carry out strict re-education on those who obstinately refused to listen. In fact, in the course of their propaganda work they arrested some of the independent evangelists preaching in the parks.

4.4 A Sermon

This is the edited translation of a sermon given in an "open" church in Guangzhou. The preacher (Rev. Tong) comes from a Chinese independent Christian background and is generally much appreciated by the Christians who go to this church.

When Jesus first started his ministry, he came to Jacob's well on his way to Jerusalem. This well was used for sheep grazing and for the nearby dwellers. But this was a famous well. As Jesus was thirsty he asked for water from the Samaritan woman. The woman then said, "You are a Jew, why are you asking for water from a woman

of Samaria?" Why was the woman so curt? The reason was that the
Jews looked down upon, and had no dealings with, Samaritans. She
recognized Jesus' Jewish accent. She then thought to herself, "Well,
this is an opportunity for me to show off."

But Jesus was not angry and continued to talk with her. There
were questions and answers. From the conversation, the woman
realized that Jesus was an unusual man. She said, "Teacher you are
a prophet." What is a prophet? A prophet is a teacher who has an
understanding of theology. Thus the woman changed her tone toward
Jesus.

"Where should we worship God? Our ancestors said that we
were to worship God on the mountain east of Jacob's well. But you
Jews said that you must worship God in Jerusalem. Jerusalem has
beautiful temples. Which of the two places do you consider to be
correct?" The Samaritan woman hoped in her heart that Jesus' reply
would be, "on the mountain." The woman would then gleefully feel
that the Samaritans had triumphed, as this mountain was situated
where the Samaritans live. But Jesus' reply was: "We are neither
Samaritans nor Jews." If someone were to ask you this question before
you knew Jesus' reply, which would you answer?

Let us talk about the Samaritan's Mount Gerizim. This is a
famous mountain. This mountain had been honored in history, during
Old Testament times. When Moses was old and about to leave the
earth, having led the people to the edge of the promised land, he
instructed his successor, Joshua, to quickly lead the people across
to Canaan and proclaim the Law at Mount Gerizim (Deut. 27:11-26).
However, there is a difficulty here. Today, we have a thousand or more
worshippers here, and, if there were no loudspeakers, even if I used
my loudest natural voice you might not hear me. According to
Numbers 2:32 Moses had counted about 600,000 people. Joshua was
to instruct the Law to 600,000 people, and even if he were to shout
his loudest, he could never make the people hear.

However, even in Old Testament times, Moses had a scientific
mind. He chose a good place for Joshua to instruct the Law to the
600,000 people. Where were they seated? Joshua's pulpit was not like
mine, above everyone, but was in the valley, between the two

mountains. And Jacob's well was situated in this valley. Earlier we
talked about Jesus and the Samaritan woman at the well. The well
mentioned was exactly the place where these 600,000 people were
given the Law. Joshua then divided the group into two assemblies:
300,000 on the east and 300,000 on the west. On the east stood Mount
Gerizim, and on the west was Mount Ebal. Joshua stood in the valley
and gave them the Law. When Joshua spoke, the echoes spread far,
with the mountains serving as a loudspeaker, so that the people could
hear.

Let us pause for a minute: a person addressing 600,000 people,
with the mountains trembling and words echoing, is indeed a
spectacular scene. Was not Mount Gerizim mentioned by the woman
of Samaria as a good place for worship? Was it not exciting? No
wonder the Samaritan woman was quite excited and proudly said,
"Our fathers worshipped on this mountain." Hence they named this
mountain the blessed mountain.

Dear brothers and sisters in Christ, how do you see this? Would
you like to be on the blessed mountain or the cursed mountain? All
right, you decide for yourself. Jesus didn't make any decision. The
woman then said that her ancestors were on this blessed mountain
and the Jews were in Jerusalem. This meant the Jerusalem temple.
Needless to say, the temple is a place for worship and has all kinds
of advantages, such as priests leading the worship and offering
sacrifices. This helped to raise the form of worship. No wonder the
Jews maintained that they must worship in Jerusalem, as Jerusalem
had its benefits.

The Jerusalem temple was not the one built by Solomon. The
temple that Solomon built was no more in existence. This was the
one built by Zerubbabel after his return. Remember four weeks ago
I mentioned the rebuilding of the temple, and that the people cried
as it was not built by Solomon. But let me tell you, during Jesus'
time even that temple, however beautiful, was destroyed. It was King
Herod who had helped to repair it.

We have already heard Jesus' opinion about the two places. In
the Scripture we read just now Jesus' words: "The time is coming
when you will worship the Father neither on this mount nor in

Jerusalem." It was not that Jesus did not see the importance of Mount Gerizim or of the Jerusalem temple, but that he wanted to reveal the truth to the Samaritan woman and to us. This truth is that it is wrong if we only seek to worship God at a specific place or location, as this limits us physically.

If Jesus had said, "Woman, you should go to Jerusalem to worship God in the Jerusalem temple," what do you think would have been the Samaritan woman's response? Let us think for a moment. The woman would then have asked how long the journey takes from Samaria to Jerusalem. Fortunately Jesus did not say Jerusalem! If Jesus had said Mount Gerizim, then, brothers and sisters in Christ, we would not have the opportunity! I would not dream of going to Israel for a visit. If Jesus had said you should worship God in Dongshan Church, then you would be fortunate. But the invalids would lament that they have no opportunity. The elderly people with their walking sticks and hunched backs would stop halfway and say that they cannot make it.

A specific location would handicap us physically. Jesus did not say we have to worship at any particular place. Looking for a place to worship God is not good, as God is with us always. God does not leave those who fervently believe in Him. When you are close to God, God is close to you. Wherever we are we can worship God and call Him "Abba, Father," and at the end of our prayer say "Amen."

4.5 Letter from Guangzhou

A young Christian in Guangzhou wrote this to a friend of his who had just left China. They used to take part in a house church together.
Dear brother in the Lord,

I received your letter as I was about to write to you. Recently members of the Body [of Christ] from other provinces have been coming. Their main purpose in coming is to obtain Bibles. From what they say, they all need the Old and New Testaments very badly, because even the "responsible brothers" [lay Christian leaders] in many places are lacking Bibles.

Two months ago a certain former pastor's wife and a sister from a northern city went up north to visit Christian brothers and sisters. When they reached Zhejiang Province, they saw how the Gospel was flourishing and also how Bibles were lacking. I think that if anyone among you is going to Hangzhou, he should take some books [Bibles] to give them. The contact address is....

Brother, in a few days some brothers may be coming from Xinjiang Province [in the far-western part of China] to Guangzhou. When you receive this letter, please send some people to bring more Bibles over right away. Inasmuch as they have come from so far away, we must not lose such a good opportunity.

Concerning the opening of official churches, since September thirtieth to this day I have gone to the Dongshan Church every Sunday. In my opinion one of the pastors, a Rev. Bing, is relatively good. It's hard to say anything about the others; only God knows. But I am rather turned off by one of them, Rev. Qing. For example, is the reopening of church due to the grace of a certain leader? Whom should we thank? I always feel that all this is part of God's eternal plan.

In his sermon today, he did not say a word on salvation. All he said was to urge the people to do good. Can a person receive eternal life simply by doing good? Anyway, what kind of a man is this pastor himself? Believers of your father's generation all know about him.

From now on I do not plan to spend so much of my time in the Dongshan Church, but plan to join the house church meetings and to have more quiet time at home. Next year I would like to travel to other places with a certain pastor's wife to learn from other house churches. But I am leaving all this to the Lord; only He orders my steps. Please pray for me, brother, for I am very weak. May the Lord lead me in how to serve Him.

> Emmanuel
> A weak member of the Body

4.6 Travelers' Tales (I)

A Christian writer made an extensive tour of China in 1979 and gave interviews to us on various topics. This one concerns building bridges of understanding with one's tour guides.

Q: What were the backgrounds of some of the guides you met?

A: As guides, we had both a young man and a girl together, except for the last city, where we had two fellows. They were from twenty-four to thirty-three years of age, the oldest being a lady in Peking; she was thirty and a mother. Several had assignments in other cities. they admitted that one of the shortcomings of the guide course was that their training was academic, learning to converse, but not on the lifestyle of the tourists.

Q: Were they Party members?

A: None of them was a Communist Party member. One young guide in Shanghai had tried for three years to become a member of the Communist Party. He was most careful to keep himself politically pure. He just didn't want any slip-ups. He was the only guide who had some reluctance to accept a gift I gave to each guide.

Q: Did you give them any Christian literature?

A: Among the Christian literature I brought in were sets of a cassette tape for learning English and a correlated handbook.

My strategy was to give this gift packet to each guide at the very last moment at the airport, so that there wouldn't be any chance of his refusing it. I would thank him in English for all that he had done and give him the little gift wrapped up with his name on it. It worked except for the last place. After we had gone out, the loudspeaker blared, "Flight 309 will be one-and-a-half hours late; please go back into the lounge." Fifteen minutes later the guide walked up, and this happened to be the guide who had applied for three years to be a member of the Communist Party. He came and said, "I want to thank you very much for the cassette and handbook, but I cannot accept the religious material.

I had already had an extended conversation with him on religion in China. He was interested to know what I knew. He was with me when we went to the foreign language bookstores and I bought books about Mao Zedong and Zhou Enlai. He knew that I was open-minded as a Christian and wanted to understand Communist ideology. I countered his objection to receiving the Gospel of John by saying that I understood from our conversation that they do have religious freedom in China. I said, with a smile, "I'll take it back if you insist, but I really would like you to have it." We approached all this with friendly ease. After thinking over that point, he said, "I guess in that case, all right, I'll take it."

Q: How else do you build up your relationships with guides?

A: I think that Western Christian tourists have a unique opportunity to converse with guides. Religion should not be the only topic, but ask a lot of questions about other things. Be interested in everything. Go as a learner.

However, don't monopolize the guide so that the rest of the tour members are ready to cut your throat because you are spending all the time with the guides. There is a fine line there. Strike a balance.

Q: Did you find the guides curious about the cross you wore?

A: I wore a small jewelry cross around my neck. I don't do that as part of my ordinary lifestyle but I did in China deliberately and it really got questions, some sincere questions that I wouldn't have gotten any other way.

Our bus driver in Peking was only 21 years old; we were with him day after day. At the end of the first day, I had to return to the bus for my camera and the young bus driver turned around to me, pointed to my cross, and said in Mandarin, "Christian cross, right?" So I smiled and we had a little conversation about it. I didn't directly ask him if he was a Christian, but I had a Good News for Modern Man in Chinese, so I gave that to him to read while we went to the Ming tombs for two hours. He was profuse in his thanks for it. Before I was out of the bus he was already reading. When we came back, he told me that he had read the whole of Mark in simplified script. He wanted to hand it back, but I told him that he could keep it. That was the beginning of a bridge.

Q: How did this bridge develop?

A: We were going to spend two more days with that bus driver, so I took particular efforts to be friendly and express my appreciation.

When we went sightseeing for hours and he couldn't leave the bus, I would bring him a cold drink or a popsicle, just quietly; they cost only a couple of cents but reinforced our friendship bridge.

Then once I was explaining to another tour member that I was going to Nanking to look up all the places in a book about an old missionary in China. I had both the English copy and the Chinese translation with me. Apparently he had overheard me talking, so he came up to me afterwards when nobody else was around and the tour guide was somewhere else, and asked me about this book. So I left it with him on the bus while we went to Tiananmen Square. He read it from cover to cover and asked to keep it overnight. I hadn't pushed a thing; our friendship had started when he noticed my cross. As we parted, I gave him a simplified script New Testament. Again he was profuse in his appreciation. Such opportunities with guides are unlimited on structured tours if you pray for wise openings.

Q: What are your general conclusions?

A: It's great when they ask questions. But I only answered them as much as they asked; just asking is not a chance to give your whole testimony. Plenty of time for that if there is a whole bridge to talk over for a longer time or by correspondence.

My feeling is that one need not be tense and anxious about forming friendships with the tour guides or the youths of China; they are flesh and blood youngsters like anybody - with normal curiosity and interests. We can take advantage of these for a wise, natural sharing of our faith and for building bridges to keep walking over, perhaps by correspondence, surely by prayer.

4.7 Travelers' Tales (II)

This interview, conducted in 1979, is with a Hong Kong Chinese man who wished to minister to his brothers and sisters in neighbouring Guangdong Province.

Q: When did you go in, and for how long?

A: I went last Saturday and stayed for two days. I came out Monday morning. Sunday I toured around Canton City.

Q: Did you make the trip by yourself?

A: Yes, alone.

Q: Why did you go then? Just to see it?

A: Christians in Hong Kong are so concerned about their brothers and sisters in China. I'm very young in the Christian way. I accepted Jesus as my Saviour in August, 1977, after an operation. So I'm concerned about them and went in. I have no relatives inside. Some people gave me the address of a sister in Christ, and so I went and visited her and left her some Bibles. My impression of China is that the people inside are very vulgar and the clothing and everything are very poor. The education is also poor. Most of them would like to come to Hong Kong.

Q: When you went in to China, did you stop at the border at Shenzhen?

A: Yes. I boarded another train there to go to Guangzhou.

Q: Did they look through your baggage there?

A: Oh, yes, they looked through our baggage carefully. They asked what we had. I answered them, "It's clothing." They let it pass. I also brought along fifteen Bibles separate from my luggage, and they asked what that package was. I said, "It's a gift, for my relatives and friends." They asked what kind of gift, and I told them it was Bibles. They said, "Oh, you can bring one or two, but fifteen is too much. You'd better leave it here." So I left all the Bibles at the border, and they asked me to pick them up when I came out; but praise the Lord that they didn't search my luggage, because I had about seven Bibles in it. So the Lord really helped me and prepared the way for me to go in.

Q: When did you see the person whose address you had?

A: I went on Saturday. She took me to see all her relatives and some of her Christian friends and asked me to give my testimony to them and share how the Church was doing in Hong Kong. I told them we have quite a lot of Christians in Hong Kong. But how many of them are really praying for them? Many of the Christians in Hong Kong still love the world, but I didn't tell them that. I just told them we have a lot of Christians in Hong Kong. I told them they are lucky inside — they lack temptations. But in Hong Kong we are so free.

Q: Do you think any of them wanted to become Christians?

A: Yes. The son-in-law is interested. I pray for him that one day he will become a Christian. He will come to Hong Kong very soon, because he's going to emigrate to the United States. He is a very fine fellow.

Q: What impression do you have of the character of the Christians in Canton? Do you think that they are a strong church?

A: Oh, yes; if they confess to you they are Christian, they have a very strong faith. They confess themselves everywhere. They are really witnessing they are Christians. On this point they really encouraged me.

Q: Do the people work on Sunday?

A: Some of them had to work on Sunday, but many people walked on the street because they had nothing to do at home. They don't have any entertainment, so they just go out and walk on the street.

Q: What were your impressions as you rode around? What about the kinds of clothes people were wearing and things like that?

A: They have very poor clothing, like that of a farmer. I think it was typical. You don't expect them to have a suit and tie like outside — anyway, you can't find any. I was very interested in the city. The people were smoking; they all like smoking. Everywhere you go you see people smoking, even children. I saw some children about 12 years old, smoking already. And they speak bad language a lot.

Q: You took in about seven Bibles. Where did you leave them?

A: One was my own Bible. I gave a Bible to the sister. She was so happy. She held the Bible and ran in and out of the room. She said to her small children, "This is a Bible." So I lent her my own Bible too.

Q: Whom else did you leave Bibles with?

A: I left two with some of my cousin's friends, but they didn't say much to me. Maybe they were worried or frightened of me. You know, a stranger came and left them a Bible. "Did you come from the government?" they asked. But they accepted the Bible. I left the rest of the Bibles with the sister and one other person.

4.8 Travelers' Tales (III)

This man makes frequent trips from Hong Kong to China for business reasons, and the interview he gave shows some of the problems apparent in the mainland church.

Q: When did you go to China, and where did you stay?

A: I visited China from January 13 to 19 this year. I stayed in Canton the whole time. I took a considerable number of Bibles and religious books in with me. There were 23 Bibles altogether, of various versions, some in English. I also took a big Bible commentary, a systematic theology book, books on church history, and some other devotional books. I had no difficulties going through customs with these books.

Q: What did you do with these books?

A: I give them to a Mr. Chan, who is a Christian, to a former minister, Lambert Kou [pseudonym], and to a small Baptist church.

Q: Tell me about Mr. Chan.

A: During my stay in Guangzhou, I saw Mr. Chan several times. I knew that he was a Christian who had fallen away from the Lord for some years. One time that I met with him, we had a Bible study. I deliberately chose to read Romans, because I feel this is the most complete exposition of theology in the New Testament books. We read the first three chapters. In this first meeting, only Mr. Chan and his wife were there. Mrs. Chan was very attentive and receptive to the words, but Mr. Chan was less enthusiastic. I explained word by word the details of the verses and the related theological terms contained in them. They seemed rather ignorant about them.

Q: Why was Mr. Chan less enthusiastic about the Bible study?

A: We held different views on the interpretation of the Bible. He was an admirer of Wang Mingdao and held fast to Wang's "Seven Epochs" dispensational beliefs. He still had some of Wang's books.

Q: Tell me about the next meeting.

A: The next day we spent two hours studying chapters four to six of Romans. Two young girls joined our group. I told them to ask questions on what they did not understand. Their questions were mostly on basic doctrines, like the trinity, the crucifixion, etc.

Q: Did you think they were born-again Christians?
A: I think Mrs. Chan was. But I was doubtful about Mr. Chan.
He often criticized others, and he held great emnity toward the cadres.
He also insistently believed that those who betrayed him could not
be saved, despite my repeated explanations of the doctrine of
forgiveness in the Bible. The two girls had been guided by Mr. Chan
in religious matters. But I was not sure about their faith. They asked
questions on parables in the Bible and on the last supper of Jesus.
Q: When was the third Bible study held?
A: The third Bible study was held on Monday evening. More people
came to join us. One of the new members was a young man called
Peter. He was an educated youth who had been sent to a rural area.
Later he became ill and returned to Canton. For the time being he
studied Chinese boxing with Mr. Chan. That evening, we read chapter
four of the Epistle to the Ephesians, concentrating on not
disappointing the Holy Spirit and on holding fast to the new hope.
They were happy about these messages. After the Bible study, we
prayed together. Through the prayers, I learned that they needed
peace, freedom to preach, and more religious books.
Q: Was there a fourth Bible study?
A: Yes, we held the fourth meeting on Wednesday evening at Chan's
home. Six young people joined the meeting; they had been led to
Christ through Mrs. Chan. A daughter of Mr. Chan was there too.
We studied I Thessalonians, chapters one to four. It lasted more than
two hours.
Q: Why did you choose I Thessalonians?
A: I believed that they could learn from Paul's warning about the
low moral standards of the Thessalonians. I observed that they had
problems with sex. So I concentrated on the biblical teaching about
adultery. They were receptive to the Bible teachings.
Q: What were these young people's occupations?
A: I know that one of the girls worked in a garage.
Q: Did you sing hymns in the meeting?
A: No, we did not. We started with prayer, and ended with prayer
too. Some of them did not know how to pray.
Q: You mentioned a Rev. Kou earlier; please tell me more about
him.

A: Rev. Kou had worked with Wang Mingdao for a time. After that, he was put in jail for eighteen years. He was very proud of that. He quoted Wang, saying that "the one who made the most troubles for the government in Shanghai was Wang, while in Guangzhou it was Kou." He implied that he was now about 53 years of age and still served the Church as a "traveling preacher." He told me that Wang Mingdao was released from jail last year. By now Wang is 78 years of age. Rev. Kou called him Peter, meaning a person who denied Christ and returned to him afterwards.

Q: What was your general impression of the Chinese Church recently?

A: It was that young people have become more interested in the gospel and in God's word. However very few of them possess Bibles. I learned that a young girl believed in Christ because her cousin in Hong Kong sent her some pages of the Gospel of John. These young people usually had to depend heavily on older people to understand the gospel and how to interpret the Bible. If the older people misinterpret the Scripture, the young generation will too.

4.9 Church Re-opened

A Chinese Christian wrote a letter to CCRC to give his impressions of Dongshan Church after it opened again.

On October 7th, I participated in the second Sunday worship service of the reopened Dongshan Church of Guangzhou. I was so excited when I was getting ready to go that I did not take a camera or tape recorder.

The number of people participating in this service was very large; all the seats were taken. I would estimate that there were over 1,300 people there. Most were middle-aged and older people; young people were only about one-quarter of the congregation. There were also some Hongkong and Macau people there, one of whom took a lot of pictures.

Three people spoke, in the following order:

1. The [Guangzhou] city Three-Self [Movement] Vice-Chairman, Ye Xiaoqing, introduced the people taking responsibility for the

restored Dongshan Church: Chairman, Matthew Tong: Vice-Chairman: Long Bingchao, Liang Naidao, and Fan Xiuyuan; along with workers Gu Shiwei and Chen Zhanglan, and so on. The announcements were that the Henan [South River] Church and Xi'an [Zion] Church were being prepared for reopening. Ye then said: "We owe deep thanks to the [Communist] Party and the government for adjusting the religious policy to protect proper religious life. We ask Christians to be patriotic, keep the laws, respect the government's regulation and 'religious regulations', and to not engage in illegal religious activities but rather to embrace the progress of the Four Modernizations under the leadership of the Party."

2. Matthew Tong said: "Because so many membership rolls of the churches were destroyed during the Cultural Revolution, there was no way to send invitations to individuals. Please excuse this."

3. Long Bingchao preached the sermon, using Matthew 16:24-28. He used the words of Jesus recorded in this scripture as an analogy for the spirit of "the older generation of revolutionary proletarians who shed their blood as a sacrifice." He only hoped that Jesus' teachings would arouse us to contribute to the progress of our ancestral land's Four Modernizations in a new Long March.

My own viewpoint:

1. Praise the Lord that this Gospel has incomparable strength. Among the brothers and sisters in the church that day were many who were moved to tears by the grace of God. They understood God's power and regarded the reopening of Dongshan Church as having been arranged by God. Some young people came, longing to find truth. We must pray that the Spirit of God will work among them.

2. The words of the Three-Self people were more "leftist" than those of the government representative. (A) is basically a bureaucrat. (B) has no gift in preaching. His use of scripture is entirely disrespectful, changing it at whim, slanting it at will. (C) still has life. Before the worship service, he said to a sister from Hong Kong, "You have come to see a place that has received much discipline; I hope that when you go back you will be able to love the Lord

more. Having gone through refining, one knows the sweetness of the Lord's grace even more."

3. I am somewhat suspicious about the registering of believers.

P.S. Rev. Tong also mentioned having ordered 1,000 hymnbooks from the Beijing Three-Self Bureau, and he mentioned that the Bible was being translated into modern Chinese by the Religious Research Institute in Nanjing.

4.10 Traveling Preacher in Eastern China (I)

Brother Paul is a lay-preacher, and this is one of a series of interviews with him concerning rural Christianity.

Praise to the grace of the Lord, which enabled me to travel through Zhejiang Province, visiting brothers and sisters.

Why did I go? It was because once a sister visited me in Shanghai. She told me about the situation of the churches there [in Zhejiang]. She said that the brothers and sisters there were very thirsty, but there were few workers. They had no way to hear the truth of God. Furthermore, there were many heresies there.

The main one was that someone came around who said that the Lord Jesus would be returning soon. Everyone should gather together to wait for the Lord Jesus' return. Then he told them to hand over their money and other possessions to welcome the Lord Jesus back. Because the brothers and sisters didn't have any Bibles and had never heard sermons on biblical truths, they thought this person was right and did what he said to do.

Some of them sold their houses, some sold their furniture and clothes, and they handed the money to this crook. He also told them to make white robes which they were to wear on the day that the Lord Jesus would return. He told them the year and month when he would be returning. Then he told them to go up a mountain all together to wait for the Lord.

The brothers and sisters obeyed him and bought white cloth to make the robes, and on the set day they went up the mountain together to wait. They waited from the morning to the afternoon, and nothing happened. So they wondered exactly when it was that the Lord was to return, and why he didn't come. The crook told them "You pray," and everyone kneeled down to pray.

Then he ran — while they were praying, the crook ran away. Meanwhile, the police of the commune saw this strange group wearing white robes gathering on the mountain and wondered what they were doing. So they surrounded the mountain top, arrested the brothers and sisters, and asked them about their superstition. They told the police the crook's name, what he looked like, and what clothes he was wearing. They looked all over for him and finally arrested him. After arresting him, they asked him where all the money had gone. He said that he had spent it.

Because these brothers and sisters didn't understand the truth, they all fell for this trick.

Afterwards, one of the sisters reported it to the government. Later, after she had come to Shanghai and told me about it, I was greatly distressed. This led me to feel a responsibility. Because I knew a little about this problem, I felt a responsibility to go to the countryside and clarify things for them.

At that time, a brother had just come from Zhejiang to Shanghai with the same idea, hoping to find a brother in Shanghai to help them. He told me that the local brothers and sisters deeply longed to understand the truth, longed to hear the truth of the Bible, and wanted to hear what the situation concerning the Lord Jesus' second coming really is.

After waiting on the Lord in prayer, I said I would tell him when I could come. God prepared a time for me and arranged everything. So I left Shanghai. Before I went, I wrote to the brothers and sisters, asking them to meet me at the train station in Zhejiang.

When I arrived, a brother came toward me and asked, "Are you brother Paul? Are you the one from Shanghai?" He said, "Thank the Lord I met you." He explained that when the train had arrived, a voice told him to approach me. I was the first one he approached, so he was glad that he found the one he was looking for. He said, "Thank the Lord for this meeting," and very happily led me to a brother's house.

From then on I was with this brother, who had been to Shanghai. I went with him, as he had arranged my itinerary in the countryside. I preached the way of the Lord to the people. My saying this is not to say that I did anything. In fact, in going to the countryside, I received much help from the brothers and sisters there. Seeing their pure faith and ardor truly moved me. Toward the end I said to them, "Don't regard the brothers and sisters in Shanghai too highly. Truly, those in the countryside are better than those in Shanghai, because God has blessed you first. Because you love and rely on the Lord, God has been gracious to you. I have seen the work and grace of God himself among you."

Now I want to give my experiences in the countryside as a testimony to everyone. When I went to the countryside, I clearly saw that God is personally at work in the countryside; this work is not due to any ability of man. God knows. God is scattering the seeds and fertilizing them Himself, and it is God Himself who is making them blossom and become established. Although we may gather His fruit and store it up, it is all His work. Truly, all the work is God's own. I will give an example.

In one place, there was a little girl called A Li. While sick in bed, she heard a voice calling to her, "Believe in Jesus!" She did not understand and thought it was an hallucination. But the voice came a second time, saying, "Believe in Jesus!"

The girl asked her father, "Daddy, did you hear it?"

Her dad said, "No, I didn't hear anything."

She told him "There was a voice urging me to believe in 'Jesus'. What does it mean to believe in Jesus'?" She didn't understand what it meant. Neither did her father. Later, the father asked his friends about it. Then he happened to meet an old sister. After he asked her about it, she went to his house and explained the saving grace of Jesus to them, and A Li believed.

When I got to that area, the old sister asked me to go to her (A Li's) house. I asked her about this matter: "A Li, had you ever heard about Jesus before?"

She said, "No."

I said, "Had you ever heard about the doctrine of Jesus?"

She again said, "I had never heard of that either."

So you see, it was God himself who worked in her and personally called her to believe in the Lord. This is just one example. There are other examples of God's personally manifesting His great power in the countryside through miracles, healings, exorcisms, etc., bringing many rural brothers and sisters to salvation.

Beside this, there is a brother whose house caught fire. He had gone out to work, and his wife had gone to the market. Somebody told him, "You must go home quickly; your house is burning!" He hurried back and saw many people trying to extinguish the fire, which was burning around his house.

He opened the door to his house, went in, and knelt down and prayed, "God, you have given me this house, and if you want to take it back, do so." After he prayed, amazingly, a gust of wind blew the fire over his house. All the houses in the area were burned down except his. The neighbors were all surprised and wondered how this could have happened.

Then a Christian sister gave a special testimony. Her husband had written to her, telling about a fire in his village. Over ten houses had been burned, but when the fire got to his house, it stopped abruptly. Whenever he told people about this, they were very thankful to the Lord: "Lord, you kept our house. We know you love us. We praise you and thank you. We need your blessings and remember your great love."

So, many people who saw this incident said, "Your God is the living God; your Lord is the living Lord." Through these miracles, God manifests His power and draws many people to Himself.

4.11 Eastern China (II)

When I was in one place, there was a sister who said to me, "Brother Paul, I beg for food."

I said, "Oh, why do you beg? Is your family situation bad?"

She said, "No. It's that after I hear you here, I go back and repeat what you say for the other brothers and sisters. And I do this in other places too. At the same time, I tell these other groups about the situation of my own village. I do not have a Bible and am not very educated, so I depend on my own memory; I put the words of God in my heart and go back and recite them for them. So brother Paul, you must come to my village. After listening to you, my heart has been truly moved."

Such a sister! Such love for the Lord! Although she was uneducated and her situation was poor, she did all this work for the Lord. So I went to her village. I only stayed one day in all the other places, but I went to her village twice and stayed a day each time. Her house was crowded with people, both inside and outside. From this we can see that the brothers and sisters there are truly hungry.

Once a sister told me about some cadres who had defied God and then lost their own lives. Sitting next to me was a brother who sang two hymns after hearing this. These two hymns were a great inspiration to me. They went like this: "The cross was heavy, the pain hard, the way was crooked, but the Lord was present, comforting him in a mild voice, 'Do not worry, I am walking with you.'"

Its meaning was that although the cross is hard to bear and the road is twisted and hard to follow, the Lord Jesus is at your side and saying to you in a soft voice, 'Do not worry, I am walking with you.' This hymn comforted me as well as the brothers and sisters who have suffered.

The other hymn went like this: "Lord, your grace is truly wonderful. You hide your grace in your bosom. When people come to your bosom, they receive your grace. You are truly like this."

There was an older brother who had been a carpenter. His nose was unusual. It was like the head of a goldfish — red and very big. I asked his son, "Why is your dad's nose so unusual?"

He said, "Don't you know about my dad yet? From the time he was young, he was a drinker. He drank wine the way you drink tea. He also loved to gamble. He sold all his possessions to pay for gambling losses. When he won, he bought wine to drink. When he lost, he would sell his possessions to buy wine because he was sad; he would drink to forget his sorrows.

"But once he heard a preacher telling the story of the prodigal son. After hearing this story he cried. He said, 'I am truly a prodigal son." He repented then and believed in Jesus. Then wherever he went he would tell his testimony."

Now he is quite old, 72. Everyone comes to his house. Whenever he sees a person coming, he silently puts his farming tools down, leads the person to his house, and prays for them. I stayed in his house two days, and this happened both days. One person would come, he would lay down his tools and pray. Then he would send the person off, and another would come, and he would do the same thing without saying anything. He rejected no one. He received them and prayed for them as they came.

Because there were all kinds of people there, God had given this old brother the gift of healing. By praying like this, he could sometimes heal these people. Thus, many people came and believed in and received the Lord.

Later I realized that there was a problem there; many people thought of the Lord Jesus as a big doctor rather than as a savior. So when I was there, I especially introduced the Lord Jesus to everyone not only as a great healer, but also as the Lord of salvation. After hearing this, they felt that their previous understanding had been inadequate.

They had a pressing thirst in their love for the Lord and wanted to hear the word of the Lord. They didn't want me to go. This was true everywhere. Their enthusiastic love for the Lord and desire to hear the Way of the Lord deeply moved me. In comparison to them, I felt I was far behind.

I thank the Lord that on this trip he taught me many lessons on many matters that I had not realized or thought of before. God taught me and made me see his great power. I really want to say to the Lord, "Lord, you truly love us, your power is truly great. None can compare with you."

Truly the brothers and sisters in those places love the Lord. They not only thirst for the word of the Lord, but also love to listen. When I was preaching there, to preach for half an hour or one hour was not enough. They always wanted me to preach more. How much time should I give them? They would say, "At least two hours, any more than that is up to you. but at least two hours." In Shanghai, half an hour of preaching is unusual, but [in the countryside] they always wanted two or three hours. In evening meetings, for example, I would start preaching at 6:30 and go on until 10:00. Then after finishing at 10:00, they still wouldn't want to go, would ask me questions on everything, and would ask me to pray for them. This would go on till 11:00 or 12:00 at night.

Because my time there was limited, I travelled from county to county and place to place. Since I wanted to go to the countryside, I couldn't sit still in the counties. Usually I would travel in the mornings, rest in the afternoons, have meetings in the evenings, and travel again the next morning, going to another village. Otherwise you couldn't get to all the villages in one or two years. So I kept a strict rule of staying in each village only one day, and going to another village the next day. Some brothers and sisters followed me from one village to another. Sometimes when there were many [Christians] in a village, bringing other brothers and sisters made it more crowded. But this gave them an even more eager spirit.

They really loved the Lord and wanted not only to hear, but also to have Bibles. This distressed me, because there was no way I could satisfy them. I had only brought one Bible, so I said to them, "I will write down your names and addresses, and you pray, and I will pray for God to provide [the Bibles]." Some wanted to copy hymns and wanted me to teach them hymns. Others wanted Bible study books. They wanted everything. They said, "We want to hear, we want to read, and, where we don't understand, we want reference books. When you're not here, we can continue to read." The urgency of their needs truly moved me.

There were some villages with no Bible at all. Some had only one or at most two Bibles, although that was rare. So they all needed them. I said to them, "You copy it by hand. Read a few characters and then copy them." But they didn't know where to begin copying. So I agreed, "After I get back to Shanghai, I will mail you outlines of the Bible and things to read and memorize."

So when I got back, I did this work and looked everywhere to find some Bibles and devotional books to send them in the countryside. When they received them, they were extremely happy.

Just today I received two letters. In these letters they wrote of their joy and of how they thank and praise the Lord. They are eager for faith. It truly moves me.

4.12 Eastern China (III)

This time, I didn't go to the countryside to teach the brothers and sisters. Actually, these brothers and sisters helped me and brought great benefit to me. They enabled me to see the great power, grace, and love of God. I felt unworthy to stand before God's face.

The brothers and sisters in rural Zhejiang have many special qualities. Every Christian has a straw mat at home. Whenever they run into any difficulty they kneel down and pray. When the brothers and sisters see each other, they seldom talk about how they are and what has been happening and so forth. [Instead,] they kneel down and pray. Thus, the might and miracles of God are frequently seen there. So I truly felt that the grace of God is great.

Previously I had thought that the rural brothers and sisters were uneducated and that we Shanghai people were generally better. But on going there, I learned that the rural brothers and sisters were much stronger than those in Shanghai. Their faith is pure, their love is sincere, and what they preach, they do. This is really different from some of the brothers and sisters in Shanghai. When the rural Christians pray, they pray earnestly; when they remember the Lord in Communion, they cry and weep. It's as if the Lord Jesus were being crucified right in front of them.

I visited ten counties, and in two places more than 800 people were baptized. I felt unworthy. Many people grasped my hands and said, "Brother Paul, we really are unworthy; we really are inadequate." These words cut me to my heart, because I am not as good as they are. These brothers and sisters were baptized in the river. Sometimes in the evening it was cold, but they were unperturbed; their fervor made them unafraid of the cold.

Now how is the general situation in the Church? They are all thirsty for the Lord. They want to hear about the Way of the Lord. Unfortunately, the number of workers is small. The crop to be harvested is great. This is the general situation.

Another situation is that the number of people who listen to the Way are many, but Bibles are few. Because of this, there are many meetings that don't have true servants of God leading them, so heresies easily arise. Some do not preach the whole truth or misinterpret names or facts. The reasons are, first, the lack of people [i.e. good teachers], and second, the lack of Bibles to read. They don't have a proper foundation. So the most urgent need in the countryside is Bibles. Next is for hymnals.

In Shanghai, few children have heard of the Way, because it is said that the national laws forbid those sixteen and under to go to church. But in the countryside it is different. There are a great many children in the countryside, and they are very eager. In one place I went to, all the children were sitting in the front and the adults stood at the back. There were more children than adults!

One little boy was very attentive, even more so than the adults. He stayed to talk with me after everyone had left. Although the boy was only twelve, he talked logically. A sister had led him to believe in the Lord, and she herself was only about twenty-three. [During the day] her husband has an outside job, while she leads the children to her house. The children are glad to have a place to go and to be with this sister. They talk together, one asking questions and the other answering. So even young children know the way to find the Lord. I preached to these little brothers and sisters about things that adults didn't think they wanted to listen to. But the children joyfully accepted it. What the adults didn't understand, the children understood. As the Bible says, "I have hidden it from those who can hear, but the children can understand it." Thank the Lord that He loves them.

So after I returned, I thanked the Lord: "Lord, Your loving and caring for me like this is not due to anything I can do. I am a useless vessel. I can only give myself for you to use." I really wanted to say to the Lord, "Lord, please mold me. In the past I stood too proudly. Please be merciful to me. Please lead me. Help me to serve You better."

When I was in each county, the brothers and sisters would cry and not want to let me go. They begged me, "You must return; you must come again." When they saw me off at the train station, they waited until the train had left and they couldn't see it anymore before going back. Even though this happened four months ago, I will never forget it. Their loving hearts, their love for God, their eagerness to serve God, all deeply moved me. I prayed to the Lord "Lord, may Your will be done."

In most places, church meetings are held in homes, because most of the church buildings have been borrowed by the communes. Some churches have been turned into factories. But the people are so many and the houses are small, and even where some homes are large the meetings are very crowded. The people aren't afraid of difficulties. They come from great distances for meetings, twenty or thirty *li*, and stay until eleven o'clock at night before returning. Even if they have to walk one or two hours, they don't mind.

Another good sign in various places is that they are looking forward to the government giving them back churches or giving them large places to use. Although the government has clearly indicated this in its religious policy, due to regulations it hasn't been fully implemented. Because of this, it has said, "The [Christian] meetings are all right. Even if you meet in houses it doesn't matter; we won't come and disperse or attack you."

The government in one difficult place is a little more strict about this, and so the brothers and sisters there still do not meet publicly. They inform each other secretly of the time and place to meet, and they meet secretly so that they don't draw the attention of the cadres or police in that area.

When we were there, truly God took care of us. We never had any trouble. Once when I had finished preaching and everyone had left, the commune cadres came. But this was true only at that place, not in the other places.

[Generally] they are good. They say, "We won't interfere with your belief in religion so long as it doesn't affect production." In the communes, they never paid attention to us. So the brothers and sisters all felt quite free.

There is one other matter now, that of localized controversies. The brothers and sisters feel that the greatest controversy is whether to cover the head or not. The second concerns the Sabbath, and the third is the form of baptism. These three controversies cause many divisions. When I went to places to preach, I would preach to them on the way of the Lord. I hoped that they would note the words of the Lord, the final prayer of Jesus for them, "Father, You have called them together as one, as You and I are one." Jesus' final command to His disciples was for them to love one another.

So I would preach on these two points to them. I would say to them, "When we listen to the words of the Lord, we have different interpretations, different opinions. But we must be polite to one another and not attack each other. We must unite and be one for the sake of the Gospel of the Lord, for the sake of those who need to receive salvation. We must work together before the face of the Lord." I urged them not to make divisions but to unite and be one, to respect each other and love one another.

They all listened to my words and felt that their past conflicts were not right. They repented, thank the Lord. There were two places in which they had fought bitterly. However, they felt that they should follow the Lord's words and do things according to the Lord Jesus' command. So they began holding worship together and even wrote a joint letter to the government saying that they were no longer divided.

4.13 Eastern China (IV)

There was a person named Su. Everyone called her "older sister Su." She was a doctor in a hospital. She said to me, "Brother Paul, as a doctor I see sick people. If we don't give them medicine, we give shots or operate. Mostly we use these three methods. I know that the brothers and sisters here always kneel down and pray when they get sick and ask God to heal their illnesses. I am quite concerned for them. Why? If God heals them, well and good. This brings glory to God. But if they don't recover, the name of God will not receive glory. So in my heart I am ill at ease. I feel that in sickness it is not good to depend on prayer. When someone is sick, he should take the medicine and shots. But once God taught me something which left me with no answer."

Once she went to the house of an old lady. Her son was called Huyao, so everyone called her Mother Huyao. The people in that area didn't call her house a house, but a hospital. Why? Because many times sick people would go to her house. After asking her to pray, they would recover. So this doctor said to me that once she was a guest [at Mother Huyao's "hospital"], and a patient with stomach cancer came and asked her to pray for her. She had gone to many hospitals, and the doctors had all told her that her illness was incurable. But she did not give up. She heard that Jesus could heal, and she also heard about how Mother Huyao had helped many sick people. So she also came and asked Mother Huyao to pray for her.

After Mother Huyao prayed for her, her stomach had a great pain. This made Dr. Su, who was watching from the side, very worried. What could she do? When she saw the patient cry out in pain, she felt very bad. Then the patient vomited. Blood and pus came out, with a terrible smell.

After vomiting, she said, "Could you please give me some porridge to eat?" She used to vomit up anything she ate, and she hadn't eaten anything for several days. But strangely now, after vomiting, she ate porridge. One bowl wasn't enough, and she wanted a second bowl. She was better. She had recovered.

Dr. Su said to me that she had seen this personally: "I could only say before the face of God, 'Father, all You do is perfect. This incident has deeply moved me.'"

In one place where I went, there was a brother named Jiaohua. The people didn't call his house brother Jiaohua's house, but brother Jiaohua's hospital. His house is big, with many mats and blankets for the visitors. Sick brothers and sisters are sent to stay there. Jiaohua prays for the sick brothers and sisters in the morning, afternoon, and evening, three times a day. God answers their prayers. Sick when they come, after a few days they leave well. They don't take medicine or injections; it is all from God's grace. God's great power heals their sicknesses. Because of this , many people in that area have believed in the Lord.

When I preached there, they listened very eagerly for the word of the Lord. When they knew a preacher was there, some came from long distances, twenty or thirty *li*. They would listen until ten o'clock at night, and then stay in his house. They have all kinds of urgent needs. They want to hear the word of the Lord; they want to believe; they want to receive salvation. So all this testifies that God uses miracles to call people to Him and to receive His grace.

Once I went to a certain county. There is a village there called Lincun. The house of one of the sisters was the meeting place. Every Sunday the Christians would come to this house, and everyone would kneel down and pray. After praying, they would leave. Why was this? It was because they did not have a preacher, no Bibles or hymnals, and the sister herself was not very well educated. So all they could do was pray.

Finally this sister said to God, in prayer, "God, this kind of situation should not be! You must send a servant to us. And if you don't send a servant, next Sunday I'm going to lock the door and not let anyone in. We will stop! I am not educated, so how do You expect me to manage? And we have no one to sing hymns of praise. What do You expect me to do? You must send Your servant." But God did not answer her prayer.

The next Sunday, at the worship time, the Spirit of God filled her. She stood up and preached to the brothers and sisters in Mandarin. When she started to preach, a sister next to her said, "Don't speak in Mandarin; use our dialect. what are you trying to do, speaking in Mandarin?"

But she said, "Impossible. There is fire inside, and I can't control my tongue; I have to speak this way." And she preached a fine sermon to them. The brothers and sisters were all deeply moved. Also, she sang a hymn of praise very well. After the service was over, everybody was surprised at what had happened and wondered about what could have caused it. So they asked the sister, "Why don't you use your dialect to preach to us?"

She said, "It's impossible. About this, I...." And before she finished speaking, she began using their local dialect.

The next week, the same thing happened. The Holy Spirit filled her; again she preached and sang a beautiful hymn. After this happened several times, some of the brothers and sisters began to feel a bit uneasy. "Is this really the work of the Holy Spirit?"

So they went to consult an old brother. This old brother was blind but still very alert. They told him about the situation and asked him to come and listen and ascertain whether her preaching was right or not, whether it was really the truth of the Bible, and whether her hymn-singing was right. This blind brother arranged with another old brother to go to the service together.

The sister preached as usual and led them in a hymn. After the service, the brothers and sisters gathered around the blind brother, "Brother, is her preaching right?"

The old, blind brother said, "Absolutely correct. It was entirely Biblical truth. As she preached, she didn't tell you the chapter and verses to look up, but recited the scripture passages character for character from memory. Her hymn was also this way."

They asked, "Was the hymn right?"

The old brother said, "Right," and he told them what number the hymn was, and to look it up. So they searched for a hymnal and found that she had sung it right, character for character.

So, many brothers and sisters in that area came. Those attending the meetings filled the house, with some standing outside the windows and the door. This was the situation as she preached about the Lord Jesus, and everyone enjoyed listening to her.

Unfortunately I didn't ask her name. When I finished speaking there, she stood up and prayed in Mandarin, praising the Lord with "Praise the Lord; thank the Lord." I thought it was strange. Why does she only say these two sentences? When most of the brothers and sisters prayed [in the countryside], they talked about things in their hearts that moved them. Why did she only use these words of thanks?

Afterwards I asked about it, and they said, "This is that sister." So I thanked the Lord that this ordinary, rural, uneducated woman was used by God in this way. Why? Because she had a faithful heart, a willingness to work for the Lord, a heart of love for the Lord. She not only felt a burning desire to do the Lord's work, but was also like a fire to the hearts of the brothers and sisters who came to the meetings. So God used her in this way and manifested His great power and love through her, drawing many to turn to God. Wherever I went

I saw the work that God was doing in the brothers and sisters.

God exorcised evil spirits the same way. When I was in Changduan, there was an old brother who loved the Lord very much, who had suffered much for the Lord. So God gave him special grace so that he not only received the moving of the Holy Spirit and could preach the truth of God, but could also have the gift of healing and exorcism.

One time, someone asked him to come because there was a person possessed by a devil. No one could draw near him because of his great strength. When the old brother arrived he said. "In the name of Jesus Christ, you are not permitted to move." The man didn't move at all. The old brother then continued, "In the name of Jesus Christ, your hands are tied up." Then the possessed man raised his hands and crossed them as if they were really bound by a rope and could not be pulled apart. Then the old brother spoke several sentences to the possessed man and said, "In the name of Jesus Christ, I command you to come out of the man!" The man then regained control over himself. This incident had a great effect on the people there. They loved to listen to the old brother preach. Everyone called him "Uncle."

From his long experiences, you can see the great power of God in his life, and you can also see how God does not mistreat His servants. He always gives those who serve Him sufficient grace and uses them to manifest His own love and power. It is this way everywhere; you can see how God Himself calls and saves. It is just as the Lord said, "I have come to seek and to save the lost." He personally has sought and saved the lost. On this trip I wanted to help gather into the storehouse those whom God has personally found. But I didn't need to use any of my own strength. It was all God's own work and personal action.

In another county, there was a sister who had "worn a hat" [as a criminal], but she took this hat as God's blessing and was happy in her heart. So when she walked down the street [as a criminal], people thought it was strange. "Why is she smiling like that?" The people felt that walking the street was a bitter experience, and wondered why she was so happy.

So God blessed her, and whoever she prayed for would recover from his illness. Once there was a sick person who asked her to pray. It was three o'clock in the morning.

There was another sister who couldn't sleep that night. She heard a voice calling across her room. What was this voice? It said, "God, have mercy on so and so. She is ill. God, show your mercy!" Where could this strange voice have come from?

The next morning, she got up and went to the sister. She said, "Last night I heard a voice at three o'clock, which said, 'God have mercy no so and so.' I thought it was strange. It went across the room from the east side to the west side. What could it have been?"

The sister said, "At three o'clock I was praying here. But how my voice have reached your house? It's quite far, more than ten *li*, isn't it?"

So God loves those brothers and sisters; He manifests His great grace and love in their lives, and uses them to do His work.

4.14 Cantonese Epistle

This letter is from a young man who came to Christ through a Chinese Christian traveler and then dedicated himself to propagating the Gospel. This is part of an account of a trip he made to northern China.

Dear brothers in the Lord: Greetings!

Thank the Lord, my trip up to the north went well. I will briefly discuss the events of this journey.

I went to Longzhan and lived in a Christian brother's home. After I saw the situation of church revival there, I truly felt grateful to the Lord for His grace — for allowing a man of small faith to witness His mighty acts in person. I should praise the Lord our Heavenly Father. What we human beings cannot do, God can. The situation of the church in Longzhan is a beautiful testimony to this fact.

The Longzhan church revival began in 1965. During the Cultural Revolution, many young people were moved by the Holy Spirit and rose up to preach the Gospel. Some were arrested, others struggled against, and still others persecuted. But, nevertheless, they did not forsake the faith; on the contrary, their faith became even stronger. These people today are the pillars of the church in Longzhan. They are the so-called "responsible brothers." When the Lord revived the Longzhan church, He began to protect them.

Today in Longzhan there are no officially open churches, but house churches are everywhere. In each of these house church meetings, there are maybe twenty to thirty, fifty to sixty, over a hundred or sometimes even two hundred people. The government knows about these meetings, but it is said that the government does not bother them.

I am grateful to the Lord for miraculously permitting me to participate in a few of these house churches in Longzhan. I saw how the brothers and sisters who preached came from all kinds of vocations and across other boundaries; there were workers, teachers, cobblers, and others. Among them were many young people, but they have tremendous gifts of preaching. The brothers and sisters who attended those meetings loved the Lord very much and they sang very well. Some of the hymns they composed themselves.

There is a house church whose responsible brother arranged for no more than six persons to give their testimonies. But after these six had spoken, there were still many who wanted to stand up to give their testimonies. Their testimonies came from the bottom of their hearts, and they each spoke one after the other with naturalness and with a certain kind of restraint, until it was quite late, so that the responsible brother had to ask the remaining ones to speak next time.

Longzhan has a population of around half a million. Those who believe in the Lord number 50-60,000, and among them Christian sisters are the majority.

4.15 Hainan Island

This young brother now lives outside the mainland but visits Hainan quite often.
My dear brother in Christ,
We are all bathed in the grace of our Lord Jesus. Therefore, first of

all, let us together give thanks to our mighty Creator. I am anxious
to tell you my experiences during my visit to my home village in
Hainan.

The Lichi [Commune of Wanning County] is the place where
Christians are most active in the eastern section of Hainan Island.
In that area there were churches even before liberation. Believers there
were able to conduct normal Christian life until the Cultural
Revolution. But during the Cultural Revolution churches were
destroyed, and now the believers are seeking to rebuild them. Of
course, during the Cultural Revolution period Christians could not
carry on the usual activities. During the past two to three years, after
the arrest of the Gang of Four, believers have been able to conduct
semi-open types of Christian activities. More recently believers have
been meeting openly. They usually meet every Saturday and Sunday
evening. Their meeting programme is as follows:

1. Silent prayer
2. Hymn singing, somewhat like a choir
3. Giving testimonies one by one (Because there are no pastors
   and no one to deliver a message, each one gives testimonies
   to the others.)
4. Hymn singing
5. Offering

The content of their testimonies usually includes thanksgiving for
having been called into the Kingdom of God, explanation of how
they led others to the Lord, and testimony of how by the power of
the Lord they have been able to heal the sick. Earnest believers in
that area have erected a *spiritual* hospital in the name of the Lord
and healed many by the Lord's name, and it has been very effective.
Therefore, many have been led to the Lord through healing, and it
is also the most powerful testimony that they have rendered.

The number of people gathering for these house church
meetings is several dozen, and sometimes it reaches over a hundred.
They divide their work or meeting places into several meeting spots,
with each spot at the home of a certain believer. In the county of
Wanning alone, the number of believers reaches several thousand.
Other places where Christians are known to have activities include

Wenchang County in the northeast section of Hainan, the Liangchong County in the central part, and the Chan County in the northwest section. In the Chan County there are pastors. Brothers and sisters in Haikou City conduct Sunday services regularly. A few months ago when the churches in Shanghai were opened, they sent letters of comfort to these brothers in Hainan.

4.16 Beijing and the Provinces

A middle-aged academic believer wrote to the Center periodically to give us news of the Church.
Dear Brother,
The church of the Lord is flourishing greatly everywhere, although it is difficult to get enough concrete reports. Here in Beijing we have a weekly Fellowship Meeting at Rice Street (the official church). About twenty to thirty earnest Christians come together to pray. Often with tears running down our cheeks, we pray for the church in Beijing and for all the churches throughout China. We earnestly plead with the Lord for the revival of His Church in China. Occasionally some believers attending our Fellowship Meeting come from other provinces, and from them we can hear something about church situations outside Beijing.

Yesterday a Christian brother from a certain prefecture in Hebei province brought his son and daughter to the Fellowship Meeting, and I gave him a copy of the Bible. He said that just in the one fellowship group that he attended there were more than 500 brothers and sisters.

I was baptized in Shanxi Province in 1950. I still maintain good communication with brothers and sisters there. According to them, each time they meet, more than 100 people come. Last year more than thirty were baptized and added to the Lord. There are four brothers in charge of that fellowship. In the city of Yuan, more than ten young people were baptized. In Lingbao County in Henan Province, there are more than 10,000 believers. In one particular commune, there are more than 2,700 believers. They have fellowship with brothers in Shanxi. In most cases rural churches are more prosperous than urban churches. May the Lord have mercy on the spiritually poor and thirsty in the villages, for the Gospel is for them (Matt. 11:4-6). I can bear witness that God cares for the poor and is the God of widows and orphans.

Beijing

The situation in the Beijing official church on Rice Street is as follows: In April 1979, there were less than twenty Chinese Christians attending the Sunday service. The first time that I attended was on an Easter Sunday. I wept throughout the service. Afterwards I discovered that many other brothers and sisters had wet eyes — like me, they were greatly moved. For nearly twenty years, we had been like orphans. As Romans 8:36 says, "for thy sake we are being put to death all day long; we are accounted as sheep for the slaughter." But thanks be unto God, He has not forsaken any of His children. He is going to save us to the end. Even though the Beijing church is still very barren when compared with churches in the provinces, yet the little church in the former Bible House is packed to capacity every Sunday — both the upstairs chapel and the downstairs reception hall. Right now the pastors are thinking about adding a public address system and putting a speaker downstairs so that the people [who have been worshipping in silence]can hear what is said from the pulpit upstairs. It is reported that the government has returned the Gangwa Street Church for Christian use, but it will take some time to repair it. The number of people attending the Beijing Church increases each week. We also heard that the former YMCA building may also be restored to Christians. All is in God's hands. Church services have begun in Shenyang, Tianjin, Zhangjiakou, Guangdong etc. God has opened a door for China which man cannot close.

From December last year [1979], the Beijing Church has had preaching services. [From 1972 to late 1979, services were conducted in a liturgical manner followed by Holy Communion, without preaching.] Sermons have been preached by Rev. Caleb Yan [formerly of the "Local Church" in Beijing — Watchman Nee's system], brother Shi Zhesheng and Rev. Tingzhuo.

4.17 Visitors from Abroad

An account of a visit to Nanjing.

Q: How did [your friend] know the believers?

A: She had corresponded with the pastor. Thirty-three years ago she was in China, only for two years, and then the Communists took over.

Q: Was she a missionary?

A: Yes, and so she knew the pastor. He had been a foreign student in America years ago, and he took his theological training there. When he got his degree he was offered a church, a nice Chinese church in the States, and he said no, his people needed him. So he cut off ties with the United States and went back. He has served in China as a pastor ever since, and he suffered greatly in the Cultural Revolution. He's crippled because of that.

In the Cultural Revolution the Red Guards took all of his theological library and burned it. They took all the Bibles he had, and all the books, and had a fire in the courtyard that lasted a day and a half. The Red Guards shut him and his wife up in one of the bedrooms and locked the door. They watched the fire through the windows.

Q: His church was always independent then, I take it.

A: Yes, it was an independent church, so he wasn't closely associated with a mission. Then through the Cultural Revolution the groups splintered up, spread out. They must have met in some church buildings before, but we didn't have enough time to get into all that. He is still more or less the shepherd of the groups, but all the other people are deacons and elders of his church.

Q: So they gathered together with you.

A: They gathered together with us. I have their testimonies on tape in Mandarin, in which they told us about how the group started and about some of the miracles and healings that had taken place among them. One of the fellows' father committed suicide. He was a Christian, but the pressures of the Cultural Revolution were too much. He jumped off a bridge. He was educated as an engineer in Tokyo, a well-balanced Christian.

They wanted books on theology; they literally want to go into full-time Christian ministry. And there are a lot of them around, apparently. In this group there is a heavy concentration of young people. Of course, a lot of the leadership are of the forty-to-fifty age group.

Their leadership and their group is made up of both workers and teacher-level people. That's about the highest social level. There are not really any doctors, lawyers, or other professionals, but they have teachers of one kind or another. They freely gave me their addresses.

His daughter-in-law was our contact to come and get us at the hotel and pick us up. Then we walked for almost an hour down little lanes and alleys to get to the pastor's house. One of the pastor's sons is married, and he's in prison. I didn't press for the reason why, but I got the drift that it had something to do with his position as a Christian. They have two boys.

Q: Has he been in prison long?

A: Yes, he's been in two and one-half years and he has two and one-half years to go. He's in the middle of it.

Q: What happened at the meeting?

A: There were 200 people who came in the middle of the afternoon because we were there. They didn't treat us preferentially. We weren't foreigners held in high esteem, nor did they look down on us either. We were the first foreign Christians who had contacted the group since before the Cultural Revolution.

The pastor had been writing freely to Christians outside that he knew and to the mission that he knew before, saying that he had no Bibles for all these groups since the Cultural Revolution and asking to borrow one in some way. If somebody could bring it in, they would copy it and be sure to hand it back again if they were in short supply outside. So it was in response to this that my friend was delivering a Bible. He knew that she was coming, as he had invited her. Otherwise, when she told me, "Hey, there's a Christian group that I would like to contact; do you want to come too?" I would have said, "No, we mustn't touch the Christian groups. This is for our Chinese brothers and sisters to do." She told me this is different because they requested the visit and that we are not endangering the group because the pastor has freely written outside.

Q: Can she speak Mandarin?

A: Well, she studied Mandarin for three years, but she didn't even want to try to speak it. But the pastor speaks passable English because of his background.

Q: Did you only take one Bible to him?

A: She brought a Bible; but I had a whole suitcase full of stuff. Well, I didn't know what the Lord had in mind for it, because I wasn't going to stand out in front of the hotel and hand out Bibles. But I took Bibles, Testaments, everything I could with me; that's why I kept appearing in one set of clothes there. I didn't take any more clothes; I just loaded up with this stuff, trusting that God had some reason for it. And this was the reason for it, because she had brought along only one Bible for the pastor.

Q: She came all the way to China and only brought one Bible?

A: She was a tourist, just going on holiday. After she had given him this Bible in the old script, I dumped out my stuff too. When he handled that Bible, the tears just fell all over it. He said this was the first Scripture he had had in years.

Their group numbers thousands of baptized believers meeting in many locations, and this is only *their* group. He says there are dozens of others, hundreds of other house churches. He also says there are about twice as many unbaptized believers as baptized ones. But they are very slow to have them baptized; they want to be really assured, especially [about the] young people.

Now they had this meeting of 200 people, with loud singing, testimonies, and preaching, and all in the middle of the day, and I asked the pastor, "Aren't the government authorities going to come by?"

And he said, "If they do, they do. Now is the time for us to preach the Gospel. They promised us a little more freedom of religion, and we're going to take what we can get." And he said that if they do come, "We'll just tell them we're celebrating a birthday."

"A birthday?" I asked.

He replied, "Well, we can celebrate Jesus' birthday anytime.

Not just Christmas."

They kept sending us from house to house for meals. We knew
that this food was rationed. They must have spent all their ration
cards for months on us. We kept saying, "No, the important thing
is just to have fellowship and prayer together; you don't have to feed
us. We're overstuffed as it is." But they wanted to do it.

On the very last night, when we were ready to leave, we had
prayer together. The pastor laid his hands on us and prayed for us.
He thanked the Lord for bringing us as the first overseas contacts.
He asked us to bring back the message to Christians on the outside.

They wanted to know so many other things. They wanted to
know, are there any Christians in the rest of the world? Are there
any churches in Hong Kong? Do any Westerners believe in God? Is
there public worship? Are there any Chinese churches in America?
I had brought certain photos along. I was prepared for the
unexpected, and showed them pictures of large groups of believers
like in a football stadium. I said, "There are 55,000 people in this
picture."

They said, "Watching ball?"

I said, "Not watching ball, worshipping God."

"In public, all together?"

And I said, "Yes."

And they said, "From what church?"

"Different churches, it doesn't make any difference." It just blew
their minds.

Then I showed them pictures of Chinese Bible study groups
in the States and told them how many Chinese churches there are
in North America. I told them that God is working among Chinese
in Asia in church growth and building up the churches and uniting
the churches to work and pray together. They couldn't believe it, that
God was working *this much* in the world today.

They said, "Are there any intellectuals who believe? Are there
any students and university people who believe too?" Apparently they
had been told that only ignoramuses believe these superstitions. "Are
there intelligent people who believe?" Questions like this really made
me weep.

They nearly wore out my photographs by passing them around and telling each other, "These are Christians here."

The bottom line came when I told them that the Christians had remembered to pray for them all these years. Then it was their turn to weep. They said, "Christians outside have been praying for us all these years?"

And I thought, "Oh God, keep me from being a hypocrite. A lot of us have forgotten and a lot of us weren't diligent in prayer."

But then they said, "Well, no wonder the Lord kept us through all of this, because they were praying for us." They said, "Go back and tell the brothers and sisters all over: 'Thank you and don't forget to pray for us now, because we are in the greatest crisis we have ever been in, with these opening churches.'" They didn't want to have anything to do with them.

Q: What kind of information did they have about what the Religious Affairs Bureau would be doing?

A: Oh, they were knowledgeable. I just heard that this group was actually so bold as to appeal to Beijing for more religious freedom for Christians in China. Apparently they, through official channels, had said, "Okay, now if you really mean it, give the Christians more liberty."

But this is a bolder group than some of the others. You have to recognize that this is not a typical group, because they are so open to foreigners. Now they want more Bibles and more Christian materials. Specifically they shared with me what they need, and they gave me addresses in Chinese to try to send little packets first to see whether they arrive, and that sort of thing.

I am hoping to get them a cassette recorder, so that I can send messages from Chinese Christians and so forth, or so somebody can carry them. It is a very live contact. The last thing that the pastor said to us was that he was so thankful that he had committed to faithful men the work of the Gospel, so that at any time he could go and all the groups would be taken care of.

Then he said that, in his long ministry, the last two years have been the time of the greatest ingathering of Christians that he has ever experienced. The groups have proliferated in just the last two years, and a lot of them are young people. That's really something.

Q: Yes, that is, because the same thing could be happening all over China.

A: Yes, sure. It's more than one isolated case. There is a vacuum right now. When we were there, as soon as I dumped my Bibles out on [the pastor's] bed, three men from Anhui Province came in, you know with straw hats and staffs. They had come by river boat and traveled at night, just because they heard there were some foreign Christians that came to this other group, who brought news of Christians from the outside, and that may have brought some Scriptures. And they appeared at the door one morning while we were there, and the pastor recognized them when they came in, and he told us that these men were from a brand new group in Anhui Province out in the countryside. It was only four months old. He didn't mention how many, but he said it was a large group of believers. They didn't have any Scriptures, and they'd come just because they heard there might be some Scriptures. So the pastor picked out a whole New Testament from the bunch of stuff that I brought, one in old script because these were country folks. And he gave it to these guys. And one of them had a sweaty towel around his neck. He took off his sweaty towel and spread it out there and put this Bible, this testament, on it and wrapped it all up in this sweaty towel and put it in his bag, just grinning and saying, "Thank the Lord." The pastor said that if he hadn't picked it out and given it to them, they might have taken everything. So he instructed them to be sure that every member of the group had his turn in reading the Scriptures. He said to memorize the Scriptures.

4.18 Prisoners' Words

This interview with Wang Mingdao took place soon after his release from prison in 1980.

Q: When did you leave prison?

A: On January tenth I came to Shanghai. So it has been exactly two months since I left prison. They wanted me to leave the prison, but I refused to leave. I wanted to stay. I did not want to leave until my status was clarified.

Q: I have a question to ask you.

A: If the question concerns faith, I will answer you, but if it concerns politics, I will refrain from answering you.

Q: How many years were you in prison?

A: The first time it was nearly fourteen months. The second time was twenty-one years plus eight months; altogether I stayed in prison more than twenty-three years. I entered into a great University, and there I learnt many many great lessons. Throughout these twenty-three years of imprisonment, my faith has become stronger than it was before I entered prison.

Q: Do you have any words of encouragement to Chinese Christians overseas?

A: Well, there are many indeed. Most of my books have been published overseas. One of them is called *These Fifty Years* which is an autobiography of my life written for my fiftieth birthday. There I wrote everything I experienced from my birth to my fiftieth birthday; there I recorded my entire faith, my call and my work.

Q: Many Christians in the West find forgiveness a serious problem, and we have not even suffered. How are you able to forgive?

A: I don't remember any of the faults of those who have offended me. I can thoroughly forgive them because Jesus told us, "If you will forgive those who trespass against you, your Father in Heaven will also forgive your trespasses; if you do not forgive others, your Father in Heaven will not forgive you." Therefore, we should not hate anybody. Anyone who has hurt me, I am able to forgive. This should be so, because I am a great sinner myself. If God has forgiven me, can I not forgive others?

Q: Were there other Christians in the prison where you served? How did you mutually encourage each other?

A: There weren't many believers in the prison except for one Roman Catholic doctor with whom I could talk. He was sentenced for fifteen years, and just before he was released he committed suicide. So there was just one true believer that I knew. Besides him, I did not meet any Christians.

Q: Wasn't there a pastor who struggled against you?

A: Oh, he was a rice-Christian — I mean one who used to preach
the Gospel for employment. His conduct was terrible.

Q: Did you have any Bibles in prison that you could read?

A: No, not a single Bible in the twenty-three years and ten months
that I was there. I never saw a Bible even once during my
imprisonment.

Q: Did you memorize the Bible?

A: Yes, I memorized many passages from the Scripture. I would
not consider myself as one who knew the Bible the best among all
people, but I am one who knew his Bible well. I had trained myself
to memorize Scripture in long passages consisting of many verses,
which I could readily recall during my imprisonment. Thus it did
not matter that much whether I had a Bible with me or was without
a Bible. Even though I did not have any Bible, I had the Bible in
my head, and so it was as though I had a Bible with me during my
imprisonment. Of course, it was not as good as having a Bible before
me to be able to read every detail of the Scriptures. But I remembered
the important teachings and promises in the Scriptures and I could
dwell on them often. Thus, to have a Bible or not have a Bible did
not differ that much with me at that time. I was also able to memorize
many hymns, both in English and Chinese, although I could not
remember them in their entirety — usually one or two verses. For
I never dreamed of spending such a long period of time in prison.
If I had known that, I would have memorized many, many more Bible
passages and hymns.

Q: Did you sing hymns while in prison?

A: Yes, but I would only sing in a low voice, alone, not wanting
to disturb others. I would walk around the courtyard and sing in a
low voice to myself.

Q: What has kept your faith going all these years? Are there special
verses which kept your faith stronger and stronger as the days went by?

A: There are many passages from Scripture which helped me.
Actually I can recite many passages from Scripture.

Q: What was the most blessed time you had while you were in
prison?

A: The more often I was tried and attacked, the more abundantly

I received His grace. The words of Scriptures became my strength after I had fallen; God, through His word, enabled me to stand up again. Peter cried bitterly after he had denied the Lord three times. Peter fell only for one day, but I fell for several years. Thanks be unto God. Peter was forgiven after he had bitterly cried in repentance. I did not shed tears, but in my heart there was severe pain. I confessed my sins, and I repented, and my Lord also forgave me. So, like Peter, though I had failed miserably, yet I was able to rise up again. Peter's case gave me great comfort, because it shows that, as a man falls, he comes to know his greatest weakness, and the Lord is able to change his weakness into strength.

Paul said, "In my body there is a thorn; I prayed often to the Lord that He might cause the thorn to be removed from me, but the Lord said to me, 'My grace is sufficient for you, my strength is made manifest in your weakness.' I like to boast over my weakness for it is in my weakness that I become strong." I have gone through a long period of failure, but, thanks be unto God, from my failure I have turned to victory.

Even now I can only boast in the Lord. Jeremiah said, "The wise should not boast over his wisdom, the rich should not boast over his riches, the warrior should not boast over his strength; he who boasts should boast because he knows that I am the Lord and knows that I perform justice and righteousness on the earth. Therefore I boast, says the Lord." Only after I had experienced severe failure, did I know how to trust my God. Therefore, today I can only boast in the Lord, not over how strong I am, but in that, after I had fallen, the Lord enabled me to stand up again and made me become a strong man. I am now stronger than I was over twenty years ago.

Q: During all these years did you have any word from other believers?

A: I did not receive any news, not a single letter from anyone except for letters from my wife and my son. But even they could not say much. Neither could I write much, and, if I did, it would not be sent. So I was totally cut off from outside news.

Q: So the Lord allowed you to stay in prison out of His own will; He did not make a mistake, did He?

A: He did not make a single mistake. We know that "all things work together for good to them that are called according to His will."

Q: If you had not been in prison, wouldn't you have done more work for the Lord?

A: No, the work that I did by staying in prison is greater than what I could have done by not being in prison.

Q: What work did you do inside prison?

A: I received training and exercises from the Lord. That is my greatest gain. If I had not been in prison, I would not have the privilege of giving so many testimonies, and neither would there be so many people who respect me. Although I could not do much work inside prison, by my being in prison my books were circulated throughout the world. Before, I only served the Lord inside China; I had never gone outside of China. Then God circulated only a small portion of my writings outside China. These twenty-some years in prison enabled my books to be read overseas; the result is greater than if I had been preaching myself. So I did not stay in prison in vain. The work of the Lord was expanded and I myself made considerable spiritual progress. Through trials and sufferings, I have gained much maturity. If I had not gone through these many trials and sufferings, I would not have achieved the kind of maturity that I now enjoy. Neither would I be as strong as I am today.

Q: What benefits have the past thirty years of suffering brought to the church in China?

A: There are great benefits. Through trials and sufferings those who did not truly believe in the Lord have been eliminated. The remnants remaining are all very strong ones. It has been a great purification.

Q: Any other benefits?

A: I do not know what benefits others have derived from their experiences of suffering, but mine are as I said: one is that my writings have been circulated overseas, and the second is that I myself have experienced progress in maturity. Although I was not able to preach, my books continue to preach. If I had not gone through these twenty years of suffering, I would not have made the kind of progress that I made.

Q: Are your co-workers around nowadays?

A: My wife has been out of prison for two years already. From her I learnt that some of our former co-workers have stood firm, while a few others have fallen. Still others have died. During the thirty years that I preached in China (before Liberation), I never talked about politics. Although I was aware of the political situation and trends, yet I did not talk about or get involved in politics. This is because a preacher should preach only the word of God, and if he mixes his preaching with other things, the preaching will not be pure. I watch political movements and know about trends, but I do not talk about them. In the future I will continue to preach the Word and refrain from touching on politics. In prison I talked a lot about politics because we were all forced to talk about politics. I will continue to be this way in the future.

The present situation in China is leaning toward the good. It seems that the door for the Gospel is opening. The government is not prohibiting the preaching of the Word, and problems confronting believers are fewer now. For some there is no problem at all. If the political situation in China were not turning toward the better, I would have remained in prison until the day I died. Now the political situation has changed, and the door to preaching the Gospel has opened.

But within the church the situation is very complicated. It is not something that I can say in a word or two. From now on, there is need for someone to lead the church in China toward the right path, the correct path. It must not turn to the left nor to the right, but walk in the right path, as the prophet Jeremiah said. Today there is a need for leaders to lead the believers in China to walk on the right path. I am neither a leftist nor a rightist; I am walking in the orthodox path. The orthodox path is to preach the word of God to the believers. For all of them love to hear the truth, leaning neither toward the right nor to the left. If someone asked me, "From now on, whose path should we walk?" I would answer him, "Walk the path of God; that will be correct."

Q: What, then, is the right path, on which we must instruct the people to walk?

A: The correct path is not to deviate from life, real life. It is useless to talk about things in the air, about things and theories that have nothing to do with life. Such talk only makes one's head big, and it makes one' feet very small. As he walks, he falls very easily. If he talks about teaching concerning ethics and life; well, what we teach ought to be useful in actual life. I have written a small booklet called "How Should Believers Live in the World?" It contains the general idea of what I am talking about, teachings on life and ethics. If we can be good persons, we will be able to glorify God; we will be able to bear witness for the Lord. But if one talks about doctrines and theories, no matter how high and how sublime they may be, if they have nothing to do with teaching man how to live they are useless. For, if one does not live by life, he will give others excuses for attacking him.

People used to criticize me and say, "Mr. Wang, you always preach about ethics and life and you do not teach spiritual things." I used to say to them, "That is spiritual teaching. Teaching which is related to man's life is true spiritual teaching." During the 1920's and 1930's, there used to be a saying circulating among the churches in China, "Pastor Jia Yuming teaches *Daoli* [doctrine]; Watchman Nee teaches *Daolu* [the way]; and Wang Mingdao teaches *Daode* [ethics]." Now Pastor Jia has died. Watchman Nee has fallen. And I who used to teach ethics am still here teaching ethics. In the future, I will continue to talk about ethics.

I am a disciple of Christ, but I am also a good follower of Confucius. I became a Christian at the age of fourteen, through a classmate of mine. His character and ethics were of a high caliber, and so he influenced me greatly. He left a deep impression upon me, and so when he shared the Gospel with me I was ready to receive it. That's how I repented of my sins and became a believer. But after thirty years of preaching I came to realize even more that, unless one has a high standard of morality and has blameless love, one cannot bear witness for the Lord. If you do not have a sublime character and genuine love, no matter how hard you preach, people will not feel deeply moved.

It would be like a sounding cymbal, as Paul said in I

Corinthians. Bang! A big sound, and then it is done; it produces no effect. That is what is important, ethics and love. But what is the basis of Christian ethics and love? In my booklet on *"How to Live in the World,"* the opening sentence goes like this: "The fear of the Lord is the foundation upon which to erect one's life. The love of one's labours is the method by which to get along well in the world." The concluding two sentences go like this: "In every thing, think on behalf of others; in every event, seek the glory of the name of the Lord." Faith and life cannot be separated.

In Chinese, ethics is called *Daode*; that means there must first be *Dao* [doctrine], and then there will be *De* [conduct or virtue]. Without the *Dao*, there would not be the *De*, without the word, there would not be ethics. When you have the word, then you have ethics or virtue. If you talk only about the Word and have no virtue, then it is like water without salt or a road without origin. If you have *Dao*, you will surely have the *De*. If you only have *Dao*, but without the *De*, your *Dao* will be like wind blowing and will have no effect. It will be like a sounding cymbal; after its sounding then everything is gone. Therefore there must first be the *Dao* and then the *De*.

Before my twentieth birthday I was not called Wang Mingdao; it was in the summer of 1920 that I changed my name. Mingdao does not mean "to understand the *Dao*," but "to testify of the *Dao*." I wanted to testify to the word of God in this generation when the true word was being obscured. This responsibility I carried for thirty years. Even though I fell thereafter, I was able to rise again. Even today my job is to be the witness of the word. This is my responsibility in the future.

Q: Were you ever physically beaten while you were in prison?
A: I am sorry, I cannot talk about this. I don't want to let the world know about that aspect. God knows everything. Now, since the government is turning toward the good, I will not mention anything of the past. I don't want the world to have a bad impression of our government. Since the government is turning to the good, why should I recall past things?

4.19 A Cantonese in Henan

The writer met a Henan man at the Guangzhou Railway Station and talked to him at length. When they met again, he became sure the Lord wanted him to go to Henan. This is his account of that trip.

When I arrived at his home in southern Henan by train, I learned that his mother was a believer, although she had never been baptized. The family which his sister married into lived in a nearby village and were also believers. On the third day of my stay there, his brother took me to the village where his sister and her husband live. There, through her mother-in-law, who also has believed but has not yet been baptized, I came to meet a few Christian sisters in their forties and fifties. In the beginning they would not open themselves to me, but, after praying together, they took me into their trust. I was then invited to attend a family worship, which fifteen to sixteen people attended. Most of them were women, although there was a young girl in her early teens.

The meeting followed the usual house church model: hymn singing, prayer, and fellowship. Even the children know how to pray. The singing and prayers were indeed very spiritual, although the level of spiritual understanding appeared to be low because of the lack of Bibles and of educated preachers in that area. I left my only personal pocket New Testament with them.

On the fourth day of my visit, my friend took me to his great uncle and his great aunt's place. Both of them were believers in the Lord. The old lady had been ill in bed for a long time, and they asked me to pray for her. The old man asked me to go over to his house to pray, and when I arrived there was a small gathering of about ten persons in his house, mostly women. The form of that meeting was also about the same as in most other house churches. After this meeting, I was asked to attend another house meeting, which a larger number of people attended. They sang hymns and prayed. Their singing and praying were exceptionally earnest and spiritual. There was a small boy who was a fourth grader, and his prayer was exceptionally moving to me. I would say that the zeal which this boy displayed by far surpassed that of those in Guangzhou who have had theological training, believed for many years, and are now leading others in the things of the Lord.

My friend's great-aunt was so ill that she could not get up from her bed. She was more than sixty years old. She had believed in the Lord for a long time, but in her sickness she was still carrying heavy burdens of sin. When I saw that she was feeling great guilt in her heart, that she felt that the Lord might not forgive her, and that her faith was weak, I prayed for her, kneeling down in front of her. I prayed once in the morning, and I prayed for her again in the evening. On the following day she was able to eat and regained her appetite and strength. She wanted me to pray for her once again. After praying for her, her husband took me to meet a preacher who lived a mile away.

On January 15th, I met twelve "responsibile brothers," or house church leaders, who were doing the work of the Lord, and we had a wonderful time of fellowship. We prayed together till noon time. We also discussed ways to do the Lord's work.

That evening I went to bed early. As soon as I went to bed, the old man came and told me that several younger Christian brothers had just arrived and wanted to see me. They had come from five different villages. The oldest of them was thirty years old and had been baptized eleven years earlier. The youngest one was only fourteen and had not yet been baptized. After we met, they earnestly pleaded with me to preach God's word to them. I replied that I could not preach; I didn't even have a Bible in my hands. The thirty year old man brought out a portion of Scripture which he had copied by hand and gave it to me, asking me to preach. I was not able to refuse them, and so, after prayer and receiving permission from the Lord, I preached a portion of Scripture to them. Thereafter, I told them that the local preachers all preach very well and recommended that they listen to their preachers more. On the several occasions that I attended the house meetings, they always asked me to preach. Each time it was only after much prayer for the gift of grace and the presence of the Holy Spirit that I dared to preach. For I knew that until then I had not yet received the gift of preaching, and I felt unworthy.

Some General Observations

Basically I was able to understand the church situation in southern Henan. I came to know the needs of the Body of Christ there, and I was able to establish fellowship and communication with house church leaders.

Church Situation

The churches in southern Henan that I visited are quite spiritual. In that area, as well as in neighbouring regions, all churches seem to have a good spiritual foundation. The number of believers appears to be large. There are no official, institutional churches. All are household churches. In practically every village , there are "meeting points." The age groups among believers are well balanced: the old, the middle-aged, the young, and teen-agers. Male and female attendance is also quite balanced. Their faith is orthodox. Most of them meet at night. The content of their meetings consists primarily of singing, praying, testimony-sharing, and prayers for peace and for healing.

In the smaller household meetings, there were times when they would first bless steamed bread called "man-tou," home-made flat noodle soup, and even candy, and then divide these up among the participants to eat. Those who requested prayers for peace or for healing were the ones who brought the food. This situation was probably due to the fact that in that area there was a serious lack of Scripture and of preachers.

In the larger household meetings, there were preachers who preached sermons. Most of the women did not appear to know the Christian teachings very clearly, but their prayers were very spiritual and earnest, and this was true all over. Bibles were extremely scarce, and those who did Christian work all depended on copying the Bible by hand. Most of the believers have been baptized, and I suppose baptized by preachers. Basically those who have been baptized were very clear in their doctrine of salvation. Throughout the area that I visited, believers were extremely eager to search for and practice the righteousness of the Kingdom. The places I visited were formerly connected with churches belonging to the "Chinese Gospel Self-

Propagation Association," the *Zhonghua Fuyin Zichuanhui*, and with churches that used to belong to the former China Inland Mission.

Since 1958, there have been no public church services. The influence of the restored Three-Self Patriotic Movement has not yet extended to these villages.

Preachers

The preachers were practically all farmers. They worked on the farm in the day and did the Lord's work at night. This time I met four preachers:

Preacher Zhou is an elderly man of seventy-seven. He used to be a deacon in a small church belonging to the Chinese Gospel Self-Propagation Association. In 1957, he was labelled a "rightist" and consequently had to do labour work for several years. He is now single. He has not yet been exonerated from the "rightist cap." His occupation was small peddling — he carries a small basket around and sells miscellaneous items here and there all day long. But as he goes hither and thither, he communicates the Gospel. Wherever he goes, he is taken care of by local Christian brothers and sisters. His spiritual foundation is quite good.

Preacher Li, fifty years old, used to preach the Gospel before the Cultural Revolution. During the Cultural Revolution, he was accused five times, but he never denied the Lord. He is still a farmer, working in the day time and serving the Lord at night.

Preacher Wang, around forty years of age, is also a farmer, working on the farm in the daytime and preaching at night. His educational level is not very high.

Preacher Jing is in his early thirties. He is also a farmer, working on the farm during the day and serving the Lord at night.

When these preachers prayed together with me, we also took food, blessed it, and then distributed it among us. Whenever there are believers who are sick, they usually call for the preachers to come and pray for them.

Deviations

There are three kinds of dubious practices that I encountered:

1. "The Way of Fasting." Those who practise it eat only one meal a day. Their number of adherents is not large.

2. Seventh-Day Adventist. When they pray, they face west, saying that they are praying toward the front gate of the Temple. Female believers must wear veils. They insist on baptism by immersion and reject sprinkling.

3. "Four Gospel Sect." This group preaches the four Gospels only. They do not use other portions of the Bible. They also criticize the Apostle Paul. The Four Gospelers are unique to this locality. The founder is called Zhang Liansheng. Originally Zhang was working as an assistant to a pastor Liu, who put him in charge of a certain village chapel. Zhang, Liu, and a certain Miao were once discussing the circumcision of the Jews, which they concluded was symbolic in nature and intended to assert their commitment to God. The three of them decided to use a razor to circumcize themselves. In a closed room, each tried to be the first to receive circumcision. Finally, it was decided that Miao would be the first. But the razor was too sharp and so Miao accidently cut off his reproductive organ, and the other two, seeing the blood flowing, fled away. Zhang then found his way to an old couple who had no children and explained to them what a mistake he had made. He feared that pastor Liu might rebuke him. The old couple said to him, "We have no children; why don't you be our son. You can change your denomination and call it the Four Gospels, and Pastor Liu will have no right to control you." So from then on, Zhang started to preach the way of the Four Gospels. He was able to deceive some, and he is still alive today.

Deceivers

Last year there was a group of young people from outside who brought a few Bibles to that village. They found some women believers who were not clear in the faith. After they met, they proposed to give more Bibles and arranged for a woman believer to send her daughter to the place where they stayed. They then deceived the young girl and led her away. Her folks had to chase the deceivers all the way to Xinyang before they were able to retrieve her. It is still not known where they got the Bibles.

Religious Policy

During the Cultural Revolution, persecution was quite severe in southern Henan. The situation is now more relaxed. There are some Chinese Communist Party members who serve as secretaries in the communes or who belong to the production battalions and believe in secret like Nicodemus. For the last two years, most house churches have been experiencing revivals. Last year a representative from the county office of the United Front Work Department came to see the former pastor Liu, who was sent down to the countryside and who is now in his late seventies or early eighties. The official invited him back to the city where he used to live and discussed religious affairs with pastor Liu. It is said that plans are being made to open a church in the county city. Liu is now living in the city and takes care of his own room and board.

V   Clamping Down
(1981-1984)

INTRODUCTION

The years 1981-1984 were characterized by a dual policy in China. On the one hand, there was a continuation in these years of the open policy toward economics and foreign participation in China's development. On the other hand, domestic control of thought and culture tightened.

The opening of the society continued on the course charted in 1978. The responsibility system, whereby peasants contracted for a specific piece of land and kept all profits after a state-set quota was met, continued to be pressed. Industry as well as agriculture were urged to adopt the system. Specialized households and self-employment were allowed for a few, and some glowing personal success stories appeared as the Chinese took advantage of the new system.

The overall growth in China had been good, although in terms of its currency China still remained a poor nation. The open policy also encouraged foreign investment. Although the Chinese were cautious about allowing any foreign control of enterprises in China, many foreign investors were lured to China by the promise of high returns and a large market. China also pursued a vigorous foreign program of making friends with as many nations as possible, reserving only Israel, South Africa, Vietnam, and South Korea as enemies.

The closing of domestic culture was signalled near the end of 1980, when Deng gained ascendancy over Hua Guofeng. In December 1980, at a Party work conference, political studies were restored, every adult being expected to attend political study sessions under the leadership of Party members. Also at the work conference, Deng introduced the "four insistences:" 1) insist on socialism, 2) insist on the people's democratic dictatorship, 3) insist on the leadership of the Communist Party, 4) insist on Marxism-Leninism and Mao Zedong Thought. These four basic principles are still the principles by which allegiance to the state is tested. Deng discussed the third principle at length and thus signalled the return of Party control over society.

These measures were followed by discussion of ideology in public once more. Admitting that many youths had lost confidence in socialism, the Party set out to win them back. At the Twelfth Party Congress in September 1982, one of the major themes was socialist spiritual civilization. The Party leaders put forth the idea that a Chinese socialism should be the spiritual frame of reference in all higher cultural spheres, such as education, arts, communications, ethics, etc. This was followed a year later by the flipside of this coin, the campaign against spiritual pollution, begun in October 1983. Attempts by competing ideologies to interfere with socialism's leadership in culture, and even unintended foreign cultural influences — especially in the fields of music and art — were labelled as spiritual pollution. Although there were some factional difficulties in the Party's conduct of this campaign, the intent was clear — the Party's leadership in socialism was not to be contested by competing ideologies.

To ensure compliance with the major policy changes initiated by Deng Xiaoping, the Party also began a rectification campaign among its members. This was begun in October, 1983. These campaigns were accompanied by a special focus on economic crimes in 1983 and a more general anti-crime campaign that began in August 1983. These campaigns were clearly intended to intimidate both Party members and non-Party members. The leadership of the Party was not to be challenged with impunity.

In the church the major trends in society were also followed. The leaders of the TSPM and CCC began cultivating a large number of foreign contacts. They made special trips abroad — to Montreal in the fall of 1981, to Europe in the fall of 1982, and to Australia and New Zealand in the spring of 1984. In the meantime, many more delegations from all over the world called on the TSPM. The TSPM became very conscious of its image among both liberal and evangelical Christians around the world.

Within China, the TSPM and the CCC began to pursue a policy that they hoped would lead to all Chinese Christians coming under their leadership. They opened churches at an increasing rate, until 1,600 were opened by the spring of 1984. This represents a rate of about two per day from 1982 to 1984, and this rate increased so that some 4,000 churches were open by the end of 1985. The congregations of these churches were composed of people who met in their homes before the reappearance of the TSPM and gradually were persuaded to join the TSPM. Throughout 1982 and 1983, the TSPM worked at local levels persuading house church leaders to join them, with promises of assistance, training, and some legal status. They also gave instructions on conduct with the "ten don'ts," issued in slightly varying forms around the country. These "ten don'ts" restricted worship in places other than churches and restricted youth work.

At the same time, local police forces in China began to put pressure on house meetings. The earliest incidents were in the spring of 1982. In Dongyang (Zhejiang province) and Fangcheng (Henan province), there were local incidents of violence in which house church members clashed with public security forces. In July, evangelists who had traveled to preach the gospel were arrested. Also in July, all house churches in Henan except those approved by the TSPM were told to stop meeting. In August, 140 house churches were ordered to cease meeting in Yunnan province.

In 1983, the police search for traveling evangelists continued. Many evangelists never returned home but traveled constantly. More and more came under pressure, until more than 100 Christians had become fugitives. In April 1983, the TSPM issued a pamphlet that denounced the activities of the followers of Witness Li, a former assistant to Watchman Nee. Li's group, known as the "Shouters" in China, was accused of theological heresies. In June, the Public Security Bureau around China began arresting members of the "Shouters" and took in a number of other house church leaders as well.

As a result of these developments, there is a several-tiered church structure in China today. *Open churches* are non-denominational local bodies recognized by the government's Religious Affairs Bureau. *Registered meeting points* outnumber the open churches by a ratio of nearly eight-to-one. They are registered with the TSPM but usually have lay leadership. Some are located near open churches, where members may go to receive sacraments and instruction from TSPM pastors. At the end of 1985, perhaps 3,000 registered meeting points had church properties and were seeking recognition as open churches. *Unregistered meeting points,* numbering between 100,000 and 300,000, are loosely structured fellowships tied together by occasional visits from itinerant preachers which meet semi-privately and which are not affiliated with the TSPM.

5.1 The State and the Church

This interview gives quite a clear description of the methods the government has used to try and control Christianity in China.

Q: Tell me about your local house church meetings.

A: We have our meetings every evening. There is no chief leader; whoever is so moved can come forward. Formerly my church had six evening services every week. Today at place A, tomorrow place B, and so on. Usually a few itinerant preachers or elderly brothers would lead the services.

Now my home has become a daily meeting place. We start with prayer for a half hour or an hour. Whoever would like to can stand up and pray. After prayer we sing until we feel like stopping. There are not set rules for spending a certain amount of time for any part of the service.

After singing we have the sermon, which usually lasts two hours. I will often preach for three hours. That is the typical meeting. It starts at 8:00 p.m. and lasts until 11:30 p.m. Often they will last until 12:00, 1:00, or even 2:00 a.m.

Q: Do you have any formal means of communication or organization with the other house churches throughout Henan?

A: Well, we have what we call communal meetings or

communications meetings every month. This system covers ten counties in southern Henan and six in western Henan. In each county, house churches meet to exchange reports and hear a sermon.

Q: How many people participate?

A: Several hundred, maybe 300 to 400. Some places have 800. The locals lead the prayer and preach the sermon; it is better this way not to let the outsiders get caught. So in each church one person is responsible for this meeting with the other churches. Usually he will spend one or two days a month on these matters.

Q: We've been hearing reports of the Three-Self oppression of the Chinese Church. Did this start within the last half year?

A: The oppression existed ever since the TSPM started in 1980. In the beginning they used the revived Church and issued their "ten don'ts" to each church. They assigned meeting points and distributed Bibles. Then the TSPM called meetings inviting many Christian brothers. They did a real nice job of entertaining them, letting them see movies and plays. In the process, these brothers were corrupted.

Others were fooled by this trickery. They considered the TSPM to be a part of the Church, their friend. So many did not understand what the TSPM wanted to do, namely, to restrict meeting points and prayer. And these believers are, in fact, carrying out the "ten don'ts." They will not pray for faith healing nor preach about the Spirit.

Q: How about yourself? Were you taken in by all this?

A: In the beginning I did not understand either. When I was in Yangcun village, I saw how desolate the church was, how desperately in need of education and leadership. So the TSPM elders said they were willing to unite with us and teach us theology. A lot of us were fooled by that. But the Lord protected us, and we did not join the TSPM.

Q: They have severely limited the number of meeting points, right?

A: Yes, and they have started to oppress the itinerant preachers. They forbid lay preachers and pastors to go outside their villages, and if they do they will be punished. They threaten ordinary believers by saying they will clear out their houses and arrest everybody. They accuse them of not adhering to the "ten dont's." These threats have been partially effective. The TSPM also forces the believers to pray faster or not at all! In some areas the revival has weakened.

Q: What is the present situation with the TSPM? How do they deal with you if you still have your meetings?

A: The TSPM uses scare tactics and fines. They release news of Christians being arrested, along with threats of arresting all house church worshippers. They announce that they will arrest so and so on a certain day. But the day comes and the believers are still with us. The Lord protects His believers.

Q: Are there any examples?

A: Oh yes, there were two Christian brothers, obviously in disregard of TSPM and the United Front Work Department's [UFWD] regulations, using speakers and amplifiers to broadcast their house service. Well, usually there are many people at their services every day, and many spend the night. But the day the cadres came not even one person was spending the night. The Public Security Bureau officials roused the brothers in the middle of the night. But the police could not find one scrap of evidence concerning Christians coming from other communes. The Lord concealed it.

Q: If they are preaching and disregarding the "ten don'ts," then why can't they arrest them?

A: You see, these "ten don'ts" are to scare the Church, not to charge believers with crimes. Often when a home meeting is begun, the police will come to have a look. They do not say a word; they have come to frighten them. These "ten don'ts," by the way, were jointly issued by the TSPM, UFWD, and the Public Security Bureau.

They have the authority, certainly, to arrest the brothers and sisters. And, in fact, they do not allow youngsters under eighteen, Party members, or Communist Youth League members to participate in the services. If you are a Party or CYL member you must first resign before attending house church meetings.

Q: Do you, then, rely on the constitution which says there is religious freedom?

A: We don't rely on the provisions of the constitution as a safeguard. Actually, they have rules in the constitution with which they can charge and arrest believers. However, charges and arrests will damage their reputation internationally. So they demand that we adhere to the "ten don'ts" but have no way to enforce their demands.

[A Christian sister interrupted, saying she had a conversation with a UFWD official.]

They asked me, last February, if I would not sympathize with them. The UFWD has recently decided, the official told me, that the present circumstances call for arrests and killing, if necessary, to completely wipe out Christianity. He asked me if I was afraid of this coming wave of repression. I said "No way."

I say that, if the UFWD sends the Public Security people, then just let them come. That is not terrifying. What scares me most is the Second Coming when all earth will be destroyed. This Public Security official threatened a Christian friend of mine saying that his seven year-old child would have no way to live if his father were killed. He replied by saying that he only cares about his loyalty to God.

Q: How dangerous is it for the house church worshippers and especially for the itinerant pastors?

A: Itinerant pastors daily risk their lives and face dangers. At any time they may be arrested. Often there are people just ahead of them and behind them trying to arrest them. They just rely on the Lord and their faith. Truly, we Christians are too weak. The Lord keeps and protects us.

Q: What is likely for the future? What measures will the TSPM use against the Church?

A: As I have seen from my local church, if they want to carry out this religious persecution nationwide, they will have to make more use of the Public Security Bureau. As it is now, the police and the UFWD do not want to get involved. It is only because the TSPM pesters them to send agents and make arrests. That is the development of the trend as I see it. But we know that if they try that, the churches of the interior will unite and fight against oppression.

Q: Has the TSPM thought about this result; that pressure will cause you to unite?

A: Right now they only consider how to make people respect them.

In the future, the TSPM will likely try to incorporate all house churches into the TSPM organization. At their TSPM meetings there are but a few older Christians, and those leaders all have to report every week to the UFWD. It is also possible that the TSPM will use the China Christian Council to unite the house churches with the TSPM.

But you must understand this point: the TSPM is a tool, a kind of cosmetic put on the face of a whole range of developments in foreign policy and international relations.

Q: Do you think the TSPM will be successful in carrying out this oppression?

A: They won't succeed. They can't succeed in Henan. We believe the Lord opened the churches and no one can close them. They oppress us now, but they are not part of God's work, and their time will come. The nation will realize they are of no use, severely restricting religions like they do.

We believe the Chinese Church will revive; if we rely on the prayers of the brothers and sisters at home and abroad, if we are under the leadership of the Spirit, the Church can revive. The Lord can open the heavenly gates to China's 900 million unbelievers.

Q: What is the house church response or attitude toward the TSPM today?

A: We try to expose the TSPM to those brothers and sisters who still don't understand. We're trying to pull them away from the TSPM, and we think we can do it. We're praying with all we've got, and we tell those brothers not to unite. The TSPM actually only has a few top officials pushing this persecution. They can't go all over to take care of things. What can they do if their underlings don't follow orders?

We also have the problem of those believers who are employed by the TSPM. They will never come back. Those believers are rather poor and do not have the guts to go off the government payroll.

So we call them — the TSPM and the Christian Council — whores, partners with Judas. They are the church of Baal. We must kill that whore so that all will know they're not of the Spirit. Last year, we held prayer meetings praying that the Spirit's power would come to burn that whore to death.

This problem is not confined to Henan; it's nationwide. Actually, the TSPM's power in Henan is relatively weak. In the big cities — Shanghai, Beijing, Guangzhou — the TSPM has the upper hand. Therefore, we need every brother and sister to pray.

5.2 The Danger of Heresy

In our province there is a mountainous area where the borders of three counties meet. There are eight communes in this particular locality. Many people there thirst after the Lord and earnestly seek after Him. But there were no preachers there, neither were there any Bibles. So the people asked a sixty-seven-year-old man to preach to them. Although the old man was enthusiastic, he did not understand the Christian doctrine, and what he preached turned out to be an absurd heresy!

The old man used to teach Chinese classics as a private tutor when he was young and was quite knowledgeable. Feeling empty and meaningless in life, he once joined the "Kneel and Incense Sect." Later, he felt the sect to be lifeless and joined Christianity. But he never solved the problem of his faith, which was a mixture of Confucianism, Buddhism, and some points of Christianity. After he joined Christianity he was quite zealous for some time but lacked true knowledge. Once, after he had prayed for a lunatic, he tried to fumigate the nose of the lunatic person with the incense smoke and burned the person's face as a result. He was sent to jail for it, and later on he no longer confessed his faith openly. When the number of inquirers in this mountain range grew, his popularity increased. The people thought he was persecuted for the faith and admired him greatly. He first declined their invitation to become their preacher, but as they persisted in their request, he finally complied.

Since he had no Bible, he had to preach from his memory. He said he obtained oracles from the Holy Father which permitted him to go to heaven once a week, that he saw all kinds of spectacles in heaven, that he saw the oracles of the Holy Father written on the tablet, altogether 1000 words — no more, no less. He had copied this down as the revelation of the Holy Spirit.

He compiled quite a few hymns, which he taught the people to sing from place to place. These hymns were all repetitions of meaningless phrases. For instance, one long hymn entitled "How to Pray" goes like this: "How are you going to pray? By piously kneeling before the cross. Close up all six windows and doors, and tightly fasten up your mind.... In there shines the spiritual light, and there the spiritual sister communicates in a dream. With the guidance of the spiritual light, you may go to heaven to have a look. The heavenly sight is really great; all these you may obtain by faith." Another hymn, "The Good Pluto," tells about his encounter with Pluto after he died, when the "cow head" and "horse face" brought him to hell. Pluto had compassion on him and allowed him to return to the world to believe in Jesus and to preach the Gospel. A third hymn says, "Oh, Lord of Heaven, Oh, Lord of Earth, I request Jesus to come down to heal fever, cold, the lumps, and the swollen limbs..." Others had words such as "I asked Jesus to blow on my eye, ..." or "Mouth is iron, tooth is steel.... When you catch the devil, take off his skin, extract his sinews, altogether 103 sinews. Bite the devil with your teeth."

Hymns like these captivated a lot of ignorant women's hearts. Even many Christians who were enthusiastic in witnessing for the Lord were enchanted by him, saying he was one of the most spiritual people in China. Under the influence of this old man, people prayed every night for the spiritual sister. They asked him to find out on which street they would live in heaven or how their spiritual status was. Some people asked about secular things, such as the whereabouts of their lost articles, how their folks were back home, whether they would make some money, etc., and some of these did come true.

Under such circumstances, where there were neither Bibles nor pastors, there was virtually no one who understood basic salvation. Many believers stayed at the stage of faith healing. There was no church, but meeting points were established by vows of believers who had a family member sick and asked for healing. When such a person did get well, the believer built the meeting point to repay his vow. As a result, a village sometimes has several such meeting points. A lot of people came to hear the gospel, and faith healing was extremely popular.

Even when cattle got sick the owners would ask believers to pray for their animals, and this produced many incidents. For instance, once a Party secretary of a certain production brigade asked a woman believer to pray for his sick donkey (The believer's house was a meeting point). At the time when the woman was asked to pray for the donkey, it was so sick that it could not open its eyes. When she got to the house, the donkey was on the brink of death. Nevertheless, due to her ignorant zeal, she still prayed for it. But soon after she left the donkey died. With this as a pretext, the secretary went to the county security bureau [police] and the United Front Work Department to accuse her. She was taken to the commune where she spent fifteen days in self-examination. The meeting at her house was ordered to stop, and the other meeting points in the vicinity were also affected.

After we heard about these things we went to that area to preach the Gospel, the first time for two weeks, and the second time for almost a month. Everywhere we went we drew over a hundred people to the meeting, many of them being young people. Based on this situation, we designed a "Bible Study Meeting for Youth," and established a meeting point within every eight or ten *li*'s [equivalent to 3 miles] radius. We organized people into high school, junior high, or primary school reading-level Bible study groups. These included both young and middle-aged people, but with young people as the nucleus. Regular Bible study meetings were held each week. They were designed to establish the believers in the truth of the Bible so that they would not be led astray by heresy. Attendance at these Bible study meetings ranged from twenty-five to as many as seventy or eighty people, all of them very enthusiastic.

Thus two needs surfaced: 1) The need for Bibles and other Bible study materials: 2) The need for Bible study leaders. The need for personnel was especially urgent since only two persons could take turns leading Bible study at each meeting point on a weekly cycle. May the Lord increase our faith.

In one of our staff meetings we saw the need for going to the desolate frontier area where the name of the Lord had not been called on and where the power of darkness still reigns. We thank God for this Macedonian call. May the Lord prosper His own work and grant us strength sufficient for the challenge, so that His will may be done in whatever we do and think. May we become useful vessels in His hand.

5.3 Other Heresies in Henan Province

I will report to you the situation in Xi county. This county is actually one of the last counties to receive revival. Many of the nearby counties experienced the grace of the Lord earlier. Recently, six other Church leaders and I went as an evangelism team to visit fellow Christians there.

Xi County is a vast land, with only a few villages scattered here and there. There is a river running through the county. To the north of it there are 40,000 believers, to the south another 40,000 believers. The county was earlier cultivated by the Lutherans. Before Liberation in 1949, there were only 4,000 believers.

When I arrived at the Xi County seat, all the brothers and sisters welcomed me. I have many relatives there — uncles, aunts, a grandmother and so on — and they are all preachers. As soon as I arrived, they shared with me what the Lord is doing in their church.

My relatives took me to see one of the elders. Elder Wang was imprisoned in the late 1950's because he was the head of his church. Wang said that when he first entered the prison he lifted his head to look around. But as soon as he lifted his head, he was knocked down by the prison guard and forced to enter his prison cell with his head bowed.

They forced him to kowtow — or knock his head on the floor — for an hour or two every day. Then they would force him to turn his head quickly to the left and right. Even today he cannot bow his head very easily.

At that time he prayed, "Lord, anytime you want me to walk the path of the cross, to lose my life, I shall be ready. Only receive my soul and give me strength, so that I might imitate You and do what You did, and might also imitate my spiritual teacher, Brother Chun, who also gave up his life for the cross' sake." The guards often pointed a gun at him or hit his head with the butt of the gun. He would then pray, "Lord receive my soul." He lived under these conditions day after day, month after month. He prayed again, "Lord, why don't You receive my soul?" He often wrote poetry in prison, hoping that if he should die others could read his poems.

Wang served thirteen years in prison without trial. He was released four years ago and returned to his wife and children. When he entered prison, his sons and daughters were yet very young. When he rejoined them, they were grown, some happily married. During those years, his wife brought up their children under extreme hardship. Since he was in jail, few people dared to befriend or help her, fearing they might also be accused.

So our sister struggled through life with great difficulty, even losing her sight. When Wang came back from prison, he saw his wife sleeping on her bed, her hair white as wool, unable to see anything. Yet she was full of joy.

Wang read us one of his recent poems. It told of the Lord sending him to do His work. He is giving himself wholly to the hand of the Lord. As Wang read his poem, I could see tears running down his cheeks.

Wang told us that he had three requests for the Lord. The first one was that, if he was to die, he would like to die for the Lord's sake. The second request was that if the Lord liberated him from prison, that he be liberated soon. The third request was that Lord grant him the opportunity to preach again.

He said that all three were granted. He did not have to be a martyr, and he was liberated in only thirteen years. Today he is speaking to various house churches in his county. With this dedication, he is participating in the Lord's revival of the Church in Henan. He asked us to fully dedicate ourselves. Now he even wants to organize a choir!

The daughter and the son-in-law of the director of the Public Security Bureau of Xi County are zealous and faithful Christians. They are only thirty years old. After they became Christians, they persuaded their grandmother and younger brother to believe in the Lord.

When her father learned that they had persuaded their brother to become a Christian, he tied his son to the bed, beating him and not permitting him to eat. Because he persecuted his believing children, his daughter told us, he became very ill. His son also became ill. His daughter asked us to pray for the director so that he might repent and not resist God.

Recently, the Public Security Bureau issued ten prohibitions. One stated that persons must not conduct house worship privately and that those who disobeyed would be fined. The director instructed that, "All Christians must be arrested, and I am the one who authorizes it!" The director planned not only to arrest Wang but also to attack all underground house meetings. Soon thereafter, the public security officials surrounded a house meeting and chased out the worshippers.

The officers confiscated the grain and pigs of the house church leader and fined him heavily. The man's furniture was even taken, but this was not enough. The officers threw some of the young leaders into a deep dry well and then dropped cow dung all over them. The men were given nothing to eat.

Wang decided that, "Since they want to arrest me, I might as well go to the provincial authorities to seek a clarification on religious policy. If they want to arrest me, let them do so, but as far as I am concerned, I will continue to serve the Lord." He asked many of the believers to pray for him.

A few days later, he came back from the provincial capital very happy, saying that he was pleasantly received by a high official. The man expressed interest in his work and in the county's churches.

The man himself had suffered greatly in the Cultural Revolution, having been castigated as one of the followers of Liu Shaoqi, the former president of China. In his desperation, he escaped from prison and sought refuge in the home of a former pastor whom he used to persecute but greatly respected. The pastor took him in, consoled him, and restored his health. The official was recently restored to a high provincial post.

Returning from the capital, Wang was even more zealous. He called the elders together for a meeting and discussed how to take care of the nearly one hundred thousand believers in his county. Believers in his county have increased twenty times since liberation. He and the other elders felt that, since the government had established a religious policy, believers would not be imprisoned again. The elders decided to ordain more elders to care for the flock.

They quickly ordained many elders and deacons, but some were not well-prepared or had not demonstrated a willingness to follow the cross. Some sought the holy office as if seeking jobs. Objections were raised because the elders ordained some old classmates, friends, and relatives, thereby using the will of man, not the will of God.

Many of the new elders had not had any part in the revival of the Church, but once ordained they began to assume power. This group of elders arose only to serve their own interests. They did not appreciate the grace of God.

Discontent arose, and many house church leaders, who were not ordained but who were faithful, were driven out of the fellowship. They were accused of committing illegal activities because they were not appointed by the church. These believers became bitter and resentful.

Other ministers interpreted Wang's ordinations as an attempt to establish his own special group of leaders. They too wanted their own groups. Among the young people was a Brother Qing, also from Xi County. He began to visit various people, both government officials and former pastors.

Two old respected pastors, whom he visited in another county, came to see the Xi revival for themselves. These two elderly men were deeply moved, seeing the revival as the work of the Lord and seeing that He is also using the young people to sing. They felt that the Holy Spirit was doing great work through Qing and his fellow leaders.

Qing then told the two elderly preachers of how Wang ordained elders and deacons. The two pastors, upon Qing's request, ordained a group of young people under Qing's leadership.

Thus the church in Xi County began to develop two factions. Those under Wang are called the older elders. Those under Qing are known as the new and younger elders. The elderly group despises the younger group and wants to revive the Church in Xi County according to their own pattern. They say that Qing's group does not have enough theological training.

The younger group thinks that both the local church and the province-wide church should be developed according to their system. They disdain the older group, believing that they are too weak and calm.

The two elderly men who ordained the younger elders went to see Wang, hoping to negotiate peace. Wang and the older elders became very displeased with them: "What have you done?"

These two elderly men replied that it was in accordance with God's will and a revelation of the Holy Spirit.

Wang said, "I do not think it was the revelation of the Spirit." The meeting ended with few results.

Many believers feel very hurt by the split and are distressed about the older group's leadership. They pray with tears. The older group wants to work with the Religious Affairs Bureau and within the Bureau's limits. They have good relations with both the United Front Work Department and the Three-Self Patriotic Movement (TSPM). They establish churches only in accordance with the government requirements and have access to Bibles. They even informed the Bureau of our activities.

Fearing that many of their believers would join the other group because of the Bibles, the younger group began to establish relations with the TSPM. Each group tried to plead its case before the TSPM, and each accused the other. The younger group began to call the older group "old denominationalists," "old religionists," "rationalists," and "traditionalists." "They cannot be saved, cannot enter into the kingdom of Heaven, and cannot receive eternal life!"

The younger group insists on shouting out the name of the Lord, believing that one can shout one's way into Heaven. They shout very loudly early in the morning , waking up their neighbors. "We will shout from the top of the hills, from the top of the trees, from the top of the train, from the top of our bicycles...."

One day, as they were riding their bikes, they shouted so loudly that cyclists in front of them were frightened and fell. Each time they meet, they shout. The nonbelievers have protested against the shouting by beating drums even louder.

The turmoil has involved many people. A certain elderly sister who disagreed with Qing became ill. Qing claimed, "She is ill because of our prayer. We condemned her!"

We tried to reason with Wang, but he is a Bible school graduate and a senior elder. He is full of zeal for the Lord now, and he feels that nobody is like him. He does not listen.

Qing seems to be acting out of the flesh. He suggested we work with him and merge with his group. If not, let us take care of the northern section of Henan, and let a certain other brother take care of the southern part of the province.

As we conducted our work in Xi County, the two factions had their own views. Neither was happy with us, especially Qing and his followers. But we disagree with Qing. We cannot join them in loud shouting. He would not listen to us, so we can only bow down before the Lord and pray.

We feel we must establish ourselves in the truth of the Bible. We can only engage in Bible teaching and the provision of Bibles — or help to write stencils for local printing of portions of the Bible. We also cut stencils and print Bible study materials.

Leaders in the house churches need to study the Bible, establish Bible study classes and prayer meetings for the young people, and establish inquirer classes for those who are seeking to become Christians. In fact, this type of work is being carried out in the five counties we visited on the way to Xi County. In each of these countries we have established Bible studies, prayer meetings, and inquirer meetings.

5.4 The Church Inside and Outside of China

When asked what kind of literature foreigners should bring into China, Brother Paul and Sister Zhang both agreed that complete Bibles were the best. The Chiristians in Henan weep with tears of happiness when they receive a Bible. It is their most precious possession. Sister Zhang had not yet read the theological literature *Study of Truth* and *Practice of Truth*), but she claimed it was very useful for the lay preachers. Brother Paul maintained that, besides bringing Bibles for the average Christians, the lay preachers and house church leaders must also be exposed to these theological training books.

Brother Paul explained the problem of Bible distribution. Surely with so many Christians in Henan and so few Bibles it is very difficult to find a fair method of distribution. Brother Paul said that some of the ministers and others bringing Bibles to Henan were not following the Holy Spirit in their distribution but were keeping them for friends or using them to obtain favors. Others were not using discretion and were giving away Bibles to anyone they met and to people they may or may not have known to be Christian. They were endangering themselves by exposing this work of Bible distribution and risked being caught by the authorities. Also, the Bibles could be confiscated. Others gave away the Bibles according to the needs of the Christian community, but often it's too difficult to decide who really needs the Bibles. For example, Brother Paul said they have a Bible study class in one county with over thirty people and only five Bibles. Some are older Christians, but many are young people who have become Christians. Who needs the Bibles the most, the old or the young? It's hard to say.

I told them about the opinion held by some foreign Christians that the house churches should not rely on foreigners to bring Bibles in, that they ought to be independent and print all their materials themselves. Brother Paul thought it might be "okay" to bring in equipment necessary to print in China, but he was not familiar with printing machines and equipment. But it was clear more Chinese Christians would be in danger doing this than by using the present system of foreigners bringing Bibles. There is really no danger to the foreigners; if the Bibles are discovered at customs, they can retrieve them when they leave the country. For the Chinese to print them legally, they must register with the police (Public Security Bureau). Trying to print Bibles is proof of their opposition to the TSPM and could lead to investigation and trouble. To do it illegally would require that several Christians find a secret place and spend much of their time printing. Their absence from the commune would probably be noticed by the authorities. If caught, the punishment would be severe. They would probably never be heard from again. Sister Zhang pointed out that the TSPM Bibles allotted for Henan were printed in Shanghai. Last year [1981] the entire province was given only 150 Bibles.

How, then, can the foreign church help the Chinese church — especially the house churches? What is the proper relationship between the foreign church and the Chinese church? Brother Paul said the first and most important thing foreign Christians can do is to pray for them. In fact, the Chinese Christians are praying for their fellow Christian brothers and sisters in the outside world. Christians believe in the power of the Spirit, that it can overcome all obstacles, that it can't be destroyed by governments or political parties. Foreign Christians, then, can ask the Holy Spirit to bless the Chinese churches and to strengthen them in their fight against political oppression.

A second contribution would be to encourage foreign teachers, students, or businessmen to spend a year or so as Christian witnesses among Chinese intellectuals. This can be especially effective among urban youth, businessmen, teachers, and even Party members. For those such as tourists who can't spend that much time, they can supply house church Christians with Bibles. Bring a few or many; any amount would be appreciated.

Another contribution would be to broadcast Bible teaching on the radio. Brother Paul said that there are specific needs that can be met via radio broadcasts. First, programs can be addressed to Christians who have just come to Christ. Bible lessons and stories can be adapted and simplified for the recent converts. Another program should be designed for long-time Christians, for those devoted to a lifetime of serving Christ. Their level of understanding and faith is higher than that of the first group. A final program could be developed especially for lay preachers and house church leaders. This would include theological training and doctrine. The three programs could be combined to be broadcast over a period of two hours. Each section could be devoted to the special needs of each group. To serve all the people, especially those who work at night, they should be broadcast in the afternoon and after dinner. That way, everyone would have the chance to hear the program.

The relationship between the foreign church and Chinese Church should be that of mutual help and spiritual encouragement. Brother Paul felt that the Chinese Church could inspire the foreign Christians as they heard of the Holy Spirit working in the Chinese Church. The Chinese Church could strengthen the Spirit's work in the foreign churches. The suffering Church in China could revive the foreign Christians' faith as they saw how clearly and strongly the Spirit works with and saves those in a very repressive society.

The foreign churches could help the Chinese to raise their theological level from simple faith to a deep understanding of the Bible's truth. They could help the Chinese to study the Bible better and more completely. This can be accomplished by radio broadcasts and distribution of literature. Also, foreign Christians could help the Chinese people by teaching English or science, thus making a contribution to the whole society. The two churches must pray for each other and learn from each other.

Brother Paul was skeptical of the effectiveness of sending Hong Kong Chinese, or other overseas Chinese, into China to lead theological training classes with lay preachers and house church leaders. From past experience, he felt that they were more interested in their church and community outside China; they wanted to use the mainland Church to make a name for themselves, for their own selfish purposes. Brother Paul said he did not appreciate those Hong Kong Christians who came and ordered them around and told them to raise their educational level. Those overseas Christians themselves seemed unwilling to sacrifice for the mainland Church.

Brother Paul and Sister Zhang emphasized the point that the urban youth and rural youth should be approached in different ways. The urban youth are more educated and have received systematic and prolonged Communist propaganda. They take as a faith-assumption that there is no God or spiritual world. One must be subtle to convince university students that belief in atheism is a faith, just as belief in

Christ is a faith. We can show them that there is an alternative to Communism.

For rural youth, one can be more direct and simple. They live in extreme poverty and have no hope for the future. When they hear there is hope, love, and salvation from a merciful Christ, they shed tears of joy and happiness. According to Sister Zhang, the young people are coming to Christ in unbelievable numbers in the Henan countryside. After only a simple introduction to the love and work of Christ, they believe and are willing and eager to work actively for Christ. They may not be as sophisticated as the urban youth, but they are sacrificing for the work of Christ.

5.5 Letters from a House Church Leader

John Li, a minor elder in the Baixin Church, formerly imprisoned for the sake of our Lord, writing to my fellow worker Fan Ermei, created by the same God, redeemed by the blood of the same Lord, and led by the same Holy Spirit, together following the footsteps of Jesus into the same glory. May He who gives eternal blessings bless you the same way. Amen.

Today, as if I were standing before you and beseeching you, I beg you to labor hard for the sake of our lack of Bibles among nearly 90,000 believers in our county. In our midst we have only about thirty Bibles, yet even these are imperfect and worn out copies. If it is possible for you to send us some Bibles, we will be more than glad to send you whatever amount of money is needed for this purpose. If you want me to go down [to Guangzhou], I will gladly go, whatever the cost, so long as I can bring back some Bibles, which are more precious than anything in the whole world. Whatever you write and tell me to do, I will do. For the sake of the 90,000 believers in our county, I am willing to offer the strength of my life. May you bear this heavy burden together with me. May you also do it willingly and with a joyful heart, running with patience the path which the Lord has placed before us. I am now sixty-six years old, but I am still in good health. In these last years of mine, I want to dedicate myself to the Lord until the day when He receives me to His eternal love.

In summary, I beg you to send some Bibles to us. Amen.

> A weak member of His Body
> Li Zhaode
> 1981,8,26

John Li, a weak and minor elder in the Baixin church, writing to Fan Ermei, a fellow member of His Body who was called, who received suffering and who will enter into glory together with me. May the God who created man out of dust, the Savior who redeemed man by His blood, and the Holy Spirit who leads us, bless you and all those who send the heavenly bread [Bibles] to us.

Earlier I wrote to you briefly about the church in Baixin. In accordance with your request, I will share more [about our church] with you.

The Baixin Church was originally founded by a certain mission. By 1947, when Baixin was liberated, the church already had a long history. Because those who were in charge greatly loved the Lord, they had all believers study the catechisms to learn the essential teachings of the New Testament, memorize some important verses, the Ten Commandments, the Lord's Prayer, and the Apostle's Creed, and receive baptism and the Lord's foundation. In 1947 there were about 4,000 believers, 800 inquirers, three to six foreign missionaries, three to four Chinese pastors, ten elders and thirty deacons for the entire county. Besides twenty churches within the city wall, there were some 300 meeting places in the county. In those days we used to have Bible classes lasting three to six months. Our church also had a Bible School in another province, which offered study courses lasting three to five years. I studied there in the thirties.

By 1950, three years after liberation, the visible church had ceased to exist. But God's love is eternal and never changing. He continued to send His own children to work for Him quietly. Therefore the Lord has been adding those who belong to Him daily, especially in recent years. Even though it is not like Pentecost, yet the work of the Lord continues to flourish. Now we have added twenty-two new elders and about one thousand deacons (men and women). There are over 1,200 meeting places attended by nearly 90,000 believers. All this happened to us because of the grace of the Lord. Every day we [elders] give glory and praise to God. Presently we have five people who received Bible training before Liberation, and, of course, they are all quite old now.

Because our county is not yet an "open district," all meetings are held in homes. Because my house is suitably located for transportation, all Bibles and Christian literature are received and distributed here.

A week ago I received a copy of the New Testament, and yesterday I received four Union Version Bibles, fifteen New Testaments, ten Gospels of John, and eight copies of the *"Sayings of Jesus."* For all these please accept our thanks.

In your letter you mentioned that in Jindun County some poeple took advantage of the Bibles which you sent to them for their gain. When we heard of this, our hearts felt deeply hurt. Therefore, the five of us elders in church have resolutely decided to inform every commune to be alert and have requested the responsible brethren in each commune to guarantee [safe conduct in their district] to prevent any such thing from happening in our area. You have done your labor of love, offering your time and postage costs to send us the bread of life. As usual, we have distributed them to those brothers and sisters most thirsty for the Word. Amen and Emmanuel. From the responsible brethren of the Baixin Church.

5.6 An Easter Sermon

Prayer: Heavenly Father, you know what is in man's hearts. Oh Father, I do not deserve to be in Your temple before Your people preaching Your Word.

[The sermon begins with a list of the Scripture texts.]

Mark 16:9 says, "When Jesus rose early on the first day of the week, he appeared first to Mary Magdalene, out of whom he had driven seven demons."

Luke 24:6-7: "He is not here; he has risen! Remember how he told you, while he was still with you in Galilee: 'The Son of Man must be delivered into the hands of sinful men, be crucified and on the third day be raised again'."

I Corinthians 15:3-7: "For what I received I passed on to you as of first importance: that Christ died for our sins according to the Scriptures, that he was buried, that he was raised on the third day according to the Scriptures, and that he appeared to Peter, and then to the Twelve. After that, he appeared to more than five hundred of the brothers at the same time, most of whom are still living, though some have fallen asleep. Then he appeared to James, then to all the apostles."

Acts 17:31: "For he has set a day when he will judge the world with justice by the man he has appointed. He has given proof of this to all men by raising him from the dead."

Colossians 1:18: "And he is head of the body, the church; he is the beginning and the firstborn from among the dead, so that in everything he might have the supremacy."

Ephesians 1:[19,] 20: "That power is like the working of his mighty strength, which he exerted in Christ when he raised him from the dead and seated him at his right hand in the heavenly realms."

1 Peter 1:3: "Praise be to the God and Father of Our Lord Jesus Christ! In his great mercy he has given us new birth into a living hope through the resurrection of Jesus Christ from the dead."

From the various Scripture texts we have just examined we can see that the Lord in whom we believe is a resurrected Lord. This resurrection means that Jesus cannot die, that He was willing to shed His blood on the cross for sinners, that He was willing to give His life for sinners. Although He left heaven, He still had the power to rise from the dead. As the Bible tells us in Mark 16:9 and Luke 24:6-7, He is the only true Lord, the Lord of salvation. He is the Son of God, past, present, and future. He is the eternal, omnipotent God. He knows yesterday's events, today's trials, and He controls the future.

We thank our Lord. His love and mercy is manifested even in us sinners.

Paul writes his testimony very clearly in 1 Corinthians 15. After Jesus was resurrected from the dead He suddenly appeared among the disciples while they were praying. Jesus said, "I bring you peace."

We can see that, as we are here worshiping, Jesus is also with us. We have happiness and the hope of happiness — we have a dependable hope. The old heaven and earth have passed away; now in Christ there is a new earth which has been prepared for us. This is our happiness!

After Christ arose, He appeared to Peter, to the 12 apostles, to James, and finally before more than 500 disciples. And after seven days He appeared to James and many others. Paul claimed that Christ called him. And this evening, worshiping here, there are many Christian brothers and sisters who have come before us to give that same testimony. We thank the Lord for His grace; He is our Heavenly Father, Creator of heaven and earth, Creator of man, the sun, moon, stars, and all creatures. Our Heavenly Father created man out of His own likeness and form. He is the Lord of heaven, earth, and all creatures.

Merciful Father, You have set the time when the Lord Jesus Christ will righteously judge all men. We know from the Book of Revelation that all men, all races, will receive the righteous judgement of the Lord.

Christ's resurrection gave all men a believable testimony. All the brothers and sisters here tonight know that after death there is still judgement. Hebrews 9:27 says that according to man's fate everyone must die and that after death comes judgement. The Lord has clearly shown this to us. We go through this earthly life by depending on the Lord's blessing and grace, given to us by Jesus Christ who bore the cross.

We know that the Lord Jesus Christ is Lord, the one and only true Lord. He is the only Son of God. The heavens, earth and all creatures were created by Him; there is not one thing not created by the Lord.

Do you see, brothers and sisters, that since Christ arose from the dead He will take us one by one from death to resurrection? From Ephesians 1:20 we know that our Lord is the resurrected Lord. He appeared many times to His followers in the forty days after resurrection.

When Jesus was about to ascend to heaven, He said to them,

"What you see is how your Lord Jesus will go to heaven; in the same way I will later return to you." Now all our churches, all brothers and sisters in Christ, are earnestly praying for the day our Lord returns.

I Peter 1:3 tells us to praise and thank the Lord because we all have happiness and consolation. Our peace is given to us from heaven; none can take away our happiness and peace given by the Lord. Romans 6:5 says, "If we have been united with him in death, we will certainly also be united with him in his resurrection." This is to say, we must bear the cross that Jesus did. The Bible tells us that if we want to follow Jesus we must bear the cross. Therefore, each one of us has his own cross to bear. We accept that promise which says we must suffer with Christ.

We want to follow Jesus and be resurrected disciples, be victorious disciples, be disciples honouring God's name. You must remember what the Bible says, "Faith without actions is dead." We want to be Christians doing good deeds. We want to be the Lord's servants in all kinds of charity, following the directions of the Lord, according to each one's gifts.

Beg the Lord to bless us, beseech the Lord to pity us, and look for the day the Lord comes again. Use a pious and reverent heart to obey the Lord.

We know that our Lord is a living God. We know that the Lord Jesus Christ left His heavenly throne and came to this earth. We know that He adopted man's form, absolved our sins, was put on the cross, and cursed. We know that all these things were done for us.

When we think of our Lord being put on the cross for us, when we think how man had fallen into sin, when we sing our praise before the Lord, when we see the Lord's cross appear before us, we can only fall on our knees and cry. The Lord pities us, blesses us; praise the Lord! All things have been created by the Lord! And still such great pity, such boundless love!

Jesus came to this world to save man and to fulfill God's decree. Today He brings us all before the face of the Lord. Now as we are worshiping, coming before the Lord; He leads us all to heaven. Wherever we are, God calls us. We must have reverent hearts and look forward to His second coming. We know that the first time He came

He was gentle and He humbled himself — He served man. In Revelation we see that in His second coming He will bear the image of rage and fury. We will with trembling and fear come before the Lord. We must repent and loyally serve and wait for the Lord.

The Lord says not to love this world or the things of this world, so bring all your gifts to God. If your heart loves this world, you are not in Christ. We today have already been taken by the Lord. He has separated us to be the sacred ones. Like Christ, we do not belong to this world; we belong to heaven, serving the power of heaven and receiving heavenly instructions. We are governed by God. Beg the Lord to bless us and pity us! Let us silently pray.

5.7 1,000-Mile Search for Bibles

Early this year, Mr. Zhang went to Guandong Province to visit with a brother. In Guangzhou, he met two young brothers who had come 2,500 li (about 850 miles) from Henan Province to Guangzhou to look for Bibles.

Q: Where did you come from?

A: We're from a certain county in Henan Province, about 2,500 li from Guangzhou. It takes nearly three days to get here by train.

Q: Could you describe the situation there?

A: Well, before 1958, the number of believers was very small. In 1958, after the "Anti-Rightist Movement," the "Great Leap Forward" began. At that time, the number of believers became even smaller. But soon after the Cultural Revolution began, in 1967, the number of believers suddenly began rising and now is greater than ever.

These were all young people and most of the believers still are young people. For example, in our county, many high school and even recent elementary school graduates are believers.

Unfortunately there is a lack of pastors. The believers cannot grasp spiritual things on their own, nor do they have Bibles or Bible study books. So for several years we have been searching everywhere for spiritual books.

Q: What is the extent of your needs, and why do you have these needs?

A: The last time we came to Guangzhou, we got 900 Bibles, mostly New Testaments. When we went back to Henan, there weren't even enough to give one copy to every group of several hundred believers! There were meeting places and evangelists to whom we couldn't even give one copy of the New Testament.

The reason for this lack is that, during the Cultural Revolution, most Bibles and Christian books were burned. Now, with the number of Christians having multiplied and the old generation of evangelists getting smaller, the young believers are without the knowledge of the Bible. We would copy Bibles [by hand] if we could find them.

Q: Why was there this sudden growth in the number of believers?

A: This was the Lord's doing. At that time, there was a rumor circulating to the effect that if one believed in Jesus he would be healed. Many people prayed to Jesus. Some paralytics could walk again; some dumb people could speak again.

There was a paralytic over 50 years old, who had gone to all the hospitals without being helped. Then someone told him about the Gospel, and he believed. After three or four months of praying, unexpectedly he began to be able to walk by himself. Many people were astonished and believed as a result.

Then there was also someone who had cancer, whom the hospitals couldn't heal. He was told he only had a few months left to live. But then he received the Lord, and after praying continuously his cancer was healed.

Miracles of God have drawn many to believe in the Lord, but there are also many who have believed in order to have peace or because they have close friends who are believers, especially among the young people. Some of these friends are believers and talk about it; many have believed because of this.

Q: What is the situation of the believers now?

A: Although there are many who have believed, there is a serious lack of evangelists. Furthermore, the brothers and sisters in our area are all young people. They can only gain a little truth and knowledge from studying in the Bible, yet it is hard even to get a Bible. So spiritual nurture and growth are very difficult.

Q: Where do the evangelists that you have come from? What qualifications do they have?

A: Most of them have believed in the Lord for four or five years and have had a chance to read the scriptures. They only need to be willing to offer themelves and to be able to explain the Bible, and they will gradually be accepted by the brothers and sisters. The oldest evangelist that we have is over forty, while the youngest is only fourteen or fifteen years old.

Q: What is the population of your county? How many believe in the Lord?

A: I'm most familiar with the area around the county seat. But, because the evangelists often have fellowship together, I understand that there are over 300,000 people in the county. About 100,000 of them believe in the Lord, so it's about one-third of the population. Most of the believers are women.

Q: I have heard that in some parts of Henan, it is thought that there are 2,000,000 believers in the province and that, on the average, 3,000 are baptized every day. I would very much like to know your opinion about what the actual situation is.

A: I am not very familiar with the more distant areas, but judging from our county, having 2,000,000 Christians in Henan Province would be a possibility, because Henan has over 100 counties. But as for an average of 3,000 baptisms per day, I really couldn't say for sure.

Q: Do you have baptism ceremonies in your area?

A: Yes, but we don't have any regulation about how long someone must be a believer before he's baptized. It's done according to the situation of the [house] churches in each area and the needs of the Christians. We have baptisms about three times a year on our commune, with about 300 or 400 people each time. The one who does the baptizing is a representative elected by the brothers and sisters. Because we're in a mountainous area, the number of people receiving baptism is considered to be relatively small; in the cities and their outlying areas there are more.

Q: How many [house] churches are in your commune?

A: Altogether, we have 16 meeting places. There are well over 2,000, almost 3,000, Christians. This is a fairly accurate number, because the responsible brothers in our commune often have fellowship together, so each meeting place has a definite figure.

Q: With so many believers and so many meeting places, don't the local cadres oppose you?

A: Of course they oppose us. In some places they are worse than in others. We used to have a meeting place in our commune where, when the meeting time became known, all the brothers and sisters were arrested and fined RMB ¥12 each [about a week's wages]. But where there are too many believers, even when the cadres know there is a meeting, they can't completely control it. Yet we still can't be entirely open.

Q: Do you have an open Three-Self church there? Have you been able to obtain any of the Bibles printed in China?

A: We don't even have one Three-Self church. In fact, I haven't seen one anywhere in Henan that I've been to. As for the Bibles, in June of this year a representative of the brothers is going to go to Shanghai to contact the Three-Self office. We hope we can get a few. They had said that when they were printed they would give us some, although the number was to be very small — only ten copies for the whole county. But until the time we left to come to Guangzhou, we still had not received them.

Q: Why did you come the distance of 2,500 li to Guangzhou to look for Bibles?

A: Because the last time we were helped by the brothers in Guangzhou, and we took back several hundred Bibles.

Right now the farming work is light, so the brothers and sisters strongly urged me to go to Guangzhou again. Whether we find any Bibles or not, it is worth a try. This was their will and was also the opinion of most of the evangelists. So we came to Guangzhou and talked with this brother to see if we could obtain some Bibles.

Aside from going to Guangzhou to look for Bibles, we have also gone to other places and looked for devotional food. The expenses are all met willingly. In July of last year, we had a brother who went to Zhengzhou [the capital of Henan] and spent RMB ¥2,000 to find 500 New Testaments, which he bought from a couple of speculators. But it is hard to come up with the funds to buy them. About a month ago, an older brother went to four places between

Nanjing and Shanghai to look for Bibles but didn't find a single one. So we came the short distance of 2,500 li to Guangzhou again, hoping that the Lord had made preparations for us.

Q: Aren't you afraid that the Public Security Bureau might make trouble for you when you do this kind of thing?

A: We can't pay too much attention to that. If the Public Security Bureau knows, then of course it can confiscate our Bibles. The last time, they confiscated a few copies and detained a brother for 16 days.

Q: Besides needing Bibles, what would you like the brothers and sisters in Hong Kong to do for you?

A: The most important thing is still to supply Bibles and devotional books because of our lack of evangelists and spiritual people to lead us. Aside from this, tapes of good preaching are very much needed but cannot be supplied from within China. We hope that the brothers and sisters in Hong Kong will help fill our spiritual needs.

5.8 Lift Up the Hands of Prayer

This sermon was preached by a house church leader in the Nanjing area in the latter part of 1981.

Act 12:5 paints a beautiful picture: "So Peter was kept in prison, but the church was earnestly praying to God for him." The word rendered here "earnestly" is rendered in Matthew 8:3 and Acts 4:30 as "reached out his hand" or "stretch our your hand." The stretching of a hand here is an action similar to lifting up hands in prayer. It is praying to God with urgency, sincerity, and promptness.

Acts 12:4 talks about King Herod, the grandson of Herod Agrippa I, or Herod the Great. Caligula, the emperor of Rome from A.D. 37-41, made him king over Palestine and a large piece of land adjacent to it. In order to consolidate his power, he knew he had to win the support of the Jews.

He perceived that the religious leaders of those days — namely the high priests, elders and scribes — had lost the essence of godliness and were against the Church. Out of jealousy they had killed the Lord Jesus, and they were about to stamp out the new Church and eliminate all the believers. Under the pretext of religion, they stirred up a lot of commotion against the Church, and Herod's hand was also in this.

Now, let us examine the hand of Herod in the persecution of the Church:

Acts 12:1 says that "....Herod arrested some who belonged to the Church...." He did his best to persecute the Church, and his subordinates wanted to please him, just as he wanted to please the Jews. Together with some false religious leaders he set himself against the Church and the Christians, thus upsetting all standards of right and wrong. They conspired together to do whatever they wanted to persecute the Church.

Through this persecution, the believers gained a true understanding of Herod's regime and the hand of those false religious leaders. They would never help the Church to propagate the truth of the gospel. Their goal was just to place the Church under their control. It is no wonder that the Church was persecuted and Christians suffered. It has happened in every generation throughout history, varying only in degree and duration.

"For it has been granted to you on behalf of Christ not only to believe on him, but also to suffer for him...." (Phillipians 1:20) A Christian ought to rejoice in the midst of sufferings, enduring all tribulations with gladness, so long as he is not suffering for the sake of his sin.

You are not suffering alone, you are suffering with Him. Through persecution, many Christians have filled up in their flesh what is still lacking in regards to Christ's afflictions. [See Colossians 1:24.] They willingly have given up their lives so that truth might stand. May we glorify God in our suffering with thanks and praise, so that we may be glorified with him in the future.

"He had James, the brother of John, put to death with the sword." (Acts 12:2) Herod didn't kill James with his own hand, but he gave the order, and that is just as bad. His hands were gory with the saint's blood, which ascended into heaven and is remembered by God. The martyrs regarded death as going home for the sake for truth. And this truth, the one and only truth being attested by the blood of the saints, can never be altered by any killing or persecution.

Among the twelve apostles, James was the first martyr. Once,

James had gone with his mother and brother John to the Lord and requested that they be permitted to sit one on his right and the other on his left in the kindgom of heaven. Now he triumphed: he drank the cup which the Lord had drunk, and was baptized with the Lord's baptism. He went to the heavenly home with a crown of glory.

The Lord sits on his throne of glory, and those that follow him will sit there also. When God's servants were martyred for their loyalty to him, they did not fail, but succeeded in securing that eternal life. As the words of one hymn proclaim,

"The city of glory opens for me,
With such grandeurs and delight;
The Son of God stands to welcome,
His faithful servant to come in."

The second coming of the Lord is described in John 16:1-2: "All this I have told you so that you will not go astray. They will put you out of the synagogue; in fact, a time is coming when anyone who kills you will think he is offering a service to God." Killing is a service to the devil, how can it serve God? But so said the Lord. For the slaughter of the saints, they offered laureate and flowery descriptions to lighten their blood-guiltiness.

Yet Scripture reassures us that when believers die for the truth. God will avenge them for their blood. "Precious in the sight of the Lord is the death of his saints." (Psalm 116:15)

Herod stretched out his hand to kill James, and when he saw that this pleased the Jews, he stretched his hand to persecute and kill other Christians: ".... he proceeded to seize Peter also." (Acts 12:3)

"The night before Herod was to bring him to trial, Peter was sleeping between two soldiers, bound with two chains, and sentries stood guard at the entrance." (Acts 12:6) Yet as Herod stretched out his hand to kill people, the church stretched out all her hands in prayer to save people, moving God to stretch out his hand. And when God stretched out his hand, the whole situation changed. Praise God!

God stretched out his hand. He has done the same thing to numerous saints after Peter throughout the generations. They had been put in closely guarded prison cells; for months and years they lived behind the iron bars, knowing not when those heavy iron gates would be flung open for them. *Their bodies were separated from the rest of the body of Christ, but their spirit was closer to God.*

"....And the chains fell off Peter's wrists." (Acts 12:7) "Then the angel said to him, 'Put on your clothes and sandals.' And Peter did so. 'Wrap your cloak around you and follow me', the angel told him." (Acts 12:8)

God's wonderful doings usually surpass our understanding. Once God decides to liberate his children, everything falls into place. He will take off your chains and remove your fetters. He wants you to gird up yourself and put on your sandals, for far is the distance that you must travel. He orders his angel to instruct you to wrap your cloak around you and follow him. How tender and loving his voice is!

By the strength of the Lord, let us raise the banner of truth in this generation, and be workmen that need not be ashamed in the house of God. Let us follow in the steps of the apostles in this narrow road of service to him.

On the other hand, dear brothers and sisters, you may be bearing far less holy chains. *Maybe your chains are invisible and are deeply imbedded in your heart. Maybe your chains are gold and beautiful, whose brilliance has firmly captivated your soul.* No matter what form they are, they will surely hinder you in your heavenly pilgrimage. Only the Lord can cut our chains asunder. And only when we are rid of our burdens can we have strength to march forward. May God break both the chains of Herod and the chains of our own making, and may He grant us enough strength, that we may walk fearlessly in His will.

"They passed the first and second guards, and came to the iron gate leading to the city. It opened for them by itself...." [Acts 12:10]. No matter how strong the gate of the prison is or how securely it is guarded, when the hand of God starts to move, the gates will open. Nothing can hinder the hand of God. The hand of Herod only kills, persecutes and binds, but the hand of God wakens, liberates, and opens the door. Only the hand of God "....breaks down gates of bronze and cuts through bars of iron" [Psalm 107:16].

"The Lord sets the prisoners free..." [Psalm 146:7] Dear brothers and sisters, maybe you have never entered a physical prison, but there still is an iron gate in your heart. Many times you fall into utter confusion and are confined behind a shapeless iron gate. You are deceived by the petty knowledge of the world, swayed by the practices of paganism, snared by mundane affairs, bound by the lusts of the flesh, bothered by your children's trivial arguments, and crushed under the load of worry and care.

More dreadful than all these is to be controlled by sin and become a slave of the devil. "The word of God is living and active. Sharper than any double-edged sword, it penetrates even to dividing soul and spirit, joints and marrow; it judges the thoughts and attitudes of the heart" [Hebrews 4:12]. In the presence of the Word of God nothing can be hidden, but everything will be revealed in the all-searching light of the truth. By the power of the Lord, all iron gates will disappear!

The hand of God led Peter out of the prison. "When they had walked the length of one street, suddenly the angel left him. Then Peter came to himself and said, 'Now I know without a doubt that the Lord sent his angel and rescued me from the hand of Herod and from everything the Jewish people were anticipating.' When this had dawned on him, he went to the house of Mary, the mother of John, also called Mark, where many were gathered and were praying" (Acts 12:10-12).

The Church's outstretched hand and ceaseless prayer are the motivating power that moves the hand of God to act. A group of people praying together in one accord is often stronger than an individual praying alone. God listened to the prayer of the Church, prayer that was offered with outstretched hands, and He set Peter free.

Here we face another question. Why did God let James be killed but deliver Peter from the jail? God leads His children in different ways. But everything is arranged according to his predetermined order. Certain people, in certain times, will suffer, go to jail, endure all kinds of tribulations, or even die for His name. But God is the wonderful counsellor whose wisdom no one can comprehend. For His glory and kingdom, He wants His servants to serve Him in different capacities. Some will be persecuted unto death, but they will go to their heavenly home with songs of victory!

"When the hand of God moves, the mountains are shaken and the hills removed.." (Isaiah 54:10). "The kings of the earth take their stand, and the rulers gather together against the Lord and against his Anointed One.... The one enthroned in heaven laughs; the Lord scoffs at them" (Psalm 2:2,4). The Church is God's elect, and those who persecuted the Church through the generations all came to an evil end.

The hand of God works together with the church. "But the word of the Lord continued to grow and to be multiplied" (Acts 12:24). *All the things that the hand of God achieved were the result of the believers' prayer with outstretched hands. As the Church keeps on praying to God with outstretched hands, the ministry of the Gospel keeps on prospering.*

Read Isaiah 45:11 "This is what the Lord says — the Holy One of Israel, and its Maker: Concerning things to come, do you question me about my children, or give me orders about the work of my hands?" God is really gracious to His children. When the Church gathers and prays to God with outstretched hands, she is stretching her hands to God for help, beseeching God to ordain, and committing herself to the hand of God to act. As she stretches her hands to God to pray, she is urging God to act, so that the work of His hand may proceed smoothly and the Church that He has chosen for Himself may behold the wonder of His providence. All His children in the world will see that when they come to the end of their road God Himself will begin to act. And when He acts, He will draw thousands of people to believe in Jesus Christ as their Savior, and the whole world will glorify His name.

5.9 House-church Leaders' Thoughts

The following is a report of a traveler in 1981 from Hong Kong who had extensive contacts in Shanghai, Guangzhou, and Hangzhou. The interview focused on the relationship between the TSPM and the house churches, some house church situations, and attitudes toward the TSPM by lay preachers.

I went to Shanghai on February 1 and met with two older lay

preachers. On the third I had dinner with an older Christian sister. The next evening we went together with the older lay preachers to a Christian family's house for dinner. The mother and daughter are Christians, but the father is a CCP member.

From February 5-7 we went to Hangzhou to meet some Christian friends. We exchanged stories and talked. On February 8 we went to Guangzhou, and on the tenth we returned to Hong Kong.

One of the two elderly lay preachers in Shanghai originally came from Shantou (Swatow) in Guangdong province. The other was from Shanghai. They were both arrested and convicted by the government in 1956. One was sentenced for three years; the other got four years. Their crimes were, first, spreading malicious influence in the church, and, secondly, being counter-revolutionaries. These two men, having gone through that, have a very resolute and negative attitude toward the TSPM. They spent a long time talking with me about the TSPM. They believe that the TSPM is essentially being used by the government to destroy Christianity. Thus, it will not foster the development of the Chinese Church. Even in the beginning, they said, the government used the TSPM. To begin with, it opened churches to denounce the wealthy Christians and those with foreign friends. Later, still under government control, the TSPM announced the "unity campaign" but did not permit the spreading of the Gospel. It did this to wipe out the preachers. Based on what they heard recently, these elderly preachers claimed that these things had already started before 1966, before the Cultural Revolution. In the 1950s the Shanghai TSPM brought all the ministers from the open churches together to force them to renounce their faith. They made them stand in front of their church and say, "Down with God," "Down with Jesus." Later, they forced them to march around Shanghai, starting from their churches, going up and down the streets yelling, "Down with God," "Down with Jesus." Among those were some older preachers who were unwilling to do that. They suffered greatly.

When the Cultural Revolution started, some Christians said that Christianity in China had already disappeared. There were already no more preachers, and all the Bibles had been burned up.

These two Christians said that in 1976, when the Gang of Four was smashed, the government decided there should be an atmosphere of a little democracy, so it opened a church. And so the TSPM quickly sprang up. But because [its leaders] had done such evil deeds in the past, no one now believed them.

The two older preachers spoke frankly of the situation of the Chinese church; the purpose of the TSPM has not changed, and the essence of the CCP [Chinese Communist Party] has not changed. Hence, the aim and essence of the TSPM will not be able to be changed. They also said that now the objective of the TSPM is to increase contact with international Christian churches. But it's probably not going to work out because there are too few TSPM personnel to carry this out. Therefore, [TSPM leaders] want to open even more churches. Just as long as the people come to their open churches, they can still impose their TSPM control over the Church. To achieve this goal, they must mobilize even more preachers. So the TSPM is in the midst of building its image.

Last year, the United Front Work Department of Shanghai called together all the preachers of the public churches and declared that from henceforth they could not preach on politics but could just preach on the Bible. Now, look at that; before they could not preach on the Bible, now they cannot preach on politics.

In China today Bibles and preachers are in demand. If the open churches preach the Spirit then all the Christians will come running to the TSPM churches. After the public churches have enough people, the TSPM can even better and more easily organize for international Christian conferences and exchanges.

One of those who recently came into the open is from Guangzhou. TSPM personnel came looking for him because he was rather polite before the Cultural Revolution. They asked him if he would be willing to do a few things for Chinese Christians. If the government considers that you have made a contribution to the Chinese Christians, they said, then you will quickly be rehabilitated. How was he supposed to contribute to the Church? Well, you just write a few articles for *Tian Feng* [the TSPM journal], the TSPM people said. Furthermore, you can preach in the public churches. As long as you do not criticize the government you can write about anything, and the same goes for the preaching. You can speak and preach your own personal opinions. They summed up by saying that the government now wants to mobilize all those who previously opposed the TSPM, especially those who were in prison. If they suffered, it's all the better as far as the government is concerned. Once they resurface they can have a job, but they must first prove they've already repented and mended their ways. Because these people have extensive contacts and many friends, even more will come to their public churches.

Some now say, my friends reported, that they support the Church. But there are a lot of people who say that. Actually, they are only bringing more problems and difficulties for the Chinese Church. If you help the TSPM, you are only helping to bolster their popularity internationally. This is because, as I said before, the essence of the TSPM has not changed.

The preachers also mentioned that they do not approve of those outside China who support the TSPM. For example, outsiders say on the radio there has been a new church opened in such and such a place, and then they offer thanks to God for the opening of churches. "What do they do that for? What are they trying to accomplish?" these men angrily asked. They should not be too excessive in broadcasting news and affairs of the TSPM or in saying good things about the TSPM, the men said. Sometimes the broadcasters say that we do not have to fear the TSPM and that foreign broadcasts cannot be jammed, they added.

Many are still undecided about these broadcasts. If the others are all like this, then they will not encourage believers to listen. Hence, as you can see, they oppose those foreigners who, in articles or actions, support and approve of the TSPM. They say if you support them [the TSPM] you are not supporting the Chinese Church; you are harming it.

Things in Shanghai are now a bit tight. This time when I talked with the Christians in Shanghai, they said there are very few house churches with more than ten people attending, because with more than ten they have to be very careful. The government has started to pay attention to Christians in the Communist Youth League. I asked if there were many Christians in the CYL, and they claimed there were not merely a few.

While I was in Shanghai, a Christian CYL member was approached by a Party member asking about his activities. The Christian knew it was because of his faith. Some Christians say they are not opposed to the government. They are, rather, opposed to the TSPM; they separate the two. Since the TSPM is a tool used by the government to destroy the Church, they are opposed to it.

Shanghai is a tense place because private Christian meetings are difficult. During the Chinese New Year, almost eighty young people met in one building. That is because over the holidays they have time to meet; otherwise it is too difficult. They brought some food along and spent the whole day locked up inside. After their meeting, they left one at a time. They did this for three days at a stretch. Others said that the three days off over the New Year was a great help for them. Usually they have meetings only rarely. If there is no vacation, it is too easy to be spotted by others. So during the year they cannot have too many meetings.

They also claimed that in the villages there are many Christians. But [the rural Christians] seem to pray only if there is illness. After the sickness has gone away, they do not have any need for Christ; then they will not participate in the meeting.

Once I talked with an elderly sister. Her health was poor, so she did not say much except on one important point; the Holy Spirit works outside of China the same as in China. So she opposed foreigners who supply economic aid to the Chinese Church. On this point, those two elder preachers were in opposition. It is just that now we have no Bibles or other books, they said, so we need them. The other things should be left up to the Chinese Church itself to supply and should not be brought in as gifts. Maybe this old woman was an exception. But she said that the mistakes made by missionaries should not be committed again. However, an elderly preacher from Nanjing disagreed and said the more missionaries the better. Sometimes we visited families and did not supply them with Bibles and literature, and they seemed unhappy. "Why don't you supply us?" they would ask. Then we would go to another house meeting and offer them Bibles, but they seemed insulted and were unwilling to take them. They said they did not need our things [gifts, supplies]. They already had them; they were rich. So each person's opinion is different.

In Shanghai we were introduced to one young Christian whose family is quite rich; his father is a CCP [Party] member. The daughter was in Qinghai working but has now returned to Shanghai to stay. His mother and sister are both Christians. They received me very hospitably; this probably reflects their faith in the government policy of opening churches. And it is probably the case that the father has not suffered much as a Party member, nor has the family.

We had a meeting in Hangzhou with some fellow believers from Wenzhou. They say there is a revival now in Wenzhou including more than 300,000 believers. But they too are facing problems. They want to open a public church, but the appropriate unit has been unwilling to make the arrangements, so they still have not opened the church. They have already received notice that, once a church is opened, the house meetings [will have to stop]. Furthermore, the UFWD made the statement that the Christians cannot spread the gospel to high school students. If Christian students do so, they will be expelled. Already there are some young believers who cannot attend school because they want to preach. These Wenzhou Christians said that the Party will exert pressure wherever it can. Where it cannot exert pressure, it loosens up and relaxes a little to give people a good impression.

In Canton I found out about the Bible supply situation. On my last trip a family I knew had received a few thousand Bibles, almost 10,000. Other people had accepted quite a few too; then there were quite a lot. But this time they had not received any Bibles in the past three weeks, and none of them had Bibles. Right now there are a lot of people coming from the north looking for Bibles. For example, I went to a friend's house church and six or eight Christians were found to be there from Anhui province. They were all decked out like they were from the countryside. At nearly every meeting these kind of people show up. They come hoping to carry back Bibles. My friend does not refuse them. If they come, he is willing to let them stay. However, right now in Canton there are not too many Bibles; basically, there aren't any. There are very few coming from Hong Kong, and supplies from Shantou (Swatow) have stopped too. They do not know why this has happened.

There is another matter I forgot to tell you about a moment ago. An elderly Christian sister from Nanjing said she knew of a young Christian woman who recently went traveling with some Nanjing Seminary students. They went for one week. She found out that they had never prayed before! There were probably seven or eight in all, and they went on their own during vacation. They did not sing Psalms either. Even before eating they did not pray. They just listened to popular music. She was really sad to see that the Nanjing Seminary was like that.

In Shanghai they told me that those people who often come from Hong Kong are getting to be a bother. There was one who brought some printed materials from Hong Kong. But this brother made a serious mistake. He let the Public Security Bureau know of these things. They had asked what he did and where he was from. He told them all about the original arrangements. The Christians told me that, after I get back to Hong Kong, I should tell him that he cannot come back here again.

Then there was a group of eighteen Christians traveling from Beijing to Guangzhou. They brought tapes, books, recorders, and Bibles. But at customs one of them was searched, and he blurted out the whole story. Well, customs detained them and confiscated all of their things. They asked a lot of different questions and frightened them. The travellers were afraid they might say something wrong and not be let free. They had no experience with this kind of thing before, so they told the officials everything. The customs officials gathered up all their things, the tapes, tapeplayers, and books and told them to come back the next day. That evening, they met together and told some brothers from Beijing about their problem. They advised them to go immediately to buy their train tickets. Early the next day the travellers returned to the customs office. But then an official apologized to them. He said they clearly and thoroughly investigated the case, and now they were allowed to take their possessions into or out of the country. Probably we will see more of this kind of thing.

It is my personal opinion that the present Chinese government and the TSPM have already determined the strength and power of the foreign Christian church and the power of the Chinese indigenous church. Furthermore, they have already formulated their guiding principles; that is, they are trying to build up the image of the TSPM and to evoke the sympathy of the outside church for the TSPM. Therefore, I think that in the future they will continue to do "nice" things; they'll open more churches and force more lay preachers to go to the open churches. The believers in house churches and other Christians will run to their side. Hence, in the future the Chinese Church will split over the issue of supporting or not supporting the public church.

According to certain people, if you go to the public church you are only helping the TSPM. Christians should not go to the open churches because it only serves to [support] the TSPM. So I feel there will be an even greater split in the Church. Furthermore, if we support the TSPM and say good things about it, the TSPM will develop even faster. I personally support and agree with the house churches. I feel we should not praise, support, or sympathize with the TSPM.

Q: How is Brother Li [pseudonym] doing?

A: Right now he is very busy. He himself is printing reading materials. His house church has more and more people coming. Some people in Shanghai know him and asked me if I had seen him. I said I had. I told them about the basic situation with Brother Li. Brother Li's church has really opened up now; all kinds of people can go there. But there are a lot of people in the church who are worried. Brother Li himself said that anyone who comes to a meeting is accepted. There are brothers and sisters who come from the north and Brother Li makes introductions like this: "Oh, come here. This fellow is from Nanjing; he came to pick up Bibles." He introduces people in such a way that others can hear the whole thing. He is not afraid. He very openly entertains foreigners. I brought this up with them in Shanghai, about Brother Li, which probably did not go over too well.

It seems we are now at war, and as for Brother Li it is hard to say. He is on the front lines. Probably he is a touchstone for the government. If you hold meetings, the government will know right away. If you entertain foreigners, others will ask what you are doing. What are you telling them? In the beginning I felt that they were going too far when they entertained foreigners. Maybe the government will not be able to restrain them. They feel that the Chinese government has not planned to completely control the Chinese church. If they have power to influence others, they will not be attacked. Brother Li already has contacts and influence. Local Christians really support Brother Li and admire his courage. So it is not a question of entertaining foreigners; it is a question of your attitude toward the government.

Brother Li's house church is probably the largest and most open house church in all of China. They have almost 100 people at a meeting. When they meet they sing so loud that people on the nearby roads can hear them. They have Bibles in every room. Although they are rather open, they do their printing in secret.

Q: They do not lack Bibles now?

A: In Canton, of course, they do not lack them. But there are an awful lot of people coming down from the north. They have all heard that Brother Li has Bibles. But Brother Li does not have that many Bibles. They told me that at nearly every meeting ten or more northerners come. There are also some who come down to Canton and then do not leave. They come to Li's house church meeting all the time. In one house church they have difficulty with a fellow who came from Guangxi province. They asked him why he came to Canton, but he hasn't given answers. He just stays in Canton and comes to each meeting. This house church is really worried. They cannot figure out why he comes and what is he up to. But Brother Li does not care what kind of people come.

Then there are rural TSPM ministers who send people to Canton to buy Bibles. These people say that the TSPM ministers gave them the money to buy Bibles. However, the reason for their coming is not altogether clear. There are two possibilities. The first is that these TSPM ministers are sending people to Canton to understand the situation in Canton. The second is that TSPM ministers in the countryside are not as controlled as are TSPM pastors in the city.

Perhaps it is a matter they themselves feel is necessary for the believers. Some of those who come, though, say that they use the Bibles for themselves.

There was a minister from a Henan TSPM church who came to Canton to buy Bibles. He was the one who told me all about these things. So this kind of thing happens all the time. I am not sure, but some of them may be unemployed youth.

I think this development is very complicated. Some of these people are very naive [pure-hearted], and some are using their power to go to Canton for selfish reasons, [to obtain Bibles for themselves]. Others, of course, are serving the TSPM, and still others are using their relationship with the TSPM to oppose it.

Q: Some of them who have served in prison and later been set free go to the churches. When I was in Shanghai, someone said, "There were two among us who spoke out on our behalf; one was arrested and the other was tried. One still has not changed. The government may be willing to rehabilitate him, but he says he has not changed and does not want to be rehabilitated. The other has been set free and has become a minister in a public church. People tell them, 'The two of you together issued a declaration to the government; look, one of you has already gone to the public church as a preacher, why don't you also go?' His answer is that he is his own person." So these matters are all complicated. He does not criticize, but he doesn't give any reasons either.

Q: When these people come down from the north, do they have any proof that they are sent by churches?

A: No proof.

Q: So you give them these Bibles and do not know if they are Christians. Maybe they go and sell the Bibles. Since there are quite a few like this, the problem is hard to resolve.

A: Basically, there is no proof.

Q: Do they have any hope for Gospel broadcasts?

A: I have three remarks. First, simply broadcast the Gospel; do not talk about TSPM affairs. Do not criticize or flatter. The second is that the South Korean Gospel broadcast should not have English lessons because there are relatively few villagers who know English.

Studying English is a need for the city people; the villagers do not have that need. They want you to broadcast in Chinese.

For the city folks, most have gone to bed after 9:30 p.m. The next day they have to go to the office. So for them, 6:30 — 9:30 p.m. is the best time. In the countryside they wait until after the production brigade broadcast is over, at 9:30 p.m., and then they listen to the Gospel broadcast. Also, they think the broadcast time is too short, only fifteen minutes and then a song. They would like half an hour or an hour. They like it if you preach more, the longer the better. They do not like it when, after the Gospel broadcast is finished, they list all those who contributed to the broadcast. And they do not like it when they ask the listeners to send letters to Hong Kong about their problems. As soon as they hear this kind of stuff they immediately turn off the radio because it is too dangerous to send letters.

5.10 Denouncing the TSPM

This sermon from a house church leader in southwest Henan Province gives insight into how some house churches in China viewed the TSPM.

Prayer

Jesus, our great master Jesus Christ, we seek You Lord to grant us peace. O Lord, we praise You for blessing us at this afternoon's service. We seek Your Holy Spirit to be with us; we beg that Your Word fill us and that Your spirit-filled manna appear to us. We beseech You to reveal Your word to us, to nail the mark of the cross on our bodies. We pray that our hearts may be emptied and cleansed to receive Your word, that You may purify our worship service and this assembly of worshipers.

O Lord, bless this place, cleanse this place. O Lord, we beseech You to come and listen to our prayers. O Lord, we pray that Your word may be made clear to us. No matter what we say or pray, it is all part of Your will. Praise you Lord! You have revealed Your decrees to us; we ask that You do Your work. O Lord, we are truly ignorant; we are before You with unknowing minds. We pray that

You grant us grace. O Lord, praise Your name!

We offer a common prayer for the Chinese Church and the world Church, that they become part of God's will. O Lord, praise You for the revival of Your Church, the revival of the Chinese Church and the Church everywhere. O Lord, let more and more of the saved come into Your Church through the revived Church. O Lord, we thank You, praise You and pray that Your kingdom comes. We pray that all the peoples of the world will respect Your name as sacred.

O Lord, we pray even more that You release Your gospel, that You bless the work of our Christian brothers and sisters, and that Your spirit be with them every hour and every moment. We pray that the Lord's life be always with them. As we thank and praise You, we pray that You, our Lord, keep and protect them in their different tasks. Dear Lord, we thank You that because of Your love You bless their work and families. They come before You today lacking nothing!

Our Lord, we seek You to make the Chinese Church a Spirit-filled church, a Church in contact with the Spirit, a united Church. We pray that you will bestow grace upon the Chinese Church, cleanse the Chinese Church, and remove the spirit of Judas in the Chinese Church. We ask that the Church become a spiritual Church, completely satisfied in Your heart. As You do Your work, we pray that You will lead us children in prayer, that You will release the Spirit, release Your spiritual force and Your gospel. O Lord, we hear Your gospel and believe, crawling in the dirt repenting.

O Lord — praise You — we pray that in China and all over the world the gospel is spread. Bind Satan's actions and power so that Your gospel may be delivered soon. When You come again, save our spirits.

We beg You, Lord, that You pity the Chinese Church and our church here. O Lord, lead the hearts [of those that persecute us] and do not condemn them, for they do not know what they do. O Lord — praise You — they suppress Your children. O Lord — praise You, thank You — though they restrict the Church's growth in many places, we pray that You do not condemn them, but pity them and save them.

O Lord, we praise Your name, for You have answered our prayers and blessed our work. O Lord — praise You — we know many

brothers and sisters need guidance in reading and studying the Bible.
O Lord, we need materials for Bible study; we need spiritual texts
to guide us. We pray that You do your work — that You bless this
work. O Lord — thank You, praise You — we ask You to remove
the heresies from the Church.

We offer this prayer in the sacred name of Jesus; please hear
our prayers for all eternity. Amen!

Sermon

Let us first read Numbers 25:1-9. Let us also have a look at
Psalms 106:28-31 and Revelation 2:12-15, 18-20. We will read up to
that point for this afternoon. Let us pray together.

O sacred Lord, we beg that You come to us here. O Lord —
we praise You — You reveal Your word and light so that man might
understand. O Lord — praise Your name — we pray that Your Spirit
will lead us. Lord — praise You — do not let Your children be insolent
and proud. We pray that You may accomplish Your work. We seek
You to purify our hearts and lead us in the following texts, so that
You may reveal Your own Word to us. O Lord, answer our prayer.
We praise You, Lord, for answering our prayers.

In this way we offer our prayers in the name of Jesus. Amen!

We can see from these four texts their significance for today's
Church in China and Henan. We can also determine what sort of
attitude we should have. First, Numbers 25:1-9 says that when the
Israelites went to Moab they passed through the Red Sea and left
Pharaoh behind, and the Lord was with them. Yet when they were
with the Moabites, they were defeated. Why?

When the Israelites were in Moab there was a prophet named
Balaam. When he saw the Israelites, he spoke to them in a very grand
and imposing manner. Balaam was a descendent of Abraham, but
he was not born of Isaac. If we look in the Bible, we find that
Abraham had six wives and that Balaam was born of Jeyebel.
Therefore, Balaam knew that there was a God; yet he was not born
of Isaac.

So he cursed the Israelites. But the spirit of God three times
disciplined him not to curse the Israelites. The Spirit told Balaam

that God is a jealous God who does not want His people to sin, to commit sexual sins, or to eat sacrificial food. But Balaam lured the Israelites to commit sin. He dressed up the beautiful women and prostitutes to seduce the Israelites. And it says in Numbers 25 that they ate the sacrificial food.

Since the Israelites committed adultery with the Moabite women and prostitutes, the Holy Spirit descended upon them, bringing a great plague. In one day 24,000 people died. Before that time the Israelites suffered no defeats, but then in one day so many people died. That is because the people were united with Baal of Peor and committed sexual sins. All this can be seen from the Scriptures.

But what are our present conditions in the Church? The Chinese Church is in the midst of fire and blood; there is a great struggle. By the grace of the Spirit we have both this struggle and revival. Not only in Henan, but all over, church members are put in prison and worship services are restricted. Still many people are coming to church. When the believers are oppressed, beaten, cursed, or bound, they cling to the Lord's life, to the right path. And now the church is being revived; the Spirit is being revealed, bringing more and more people to the church. This is the Lord's own work!

However, although the church doors have been opened and the doors of the gospel have been opened, the church leaders see fewer worshipers coming. When our brothers here gave testimonies last year 300 showed up. But only 100 came this spring. Recently there have been only a few at worship services. What is the reason for this?

This also is a plague. They do not say if they believe or not. There are only a few prayers. They will not allow the plague to be removed and do not allow preaching on the Spirit or repentance; they prohibit itinerant preaching. These kinds of restrictions are like those of Baal, and they are being put on our Christian brothers and sisters.

Some believers have become part of this world. They have united with the Public Security Bureau. This union is like that of the Israelites with the Moabite women, eating the sacrificial foods, just as we read in Psalm 106. They have taken and eaten all those things. They are treated like guests, treated to many things. The United Front Work Department's laws allow one to eat, yes, but not to pray. This is just like eating the sacrificial foods. They are united, completely bound together. As a result, the church has experienced a plague which has produced these present conditions.

We, brothers and sisters, must pray for them. There are brothers and sisters kneeling on the ground weeping. They are sad because the church has not been able to revive, even though the doors were open during the day, but many brothers and sisters could not worship during the day. Because of these reasons many brothers have weakened in their faith.

The TSPM worship services are not of the Spirit; without prayer it is not a service. Under these conditions, we can only see Moses cry, and many of our brothers are also crying.

What do we see? Moses cried because he had no hope. But then there was a man called Phinehas. When he saw the Israelites with the Moabites and their lewd acts, he lanced them with a spear. In that way the plague ceased. Such a simple matter and the plague was over.

As for our church today, wherever we lance these lascivious women, the Church's plague will end. Our church was alive, revived — and an exciting place; there were many older servants. Then the TSPM started up, and these old servants of Christ saw the Church uniting everywhere. Many churches were created. They assigned worship service places, which became churches. Later they experienced the Lord's revival, but only now do we understand that the TSPM is the whore that must be killed.

Another look at the Scriptures. Acts 17 and Isaiah 30 show us that what becomes part of this earthly world becomes the whore. Only after we realize this does the plague end. Many brothers and sisters have taken up the work of revival again. So we see that now we need the courage of Phinehas. What did Phinehas do? From Psalms 106:30-31, "But Phinehas stood up and intervened, and the plague was checked. This was credited to him as righteousness for endless generations to come." The Church needs Phinehases to stand up and intervene against the wicked.

Already the brothers and sisters pray for a Phinehas to stand up throughout China and all over the world, using his weapons against the evil. Our weapons are not of this material world but are of the Spirit. We use the Holy Spirit. We will use prayers and chapters and verses of the Bible as arms.

The Church has but one true head — Jesus Christ. Now, if two heads of the church appear we know the other is a spiritual prostitute. Today's Church has added another head and another prop of support. It relies on the government and the country, not on the Lord, as in Isaiah 30:1-5.

We see that today's TSPM church is not relying on prayer nor on the Holy Spirit. It is united but not dependent on the Spirit; it is not from the Spirit. Rather it is united with, and is of, this world. It rests in Egypt's shade and relies on Pharaoh's power. Egypt represents this world, and Pharaoh, the kings of this earthly world. Likewise the TSPM relies on the money and riches of the earthly world. Let us look again at Isaiah 31:1-3.

This shows us that those who went down to Egypt relied on horsemen, chariots, and the power of men. They were dependent on the riches of this world. The TSPM today also relies on the power of the nation and its powerful churches. Thus, we urgently need a determined Phinehas to stand up and crush the wicked, to lance the prostitute. By doing this, the Church in China will become a Church of the Spirit completely filled with love. No longer will the Church be separated by distance or by other divisions; we will all be the Spirit's church.

Shall we pray:

Lord of the Scriptures, we thank You. You know the situation in our churches. You know the needs of Your children; You have never forgotten us. Oh Lord — praise You — as we are in the midst of revival, let us see the implications of a union with this world. It is like adultery with the Moabite women; it brings a plague to the Church.

Many of the brothers and sisters no longer pray, attend services, or listen to the word. So many have died from this plague. We beg You Lord, that in China, and all over the world, Phinehas will arise and slay the whore as soon as possible, so that Your Church becomes beautiful, filled with Your heart. Bless Your work, and lead us to do Your work.

We thus beseech You and offer this prayer in the sacred name of Jesus. Amen.

5.11 Response to Persecution in Henan Province

Since this document has been circulated widely in China, and since the event became public news, the names have not been changed.

Fangcheng County is in southwestern Henan. The writer states that out of a population of 700,000, 300,000 [or forty-three percent] are believers. Some villages in that area are known to be sixty to seventy percent Christian.

To the brothers and sisters in other lands who bear the same burden of our Lord:

First of all, let us open our mouths wide to praise the triune God. Let us sing praises to the love of the Father and the grace of the Lord Jesus Christ and the communion of the Holy Spirit, for He has brought sinners to repentance and is giving blessings to His children.

The Fangcheng county of Henan is now receiving special blessing in the sight of the Lord. Among the seven hundred thousand in this county, there are at least three hundred thousand believers, and the number does not stop increasing. "May the Lord increase and may we decrease" (John 3:30).

This is also a county to which *they* pay special attention. They call this place a "Jesus den." The revival that is going on in Fangcheng today is a result of gradual growth arising out of more than twenty years of persecution. At this point most of the preachers are those who were released from prison in 1978-79. There is one senior preacher whose church had only several hundred people when he was first imprisoned. That church had grown to several tens of thousands by the time he went to prison the second time.

They are thoroughly surprised. They do not understand why the greater the persecution, the faster the growth. This particular old brother was in prison four times, and each time the Lord added to the number of believers. During the last twenty years of persecution, the children of God have experienced the presence of the Lord.

Even non-believers have come to believe that there is a God, for the messengers of Satan are often given their immediate recompense. Through suffering God has deepened the experience of His children. They have come to know God more profoundly, and they have come to perceive the ways of the devil. They have also learned to entrust themselves completely to the hand of the God who is faithful and trustworthy.

God has prepared his instruments for the revival of the Church today. In 1978, when a good number of preachers were released from prison, they began to preach the gospel on their way home, even before they reached their own doorsteps. They carry on their bodies scars of persecution, and with these they continue their work.

The harvest is plenteous, but the laborers are few. During the last two to three years, God has indeed blessed their work. On the other hand, the tares of Satan have not ceased to cause splits within the Body [of Christ]. Even the most experienced spiritual leaders are often hindered by their relatives at home.

Praise God! Just as we were in the midst of our worries, the Lord provided preaching tapes on I, II, and III John prepared by our dear brothers. A certain brother Chang was deeply moved by the Holy Spirit and knelt down to confess his sins before all the brothers and sisters. He was once a party secretary, a captain in the local militia, and a leader of a farm production battalion. Because he believed in Jesus, he was imprisoned from 1971 to 1978.

He knelt down on the ground and pleaded with the Christian brothers and sisters, with tears flowing from his eyes, to love one another, to have one heart in serving the Lord, and to leave no opportunity for Satan. With tears in his eyes, he said, "We have traveled nine out of ten miles. There is yet one mile ahead of us. Let us proclaim the gospel of the Lord Jesus and satisfy the heart of our Lord. Let us not forget the great commission which the Lord gave to His disciples after He rose from the dead. He has also commissioned us who live in the last days to be faithful soldiers of Christ." Everyone was greatly moved, and we all cried as a group.

Praise the Lord! This brother stood up with tears in his eyes and told us that while he was in prison the Lord revealed to him that "Fangcheng County will become a rock." He said, "I am worthy of death, for I have forgotten the word of the Lord." Those who heard him went into action immediately. From the middle of March on, they sent out thirteen teams to preach the gospel. The last group consisted of fourteen persons. The youngest of them was a girl sixteen years old. They went to Biyang County of Henan, but there were heresies in that place, and the believers would not receive them.

As a result, the fourteen young preachers had to go in to the streets to preach the gospel. That was April 3, 1982. More than 5,000 people were listening to their preaching. Shops were closed, and traffic was brought to a standstill.

Soon agents of the TSPM and the local police came and arrested the fourteen preachers. They forced them to kneel down on the ground for three days and three nights, with their arms and legs tightly bound. Those fourteen preachers fasted for nine days. Some of the authorities in Biyang became scared and decided to send them back to their home towns. The nine from Fangcheng were returned there; five others were sent back to Shechi.

There was a house church leader in Fangcheng who requested that he be bound together with them.

In the course of returning the nine persons to Fangcheng, one of the girls was pushed off the truck, and her head hit the ground. She is still in a coma today.

The health of one nineteen-year-old sister who fasted for nine days was so poor that the authorities were afraid that she might die in prison, and so they released her on the ninth day. The rest of them are still in prison [in their home towns]. Many members of the Body of Christ from various counties came over to visit them. The young girl who was released cried and said, "They bound me lighter than they did the others." Still, there were scars all over her body from being beaten.

Dear brothers and sisters, please pray for the members of our body. Please ask the Lord to strengthen us, so that our lives may grow more solidly under persecution and thereby glorify our gracious Lord.

The brothers and sisters in Henan say with one voice, "Do not

be afraid of those who kill the body but who cannot kill the soul"
(Matthew 10:28).

Praise the Lord, man is able to overcome suffering. Satan has
been shamed and forced to retreat. Although man is weak, by relying
on the Lord he is able to triumph over Satan. For we war against
Satan, the spiritual force of the air.

Emmanuel!

5.12 House Church Leaders' View of the TSPM

*This is a composite transcript of interviews with five house
church leaders from different areas of China. Each of them has had
more than ten years of experience in their respective area, and each
has a wide circle of connections.*

Q: We have heard that there are now more than 400 Three-Self
churches open. Has the number of people participating in these
services increased correspondingly or not? What is the attitude of
the house churches toward the Three-Self churches?

A.   Generally speaking, people who participate in the open church
services say that the number coming is smaller than when the churches
were just opened. For example, the Dongshan church of Guangzhou
[Canton] used to be so crowded that even a drop of water couldn't
seep through. Now, this sight can be seen no more; often there are
empty seats. The reasons are many. Perhaps it is because the sermons
do not supply enough and souls cannot be filled. Perhaps some went
out of curiosity when they were first opened.

On the surface, the Three-Self Movement is supporting and
establishing the Church, but in fact it is destroying it. This could be
clearly seen in the 1950's. At present, they hold aloft their spiritual
principles on the one hand, but on the other hand they hem in the
development of gospel work. They are two-faced but more tactful
than before.

B.   When the Three-Self Movement prepared to establish a church
in our county, a letter came inviting our principal leaders to participate
in a joint effort. After we had discussed it and prayed about it, we
first felt there was no harm in participating and in listening to the

opinions of the Three-Self people. But we ourselves already had many years experience of 'three-self" work in our area [that is, they had engaged in self-propagation, self-government, and self-support on their own initiative], and our work in church organization, evangelism, and training was already in embryonic form. Moreover, we did not need a separate leadership wing from the Three-Self Movement, so we gently refused. Our viewpoint is this: we may have contact with the Three-Self Movement and exchange ideas, but the decision-making power must lie with us. We cannot on account of them change the positions and principles which we ourselves feel we should hold. Moreover, we hope that foreign Christians do not divide us into house churches and Three-Self churches. There is only one Church with Christ as its head. A church has to follow Biblical principles. Those which do not cannot be called churches.

C.   That we at present have absolutely no association with the Three-Self Movement has historical reasons. I recall an example from a county in Henan which demonstrates the situation of all the Henan churches. But first let me add that, except for the northern region of Henan, I travel to every other place frequently and have deep interaction with the church leaders everywhere. So I know the example of this county is very representative.

After the end of the Cultural Revolution, the churches in this area had become more vigorous. However, when the Three-Self Movement appeared, its leaders took the upper hand and made a mess of the churches there. The Three-Self Movement only allows one meeting on Sunday, does not permit meetings in places outside of their designated meeting points, and does not permit propagation of the gospel. There are many limitations. In addition, in their sermons they did not preach fundamental doctrines such as the confession of sin and repentance or salvation by being born again; their messages were lukewarm. In this way most of our brothers and sisters were put to sleep listening to the sermons. Those who were very enthusiastic about going to worship services lost their excitement when they went to their meetings. They stopped going to church, they stopped praying, and there were some who lost their faith completely.

When we saw this frightening situation, we encouraged the

brothers and sisters to pray and pray. They organized prayer groups and prayed with tears for the aged ones, the brothers and sisters, and the Church. After more than a month of prayer, they gradually came to realize the reasons for the churches' universal desolation and weakness. They wanted to be the Phinehases of this age and go and pierce through the prostitute church which no longer relied on Christ but on men of the world. They wanted to be like Peter, James, Stephen, and John, to rise up to be witnesses to the Lord Jesus Christ. They wanted to be like Esther, Isaiah, and Jeremiah and earnestly pray on behalf of the churches' desolation and the collapse of the Holy City and Holy Temple. They pursued a born-again salvation and scattered the seeds of the gospel everywhere.

That church originally had only a few dozen people, and there were no young people among the believers. Now there are from two to three hundred at every service, and half of them are youths. Therefore, we can see that the renewal of this church really depended on prayer. We pray that the Lord Jesus Christ will eventually pick up his whip and throw the pigeon sellers and money changers out of the temple. Let the Lord Jesus Christ again proclaim, "My temple is a temple of prayer."

D.   Our county can also be taken as an example. Originally the Three-Self churches were very strong and had many elders. Now many in the Three-Self churches are becoming aware that a Christian cannot serve two masters or two lords. They have turned about, and all come to house churches now. When they hear the evangelist preach, they feel this is the true Word and truly a witness of God. This is the work of the Spirit of God; it is not something human beings could bring about.

A.   I would like to raise a different point of view. The situations everywhere in the country are not necessarily the same, and it is hard to generalize. To discuss it fairly, the Three-Self Movement has only destroyed, not built up, the Chinese Church; but, unless it had God's permission, it could not have come into being nor could it continue to exist. I always feel that God's vision is very broad but that human vision is rather narrow. The prophet Elijah accused the people of Israel before God, but God answered, "I have preserved 7000 in Israel who have not knelt before Baal." Although the evil of Sodom and Gomorrah was overwhelming, God still saved Lot and his family who lived there. Therefore there are some believers and evangelists in the Three-Self churches who, like Lot, are truly saved and are doing their utmost to do the Lord's work.

E.   Naturally, in the Three-Self Movement there are a few individuals who love the Lord very much, and they have truly offered themselves for the work of the gospel in China. But I think we ought to look at its basic character and from there decide the question of our stance toward it. If we focus on peripheral matters, we will not be able to see the whole picture, and we could confuse public opinion and cause the people to be without direction.

Q.   From that perspective, the Three-Self Movement's intention to bring all the house churches into a unified system would seem to be very difficult to accomplish. According to what you know, how will the Three-Self Movement resolve this difficulty?

E.   As I see it, the Three-Self Movement may pull the house churches out into the open, force them to get into the Three-Self system, and, through the China Christian Council, control the house churches, the CCC concentrating its efforts on the preachers.

C.   They cannot succeed. At present, when we hold services, the Three-Self Movement and the Public Security Bureau (PSB) send someone to listen, sometimes even to four or five places at the same time. A Three-Self official must report once a week to the United Front Department. However, this does not matter. We only preach the Bible, and we have no relations with this world.

B.   The situation in our area is about the same, except that it is not as tense as in Henan. Basically we already have a tight organization; it is very hard for the Three-Self Movement to control us.

D.   At the beginning of this year, a person from the PSB came to talk to me. He said that very soon there would be a great persecution, and was I not afraid? He also said they would kill some and arrest some in order to destroy Christianity completely. A few months ago, a person from the PSB got hold of a certain brother who was responsible for a meeting place for a few hundred people. At first he engaged him in small talk for awhile, then he discussed the question of religion. "Look at the crevice beneath you," he said. He meant that in the present situation there was already a break, that danger was coming, and that Christianity would drop into the crevice.

"This is not frightening," our brother answered. "What I fear most is that when the Lord returns, the heavens will shake, and the earth will split open. The danger of that time will be the most frightening."

The PSB man turned into the kitchen and looked around. He saw that there was rice and steamed buns and said, "You are not doing too badly."

"This is just the grace of God," the brother replied.

The PSB man smiled. Seeing that gentle persuasion had gotten him nowhere, he said, "At present, your child is still small, only a few years old. If you die, what will happen to him?"

"I am not concerned about how small my child is. I am only concerned about whether I am dedicated to the Lord." When he finished speaking, he bit into his fingertip and, in the presence of the PSB man, wrote in blood on his book four Chinese characters for "Follow the Lord even unto death."

The brothers and sisters were very moved by his unyielding stance, and all were strengthened. As I see it, there is nothing to fear in the Three-Self Movement's persecution of the church. If they come, they come; we are not afraid.

Q.   Early this year, in Dongyang and Yiwu counties in Zhejiang [Chekiang] and in Fangcheng county in Henan, there was force used against Christians. Do you think these are isolated events or a more general phenomenon?

B.   I think the general strategy is the same everywhere, although the details of implementation are different. The general strategy is that the Three-Self Movement will use any method to control the house churches. But there is a firm and a soft execution of the policy according to different regional conditions, so different phenomena have appeared. I have heard the stories of Dongyang and Yiwu in general, but the details are not clear. In our church's area, it is relatively peaceful and without incident.

C. We have heard nothing of the situation in Dongyand and Yiwu. However, we know very clearly what happened in Fangcheng. Between ten and twenty believers went to Fangcheng to spread the gospel. Five thousand gathered around to listen. The preachers were detained and savagely beaten by the PSB.

Each regional Three-Self unit has its own version of the "ten don'ts," formulated at the instigation of the national Three-Self committee. The Henan region punished believers according to the "ten don'ts." For example, the fifth "don't" says, "Do not go from work unit to work unit or from commune to commune to propagate religion." But the Lord's command is, "The gospel is to be preached to the whole world." Many hunger and thirst after righteousness; in grief and sorrow they beg to hear the gospel. We may not, indeed cannot, turn a deaf ear to them and disregard them totally. Therefore, we can only break the rule about spreading the gospel to the outside. All the brothers and sisters who travel to spread the gospel risk their lives. They can be arrested at any moment. It often happens that, when the PSB comes after receiving secret instructions to arrest the preacher, the church just happens to be finishing. Only after the evangelist leaves by the rear door do the PSB men come in the front. The Lord protects the evangelists and makes it impossible for the policemen to complete the arrest.

There is a testimony that goes like this: an evangelist in a meeting was discovered and pursued by a Public Security agent. The agent saw him slip into the house of a believer. The agent wanted to go in to investigate, but the believer stopped him at the door and boldly asked him, "What will you do if you do not find out anything today?" In the end the agent could only retreat and investigated no further. The protection and peace of the Lord often goes beyond human expectations.

There is another testimony like this: the secretary of a certain production brigade was a person who caused much harm to the Church. He energetically opposed those known to believe in Jesus. Once he heard of a meeting being held in a certain place, and he sent out the militia of the production brigade to arrest the leaders. They were bound and carried to the brigade. There the militia cursed, slandered, and whipped them, trying to get them to say that they did not believe in Jesus Christ. But, no matter what happened, the believers held on to the truth. It was not until two or three in the morning that they were released. The next morning the secretary's wife went to the outhouse and found her mother-in-law dead there, with her head cut off. It had been done by the secretary's brother, who was mentally ill. The secretary cursed him for his great evil, asking his brother how he could have done such a terrible thing. His brother replied, "Is it I or you that is evil? The Christians have done nothing to you; why do you persecute them?" The secretary was speechless. The PSB also had no way to arrest his brother, since he was mentally ill. After that, many people in that area came to Jesus Christ.

There are a great many testimonies like this. From a human viewpoint, these may be very serious matters, but God takes cares of us always and will preserve us to the end. He views His children as the apple of His eye and the jewel in His hand.

In our area there is a saying going around: "The more one crosses the Yellow River, the more frightened he becomes; the more a believer is persecuted, the more courageous he becomes." I think these testimonies show that, although persecution is not a universal phenomenon, it still exists. They also show that one becomes more courageous the more one is persecuted. However, it is not that one relies on the power of flesh and blood to confront others, to struggle, or to stubbornly resist. Rather it is because of God's comfort, care, and just vengeance that we are able to cast off the weakness of our bodies and firmly hold the vision which comes from Heaven.

A.   I have heard that the events in Dongyang and Yiwu were caused by confusion between a Witness Li faction and a charismatic faction. Then the Three-Self people sowed discord from within, causing the PSB cadres to interfere and crack down. I have no further detailed evidence.

Differences in the house churches over ritual and theological viewpoints have given rise to great schisms. In the regions of Jiangsu and Zhejiang, wherever the Witness Li faction goes, it creates confusion. The same is true in Henan, so far as I know. They attack each other sharply like enemies on the battleground. This gives outsiders another handle to grab, another place to attack, and it causes great sorrow for us.

Q.   As you see it, for this last half year and into next year [mid-1982 to 1983] what sort of developments could there be in the relationship between the house churches and the Three-Self Movement? What changes will there be in the Chinese Church?

A.   The organization of the Three-Self Movement will get tighter. Then they will increase their infiltration and control in rural villages. The plight of free evangelists and house church leaders will get worse.

In view of these circumstances, I suppose if I can somehow cooperate with the Three-Self Movement, I will. But if I cannot, then I will firmly resist cooperation.

There are many whose only opportunity to have contact with the gospel is in the Three-Self open churches, especially in the cities. They simply cannot participate in house meetings. Therefore we must take real situations like this into our consideration. We should not blindly oppose the Three-Self Movement just for the sake of opposition. The Lord Jesus said, "One who doesn't harm us is a help to us" (Mark 9:40). At least at present the Three-Self people are not audacious enough to publicly oppose Christ in the pulpit. Paul also said, "What hindrance is this? Whether it be from a true or false intention, Christ is being spread abroad" (Phil. 1:18).

B.   As for the future developments, on the one hand, for the sake of the United Front, the Party must maintain openness and become even more open. On the other hand, it also wants to consolidate the leadership group around Marxism-Leninism and the thought of Mao, so it is setting limits and controls everywhere. The situation of the churches is similar. The Party will make use of the Three-Self Movement to infiltrate and control the house churches. I will give you an example to explain what I mean. The Red Sun Church in Hangzhou was originally a well-organized place for house church meetings. The Three-Self Movement, in the guise of supplying Bibles, hymnbooks, and preachers, gradually "helped" them, until it completely replaced the original house church leadership, and the church became a 100 percent Three-Self church. This method of surreptitious takeover is a sophisticated technique. In the future they could use even more skilled methods to convert house churches into Three-Self churches.

C.   From the point of view of churches in our area, the Three-Self Movement will put forth even greater pressure, using measures even more insidious than at present. The oppression could become more severe than at present. However, the house churches might be able to eliminate their schisms in the face of a common oppression and unify themselves.

Q.   Does the Three-Self Movement anticipate this result, that, in response to pressure, the house churches might internally unify?

C.   At present they think only of themselves, just like Haman. They have not considered the consequences. Right now the Three-Self church here hasn't many people, only a few old people, and they cannot meet. In the long run, they will become cold and indifferent. The Lord will not use them; the country will not use them. Because they will not be able to hem in the house churches, they will have no usefulness and will be cast away.

E.   On this question one should look not only at the churches, but also at the development of the whole situation: the present trend in international affairs, the government's current foreign policy, and the possible changes in policy in the next year. Because the Three-Self Movement is a kind of utensil, it will change along with changes in government policy. This point must be understood. Therefore, it will not be able to suppress the house churches.

Q.   How do you react to the possibility of increased pressure in the future?

A.   The Lord once said that the wheat and the tares should be allowed to grow up together so as to avoid injuring the wheat were the tares pulled out. In the Lord Jesus' time, the temple was controlled by the evil power of priests and scribes, but the important work of our Lord was to preach the message of repentance and conversion and not to lay blame for the temple's troubles. I think that the general believer ought to concentrate on cultivating the foundation of the spiritual life. It is not necessary to introduce the issues of the Three-Self Movement and schisms within the house churches. The seeds of disharmony within the Church which are scattered in this way can easily cause others to stumble.

C.   There are two possible courses for the Three-Self Movement vis-a-vis the house churches. God may choose its members just as He chose Saul and change them from persecutors to supporters. Another possibility is that, like Herod, who listened to Herodias and beheaded John the Baptist, they may destroy or injure numerous house churches. At the moment we have taken the course recorded in the gospel of Mark, chapter 6. Herod killed John, and Jesus retreated with his disciples into the wilderness to rest. We should retreat to those places where no one has heard the gospel and where no one preaches. We should not compete with the Three-Self but should scatter the gospel in the remote areas.

If we want to revive the Chinese churches, we must exert considerable effort and pay the price. The Lord will come to the aid of the Church; He will preserve His own work. The Chinese Church is now in a dark and evil period. If we do not urgently pray, it will be lost. However, we are deeply convinced that, with the prayers of our brothers and sisters both inside and outside of the country, under God's direction the Church in China will revive.

5.13 Traveling Preacher in North China

This article is an edited transcript of an interview with an itinerant preacher in central China conducted in the summer of 1982. It reveals both how the house churches in his area developed as well as something of his personal life.

From a very early age, I was willing to serve the Lord, and I preached the gospel to young children. Soon I was traveling all over — from Henan to Hubei, from Hubei to Shaanxi, from Shaanxi back to Hubei. In the 1960s I sometimes felt such a clear calling that wherever the Lord put me I would just talk about Him. So I knew clearly that the Lord wanted to use me and train me, and hence I was willing to give my whole life as a sacrifice to work for Him.

Ever since 1967 I have been amidst Christian brothers and sisters. At that time, Jiang Qing [Mao's wife]said that Christianity in China had already been put into a museum and that there were no more believers. But we brothers and sisters knew that there were those who continued to preach from place to place. Thank the Lord that He has led His people through ten years of turmoil. The Lord by His grace has united and revived His disciples. The Lord has blessed us, telling us that, as we do this work of revival, Christ is with us.

Whenever the Church suffers great persecution, I remember what an old believer once prayed: "Oh Lord, we ask that You be with us in Your sacred work of revival. Thank you Lord." Once I heard that prayer I never forgot it. For ten years now, every time I pray I say, "Oh Lord." This is truly the Lord's grace and mercy. Although I give very little, the Lord receives my service. The Lord continues to train and lead me in the revival work as He puts me among believers all over the land. Thank the Lord for His mercy.

Just now I thought of more words the Lord had given us. The Lord does not give us worry-filled hearts; rather, our hearts are filled with peace and consolation. The Lord loves us, so what can people do to us? He whom we trust gives us strength so that we can do all this. Thank the Lord for His grace. We know we must obey our Lord, not men, because He gives us His precious power and faith. When we go preaching from village to village the Lord gives us these words to console us. We know that those who trust in Him will be richly blessed.

We praise and thank the Lord that now the powerful fire of His revival is spreading. The miracles of His power extend to all the lands. The faith in the hearts of the itinerant preachers brings that fire to all places, and then the fire spreads from one place to the next, from one province to another. We can see that itinerant preachers are being used by God to do this kind of work. They are truly the treasure of the brothers and sisters as they do this revival work. They sacrifice everything as they set up underground churches and meetings and call on the brothers and sisters to serve the Lord.

Facing Arrest

Several times over the years I have come close to being arrested.

Once, at a meeting in 1976 with a few hundred Christians, the police came in and ordered that everyone be arrested. We were right in the middle of prayer, and I was with the brothers and sisters praying in the courtyard. One of the sisters pulled me down and hid me. I wasn't sure what was going on since we were praying. Another covered me, and they took me to another place.

Once a Christian sister told me that in the event of a crisis during a meeting she knew of a small building where we could hide. If there was any danger, we could very quickly get to this place, and we surely wouldn't be discovered. We could eat there and hide out for a long time.

In another case, in 1977, when we were holding our meetings, a Party secretary who was drunk came and wanted to vent his anger. The brothers and sisters surrounded the itinerant preachers and surrounded the Party secretary too. The brothers and sisters had precisely coordinated it; they had bikes that seemed like wings as we fled. Some of the preachers were sent to the mountains to find a place to hide. Some of us were even sent to the Party secretary's house. As it turned out, his wife was a believer, along with his daughter and son. They had me stay with the son, and she told her son not to open the door when his father returned. Well, the Party secretary returned, but he didn't ask at all about me. That evening the brothers and sisters came to retrieve me and hide me elsewhere.

Revival Begins, 1973-1980

Looking at my experience from the viewpoint of the Church's revival, I remember that on the eve of the revival we had asked ourselves just who it was that we believed in. To whom was the arm of Jehovah opening a clear path? We just believed in the power of God to protect our lives. We believed that His work was to be done. I decided to proceed with faith and confidence, and the Lord gave me that faith. At that time there were no churches set up. So we left for Hubei and preached wherever we went. We had the opportunity to share with those brothers and sisters, but they were very poor and I was saddened. But the Lord gave me strength and words. God consoled me and we suffered together. Oh, our Lord is a living Lord.

Although we are often cold toward God and refuse him, our God still is a loving God. The Lord gives us strength to meet with and share with the brothers and sisters. He leads our lives wherever we travel. Although this work is very tiring and our burden is heavy, at the beginning I felt compelled to give my feet to God. Once we started, it became a year's service, then two, then three. That was back in 1974; praise and thank the Lord for His mercy.

Back in 1973 we saw how the Lord was to carry out His own work in many different places. The Lord used miracles and the Spirit to bring the fire of revival to all these places. As a result, our scope of activities expanded and more came to believe. Everybody was extremely enthusiastic. Wherever we went we were not turned away. We were truly moved as we felt their great love for us. Sometimes they wouldn't let us go. We would go there and preach, and everyone would cry. We never decided ourselves where we wanted to go. We just listened to their demands about which area needed revival next, and we would go there.

The brothers and sisters were really hungry and thirsty for the Word in those days, and it seemed that nobody could get enough. I said in my heart, "Lord, I know too little about the Bible. I feel like a sheep that has to nurse all these little lambs. My milk has already been exhausted, and they are still sucking on my nipples." I really felt helpless. There were hundreds of brothers and sisters in the meeting, and I felt absolutely empty inside. So I stood up and cried. I said, "Lord. Look at all these people. They came for You, and nothing else can satisfy them. You put me in this place, but I really can do nothing. Lord, You have pity on them, and have pity on me." Every time I stood up and cried in my prayer like this, the Lord supplied me with His message out of His compassion for the brothers and sisters.

During this period, the feet of those that preached the good tidings were a true blessing. Wherever we went, dozens of people would follow behind us and form a big crowd. It was really a moving sight. We used to sing as we marched on the mountain path, whether it was night or day. Whenever we came to a family, the host would do his utmost to entertain us. They felt honored to be worthy to receive a servant of God. Sometimes those families that did not get this honor felt hurt. They thought they were unworthy. Sometimes they even envied those that got to entertain the preachers. Satan attacked many Christians by this means.

The Return of TSPM, 1980 — present

The third period is one in which the cross of Calvary was transformed into an ornament for the daughters of Moab amidst persecutions and the roaring of the lion. Christianity was made into an ornament to adorn the harlot. For the sake of politics and diplomacy, Christianity was made a kind of showcase religion. Those Christians who had hidden themselves became enthusiastic once more. Actually, these people do love the Lord. But out of fear they confine their love for the Lord and their dedication to His work within the context of legality. If you told them it is illegal, then they would not come out. But Paul tells us that we must preach the gospel "in season and out of season." No matter the circumstances, we must sow the seed of the gospel.

There are also people who had been "church members" before but who had never really been saved. When the churches were reopened, they came back, arguing that they were the doorkeepers for the church. Why did they want to be doorkeepers for the church? They wanted to obtain legal recognition from the government so that they could transfer their residences to the city or obtain some specific position. They were willing to be ornaments in order that their conditions might be improved. These people entered the Church with ulterior motives and caused a lot of confusion. From a state of purity and devotion, She was led into a condition where She just wandered aimlessly without knowing where to go. Under these circumstances, what kind of a harlot church have we become? How can the Lord lead the Chinese Church to revival in this kind of situation?

We are still in the third period, although it might seem to have lasted for a long time. But we need to go deeper into this matter. During our co-workers' meeting, we saw three ways in which we can deal with this quasi-church: 1) We may act like Phinehas, who pierced through the harlot with his spear; 2) we may blow our horns and trumpets to warn people to come out from the evil place, as in the book of Joshua; and 3) we may grind these people-like the golden calf-to pieces by the truth of the Bible. But the present period will continue for a while.

Daily Life of the Itinerant Preacher

I didn't have time to look back before, but this year the Lord often wanted me to look back. Before the Chinese New Year, the believers at Fangmaoshan had three days of special meetings. They had been having frequent contacts with us in the fellowship of the Bible, and we felt we had a share in their salvation as well as in the building of their church. But I had not been there for a long time. One reason for this is that I have to spend a lot of time in Bible ministry, and at the same time I have to take care of my regular work. Another reason is that my mother was very sick during that time. Under their persistent requests, however, three of us brothers went to Fangmaoshan just before New Year's day. We held three days of meeting there. Each night the meeting lasted almost till daybreak. It rained and snowed on the last night. After the meeting broke up, the brothers and sisters took us to the railway station on their bicycles.

The next morning at about 4 a.m. we arrived in Tacheng. A brother who works at the Tacheng bus station took us to a sister's home with the bus he drove. After a short rest there, we caught another bus home in a heavy rain. (A brother was almost frozen.) When we got home the family had already gone to bed.

The next day was New Year's day, and we fellowshipped with brothers and sisters at home. On the second day of the new year, we went to another place to have fellowship with brothers and sisters there, which was followed by a baptismal service. Several brothers and sisters were baptized. On the third day after New Year's day I went home, and with my two sisters I went to visit my aunt, who was seventy-five years old. She had been a believer for forty to fifty years, and lately she had been expecting each day that the Lord would come and take her to heaven. On the following day, an annual co-workers conference started at Tacheng. On the first day we fasted and prayed. Messages were given on each of the following three days.

The main theme of these messages was the harlot church, and the believers were exhorted to deal with her as Phinehas dealt with the Midianite woman.

On the ninth day, we arrived at Funing in Xinsui, where a co-workers' conference was starting. The conference was conducted in a fellowship and Bible study style. The theme of the conference was the training of preachers and the propagation of the gospel. The emphasis was letting the young people testify of how they magnify the power of the Holy Spirit in their life outside the church and in their preaching of the gospel, and of how they feel the presence of God as they do this. Thank God, all the conferees saw the solemn responsibility that we have to preach the gospel and realized that He that is with us is much greater than he that is with them. They come to attack us with knives and spears and brazen shields, but we attack them with the name of the Lord of hosts. The atmosphere of the meeting climbed to a high pitch on this, and everybody's spirit got a lift.

On the tenth, my sister arrived from home. She said my aunt prayed every day, saying, "Oh Lord, please send my nephew back, for I am about to depart from this world." She had not eaten for three days. There was neither fever nor cold, and she was not suffering from any particular illness or pain. My sister wanted me to go home right away, saying my seventy-five year old aunt could die at any moment. My aunt prayed daily, "Lord, why are You keeping me in the world now that I can no longer preach or serve You? I am not anxious to go home and enjoy myself, but since I am no longer useful in the world, You may just as well take me to heaven." Her son was a cadre in the brigade and had not believed in the Lord. As they talked with her, she expressed her wish that she wanted to have a Christian funeral service after she died and that she wanted me to go back and lead the service. I had a feeling that I ought to go back.

I arrived home on the twelfth, and my aunt died on the morning of the fifteenth. The funeral service was held on the eighteenth and was attended by more than a thousand believers. In the service, we also preached from the Bible on topics like the origin of man, the redemption of Christ, and the resurrection. A brother brought an amplifier and a tape recorder. So the whole proceeding was taped and broadcast. Since the service was held by the graveside in an open field, a great number of people could hear the message, including a lot of non-believers.

Bible Studies Organized

On the eighteenth we arrived at Feng Song's place. As we fellowshipped with each other that evening, a sister named Guo with tears in her eyes implored us to go to her place. We were thinking of establishing a Bible study group in the border region in those days, and we thought this might be the leading of the Lord. So, together with Feng Song, fifteen of us started the next day for Lingbo Commune. At Annan we established the first Bible study group, which met every Monday.

Perhaps I can explain here how we set up these Bible study groups. For those young converts who were desirous of knowing more about the Bible, we organized Bible study sessions on each night of the week in different places. These sessions lasted for two or more hours each. We first trained some brothers and sisters, then sent them out two by two [two brothers or two sisters] to visit the Bible study groups, each on a different night of the week according to a pre-arranged schedule. It took them a week to complete the circuit.

In our Bible studies, we follow two principles: 1) learn basic doctrines of the Bible; and 2) provide messages that are most needed in this generation. As for visiting pastors or evangelists, they are free to preach on any topic according to the moving of the Holy Spirit. In other words, we don't want to formalize or generalize the topics of the messages. In this way our brothers and sisters are always supplied with fresh and vital messages that are most suited to the current climate. After the two brothers or sisters have released all the messages that they are burdened with, they will be led to another cycle, and two brothers or sisters from that cycle will take over the first cycle. In this way, the brothers and sisters in all the cycles will always have fresh and different messages to hear.

As they teach others, they themselves are being trained. After they have been teaching for three to five weeks or, in some cases, seven to eight weeks, they will have a recess. During the recess they will be divided into groups and assigned different Bible portions to study. Through this they gain experience not only in preaching but also in leading Bible study sessions and other meetings.

After we agreed on the basic teaching materials, we printed several hundred copies of basic Bible doctrines. Now we plan to print the "Study of the Truth," "How to Study the Bible," and "Exercise of the Truth," and to send copies of each of these to each Bible study group.

Ministering on Road

On the twentieth, we arrived at Palingmiao. There was a brother named Wan there who was quite a warrior for the truth. He was a writer before he accepted Christ. After he was saved, he didn't have any spiritual exercise and received no discipline from the Church. Out of his own zeal he went to Ningbo to get Bibles. But he didn't get any Bibles. His money was taken away, he was arrested and locked up, and he almost lost his life. Finally, he and his wife begged their way back, but the church's money was all gone. His spirit got a severe blow from this, and he was quite depressed for a long time. Later he got in touch with Brother Feng Song and was warmed up again after some fellowship with him. Now he is the pastor of that village. According to their need and our guidance from the Lord, we hurried to that village, where we had fellowship with the brothers and sisters and established a Bible study group.

On the twenty-first we got to Wangping where we established a Bible study group. On the twenty-second we returned to Annan, where we established another Bible study point. Brother Feng Song went to another place to preach the salvation of the cross. I felt very tired since I had had to preach every day before Brother Feng came. After he came, he took over the evening meetings, and the Lord really worked. I was so tired that I went to bed shortly after nine. Then I heard a sister crying aloud downstairs. So I got up and went downstairs and sat with her during her confession. It turned out that she had committed adultery since she was eight. Then she seduced her husband to commit adultery with her own sister. Her own daughter also committed adultery in order to get a job. Some of the sins she committed were really queer. But the Holy Spirit got hold of her, and she confessed her sins until seven o'clock the next morning. None of us got any sleep the whole night. As she finished her confession and was released from her bondage, she lay on the floor as if totally paralyzed, like a newborn baby.

On the twenty-fourth, while we were having our meeting in the afternoon, Lai Deliu and Peng Shengong came on their bicycles. After the evening meeting we hurried to Wendeng at two o'clock in the morning. There were about 700 brothers and sisters there. Then we continued to Wuting and entered a brother's home at about four o'clock. Since we had been without sleep for several days and nights, we all felt very tired. At the insistence of the brothers and sisters there, we decided to stay and have some sleep.

As we woke up later in the morning, they had already gathered a group of people for the meeting, and we had to preach again. I talked first, followed by Brother Feng. As he talked, I quietly slipped away. On the way I met an old lady who was coming for the meeting. So I asked her to tell the brothers there that I had gone ahead and asked them to follow on as soon as the meeting was over. Together we hurried to Tonglan, about ten miles away, where another meeting was under way. There was a young couple there that had a problem. The young woman insisted on staying with one of the men. Without approval from the church or consultation with other brothers and sisters, they began living together and exerting a bad influence on others. But they were still very fervent in serving the Lord. When we arrived the meeting started right away. We dealt specifically with this problem in our preaching according to the truth of the Bible. After some private conversations with the brothers and sisters following the meeting, we told the young couple to talk with their parents and get their understanding and permission [to marry].

On the twenty-sixth we returned to Lingbo. The believers there tried to get us to stay with them, but we insisted on moving forward. As a result of this conflict, we missed two trains, and we decided to walk twenty miles in the night. On the way, we met an itinerant preacher from Mingtang. He was a blacksmith by profession, but he also preached the gospel and led many people to the Lord. He had just returned from the mountain district when we met, and he told us that they were going to pray for a sick sister that evening. That sister also loved the Lord, but once she had thrown the Bible to the floor, and Satan had entered her heart. She got sick and was in shock, so she was sent to the hospital. There was a faint beating of her heart, but she had been lying there motionless for four or five days. Everybody prayed for her. Satan also attacked her mother. Under these circumstances the believers were so frightened that they ceased to pray, thinking that Satan was too powerful. We told him that we were coming exactly for this purpose. So we hastened to that place together and prayed for the sister. It was very cold and somebody started a fire. The doctor said the patient was going to die. According to the custom in Henan, an unmarried daughter was not allowed to die in the house. So they built a booth in the yard and put her there to die. We all knelt down and prayed with tears that the Lord would raise her up from the dead. The Lord had risen from the dead, and He also raised Lazarus from the dead. Likewise He could also raise up our sister. But, on the other hand, we prayed that not our will but the will of the Holy Spirit be done. After we prayed we hurried to Wuting the same night. Later we heard that the sister had died. The view of many on this was that when she threw the Bible to the floor she uttered many blasphemous words — that the whole incident was a warning from the Lord to the Church.

So that is my schedule. I am not alone in this situation. All the brothers and sisters who do itinerant evangelism are in the same boat. You see, we have quite a large area to cover, and it will take us a terribly long time to make rounds if we don't squeeze our schedule. We feel we have a lot of things to say to the brothers and sisters, especially to those whom we don't get to visit very often. They love to have us preach to them, and this overrides their concern for our bodies. We, too, are encouraged by their love, and with the support of the Holy Spirit we generally don't feel tired when we minister to them. Praise God for his grace.

5:14 I Belong to Heaven: Testimony of a Young Woman Evangelist in China

> I belong to heaven
> Though on earth I dwell.
> The hardships that I suffer
> Cannot my spirit fell.
> When the pain is great,
> My thoughts turn to my Lord.
> His love gives my heart peace
> And my pain a sweet reward.
>
> I belong to heaven
> Though on earth I dwell.
> Sometimes I am downtrodden
> Exhausted and unwell,
> Discouraged and despairing.
> At once His love appears:
> His presence at my side
> Takes from my heart all fears.

I learned this song while I was sick in bed for 2½ years. After I suddenly fell very ill, I was treated for a long time without any improvement. Added to that, I had a longstanding pessimism about life and society, and my mind was terribly confused. This song opened a door for me at what seemed to be just the right time and gave me a glimpse of another kind of life. That life seemed to be like a mist — it appeared for a while and then was seen no more. What would life be like for one who belongs to heaven but dwells on earth? I was eager to know.

God Tests Me

I understood very little about religion. I had an impression of Christians as always soft and weak and without abilities. My parents had become believers in Jesus in 1976, and my family lives near Puxian county in Shandong, where the number of Christians has grown dramatically. They wished me to believe like them, but I simply could not, not even in extreme distress.

Nevertheless, as I recalled a vision I had seen, I felt that it could not have come from myself. It must have been God testing me, giving me both grace and fear to make me belong to heaven. I would like to tell you about a series of miracles that I have actually experienced.

One evening in the fall of 1979, I was on my sickbed with my eyes closed, about to go to sleep. Suddenly I heard a loud voice by my ear saying, "Now I shall have to whip you to teach you a lesson. If you keep on refusing to listen to what I say, I'll beat you with canes!" I sat up in alarm and looked all about me carefully for the source of the sound. But all the patients were lying peacefully, quietly asleep. I was petrified and could not get back to sleep. Then I suddenly realized that this was from God, but it was not clear why He spoke to me in that way at that time.

As I mentioned already, there are many Christians in our neighborhood. During the Cultural Revolution, I saw with my own eyes Christians being struggled against and beaten. Their moral courage in facing severe persecution without giving in one bit made me admire them greatly. From them I secretly felt that I received the power of true faith. Then four years ago my mother was healed of a serious illness through prayer. After she became a Christian, it seemed that her whole person was free from the bondage of illness. She had to be careful of her environment as always, but she leads a full and happy life. For this person very dear to me, I am certain that God went beyond natural means and provided the power for healing and conversion.

For many years, events large and small were happening around me that brought me straight to this truth: God can be believed in. But these things all happened to others. I had my own ideas and ambitions and did not believe that these things had any relation to all that religious nonsense. For a long time, indeed, not until this baffling illness and that startling warning came — like a thunderclap on my head — I could not take it personally. Was it possible that, having been so patient with me for many years, God finally could not stand it anymore and attacked me for my stubbornness and haughtiness? This is something I cannot figure out, but the first time I really met God it scared me out of my wits.

I was urged by my family to come home to take care of my illness. For a few years I had been out working and returned home infrequently. But this time, because of my illness, I was able to spend much more time with my family, which could be thought of as profiting from my misfortune. Neighboring Christians often came to visit me and looked after me in many ways. Previously, no matter how sincerely they had prayed for me, I was stubbornly unmoved and even secretly laughed at them. But this time I was moved by their love for me. I came to respect and envy them more and more.

My health gradually improved. During that time I was taken by two sisters every night to attend meetings, with great results.

Born Again

The Bible describes the word of God as a two-edged sword able to pierce the human heart. On the day when the preacher preached on "born-again salvation," I really understood how true this description was. His words seemed to be a knife which mercilessly pierced and slashed at all my vital organs. "If one is not born of water and of the Spirit, he cannot enter the Kingdom of God" (John 3:5). "Born-again salvation" seemed to be engraved on my mind and became the goal I urgently pursued.

On 14 April 1980 the marvelous grace of God finally came to me personally. While praying, I saw a vision clearly. A large, white-robed figure appeared before my eyes. Written in small characters all over it were all the sins I had committed since I was born. The mud on the white robe produced in me an incomparable loathing and even hate. I really hated those sins! In the presence of the Lord I begged Him to have pity on me and wash away all the filth. It feels odd to say it, but each time I confessed a sin, it seemed there was a white brush that scribbled on that sin the word "clean," and it became white. When I had confessed all the sins, the muddy spots were all washed alway. The immaculate robe shimmered in white light. Then in a flash my name appeared in large letters — LIN SHAOQING. I felt like I was on cloud nine, as if I had just been released from prison. I was totally lighthearted. Peace, freedom, and joy came flooding into my heart. I knew with certainty that I had been born again. My name was listed in the Book of Life. I could not stop crying for joy. This second experience caused me to know God even deeper. Except for God, there is none I could love. With a light heart, I offered myself! I would no longer live for myself but for the Lord who died and rose again for me.

Receiving the First Bible

At that time there was no one in my whole county who had a Bible. I went all over to borrow handwritten copies and copied them day and night. I also memorized many Bible verses.

The following year, on a spring day in 1981, I unexpectedly received a package sent from Guangzhou. I opened it — it was a Bible! It was a complete Bible, beautifully printed with a black cover and red page edges. I immediately began to laugh and shout uncontrollably and danced around and around my room. Whom should I thank? I had never been to Guangzhou. I did not know even a single person there, and the person who sent it had only written "Guangzhou" as the return address. I had become the first in the entire county to get a Bible, but whom should I thank? Then I understood . This was wholly due to the bond between Christians and was a miracle of the Holy Spirit. This was the third experience in which I saw the grace of God far surpass my hopes.

Possessing at last the hard-to-get Bible, I read it aloud like a lunatic. The Word of God was like a sweet shower of rain, like the morning sun; it refreshed and warmed me. I took a whole year and read seven or eight hours every day, reading the whole Bible. There were times when I was tired or sleepy, but I forced myself awake by dashing cold water on my face and then resumed reading. So I understood it at one reading. Those parts that stood out I later memorized. I can recite every story in the Bible.

Preaching Begins

In the fall of that year, I went with some brothers and sisters to the countryside to evangelize. All that I tell you I saw clearly with my own eyes — I will not forget it for my whole life. As soon as it was known that evangelists had come, people came from miles around, some walking day and night so they could attend an evening meeting of a couple hours. When the preaching was finished, they begged to hear more. Don't sleep — keep going! Don't eat — keep going! They wanted nothing but the Word of God. They all surged forward, hungering and thirsting for righteousness. Wherever we looked, the fields were truly white for the harvest. I seek nothing more from God than to preach prophetically and care for His sheep.

Before each meeting I joyfully sing this hymn:

Take up and give to me
Take up and give to me
Five loaves and two fish
Take up and give to me

I strive to empty myself and be filled with the power of the Holy Spirit. God always answers me; not only does He give to me sufficiently, but the brothers and sisters also get life and strength from me and the Lord. Each time I preach, there may be some believers and some non-believers listening, but nearly all repent of their sins and believe in Jesus. His Holy Spirit is like a wind that uses our packing up and traveling from village to village to blow the multitudes back to Him.

The Leprous Girl

One night when the meeting was finished, there were some sisters who asked us to come to their mountainous area to preach. According to our plans we were to go to another place. But they persisted, begging us to come. We were moved, and after a brief discussion we decided to go with them that very night. The area was really remote. Groping our way in the dark, we crept up the mountainside. All the way, roars of various wild animals were heard, enough to terrify a person. Along the way several large rivers were flowing down. An autumn chill had come and the waters were both icy and swift; we were shivering from the cold. Many times one of the sisters felt me tremble, and she reached out to embrace me. I thought there was something strange about her hands, kind of cold and clammy as if they had been in icy water. But I couldn't imagine why this was so.

At dawn the next day, I saw what the girl looked like; she gave me a start. Her eyebrows and eyelashes were gone, her face was mottled red, and her rotting flesh was oozing in patches — she was a leper. She waited on us gladly. In her hands she carried sesame seeds and shelled peanuts. The food rolled around in her palm, and she handed it over to us, moist with sticky pus. But, moved by the love of God, we were able to eat it normally and tasted only sweetness, nothing foul.

Then we sat in a circle, eating and listening to her tell us her story. When her leprosy first appeared, the hospital decided to send her to the mountains to separate her from other people, but she was adamant and refused to go. Fortunately, a Christian prayed for her, and God healed her. Later she went back to the fields to make a living. Then she stole some corn from another's field. Her leprosy returned, and she could not be healed again.

After she heard the sermon that day on "How to deal with sin," she wept bitterly as she related how she had neglected to pray for forgiveness. No wonder God had given her such a severe discipline. As she was confessing her sin, she never ceased scratching. Everywhere she scratched, blood and pus dripped out. "O Lord, my mother and father have aching hearts when they see me itching and hurting all over. Have you not the least heartache for me?" Crying like this, she turned and begged us to pray. We all sympathized and had pity on her. After we laid hands on her in prayer, her itching stopped for a while. When it was time to go, she expressed a desire to go with us and asked that we keep on praying for her. Perhaps God would heal her this time.

For the next five days she went with us, eating, sleeping, and spreading the Gospel with us. When we were not preaching, almost all of our time we spent laying hands on her in prayer. How much we hoped that, through healing, this sister's spirit might be revived and her love for God be increased. We thank our compassionate God that He really did hear our prayers. In just five days, we saw her healed. The blood and pus no longer flowed. Scabs formed and then dropped off. Finally her skin shone just like that of an ordinary person. In just five days, a leper — weak, miserable, helpless, and hopeless — was miraculously given a new life. When we watched her return home with burning tears in our eyes, our hearts were thankful and full of praise. It was really indescribable.

The Brigade Party Secretary

In the past three months on my evangelistic journeys, I went to almost every mountain village in this area. Every day was almost the same; travel and preach, preach and travel. When, by chance, there was a day when I neither traveled nor preached, I went to a quiet mountain spot to meditate and pray. These days of crossing mountains and fording streams were rather hard. When we reached our destinations, we were always dog-tired. On an average day, each of us got only two hours of sleep. Liu Dashou (the leader of our evangelistic group) once went for eight days and nights without laying down to sleep. Yet no one complained of tiredness, and none of us became ill. We needed only to see the brothers and sisters swarming in to hear the word, we needed only to see the light in their eyes, and our hunger and thirst would vanish. Our enthusiasm would well up once more.

On the day we went to Choudi commune, four of us were gathered together singing hymns and reading Scripture. Someone informed the brigade Party Secretary and the brigade head. They sent officials over to get us and they took away our hand-copied Bibles and song books. They interrogated us harshly and said we would each have to pay a fine of ten yuan or we would be sent to the commune for investigation.

Seeing that neither side wanted to give way, I tried to break the deadlock: "You don't have to get angry; we are doing nothing wrong. It is only because we believe in God that we have this difference with you. If we were not believers, we would be just like you."

"If you stop believing," one answered, "then I'll have you over to my house for a feast. But I cannot stand this talk about believing in the Lord. I cannot allow you to believe, and I cannot allow you to come here." He finished with a coarse laugh.

Liu Dashou stood up. "According to Article 147 of the criminal law, if an official interferes with freedom of religion, that Party member will be sentenced to two years in prison. If you send us to the commune, there is no benefit in it for you. As for the fine, we have only traveling money. We do not have enough for your fine."

The brigade chief asked how much we had. Liu Dashou pulled out her money and let him see. There was only twenty-three yuan. The brigade chief said, "Twenty-three is enough. You keep three and hand over twenty."

"OK," Liu answered, "but you have to write a note saying that you fined us twenty yuan because we believe in God."

Two months later a sister told us that they had privately divided up the fine between them. Not long after, the old sow owned by the brigade party Secretary died. He took ten yuan from us, but lost several hundred. Then the brigade head caught a strange illness and died soon afterward. With God as your enemy, you get great punishment like this in the end. It makes me both fearful of God and sorry for them.

Mark 16:20 says, "Then the disciples went out and preached everywhere, and the Lord worked with them and confirmed his word by the signs that accompanied it." A person from heaven has the supernatural power of heaven. Although this stretch of preaching was rather short, because of the great and small miraculous signs that I have experienced, I have an even deeper and fresher conciousness of God's nature, and I want even more to give Him honor and praise.

Love Never Fails

The Scripture says, "For everyone who exalts himself will be humbled, and he who humbles himself will be exalted" (Luke 14:11). "God opposes the proud but gives grace to the humble" (I Peter 5:5). Just when I supposed myself to have reached a spiritual peak, to be fervently serving and swiftly advancing, a little test came that I failed and that caused me to lose the title of evangelist.

When I returned from my evangelistic journey, the brothers and sisters were all busy and we met rather infrequently. I was only responsible for house meetings every night and on Saturday and

day. Compared with itinerant evangelism, there was a lot of free
e. After a few months the head of my former work unit suddenly
eared personally at my door and said I should return to work.
He thought that people like me were only advocating "religious
superstition." What a pity! Moreover, he said, orders had come down
that religious activities should be restricted everywhere, so that at least
people could make an enlightened choice before it was too late, and
thus avoid the influence of religion in the future. He also said that
if I went back to work now they would be able to pay me eighty
percent of my annual salary, even though I had been on sick leave
and without salary most of the year. My wages each month were sixty
to seventy yuan. I would get hundreds of yuan for nothing! For the
next few days the leader came back to my house in his spare time.
I put aside my thinking and study and dreamed about money. I
couldn't put the thought of those few hundred yuan out of my mind.
I finally decided to tell the other Gospel workers, who had endured
suffering and danger, that I was going back to my work unit.

First of all, I went to inform my fellow workers. When I went
to Liu Dashou's house, she was eating breakfast. When she heard
that I was going back to work, she blurted out something that had
just dawned on her, "So that's it!" It turned out that a few days before
she had gone to Faxiang Commune to preach. She was extremely
depressed and heavy-hearted. Her preaching and prayer had no power;
she couldn't get across what she wanted to. She was certain that some
brother or sister was doing something, so she urgently prayed for the
Lord to protect the one concerned. After a while the heavy weight
on her heart was lifted. She knew that the Lord had preserved that
believer, and she let out a sigh or relief. Not until that conversation
did she realize that the heavy weight on her heart was really for me.

She went on, "The Lord has already moved me to tell you that
you should not go back to work. You have not suffered for Christ,
and this you should count as the Lord's great blessing and walk
according to His will." She prompted me to recall how I had been
born again, how I had pressed on, going up and down the mountains
to preach the Gospel, and how, as a result of preaching the Gospel,
God had bestowed on me all His grace. But how does a person who

has received God's grace and been offered for His service suddenly turn against the Lord's will? As she was talking, she wept bitterly. I too was very disturbed, but since I had already decided, I was not ready to be pushed around by the feelings of others. When Liu Dashou saw that I was unpersuaded, she turned resolute and stood up indignantly. She pointed at me and said, "Shaoqing, I say in the name of Jesus that if you do not pray and beg forgiveness, some great harm will surely come to you."

I was very unhappy that one who knew me so well and one with whom I had secretly worked would suddenly try to intimidate me with severe language. The reactions of the other brothers and sisters were the same as Liu's. It was terribly disappointing, but everyone opposed what I had decided.

Two days before I was to go back to work, my big toe became infected. It itched terribly and at one point oozed pus and blood. After two days it hurt so much I could hardly move, so I had to put off going back to work. My mother saw me crying bitterly and said, "If you do not promise God that you will not return to work, your foot will certainly not get better."

I immediately answered, "What you just said doesn't come from God, but from man!" How weak! I felt sorry and unworthy but would not ask for God's forgiveness.

Liu Dashou prayed for me. "If our sister is unwilling to make a promise before You, Lord, I pray that You do not reduce her suffering, but that You give her more grace." Even though I was sharply aware of the pain in my foot and in my heart, I would make no promise.

Just at this time Liu Dashou wanted our team to go to a neighboring commune to spread the Word, and she urged me to go too. Being alternately cajoled and threatened, I finally agreed to go. My foot was terribly swollen. When we were on level ground, Liu pulled me on a cart. On the mountain paths, the brothers and sisters alternated carrying me on their backs. They carried me to meetings, they carried me across rivers, and they carried me to the toilets. They were puffing and panting, but they did it all with a look as if it were nothing at all. Whenever they did anything, they thought about me, about whether it was good for me. The attentive love of the brothers and sisters were coals of fire on my head. Surrounded by their fervent love for one day, two days, ten days, twenty days, I felt more and more that I couldn't take it. Who in the whole world was able to give me care like this? Who was able to show me this kind of warmth? I could bear it no longer. I prostrated myself before the face of God to plead for His mercy. I am only a sinner, a weak and proud sinner. The punishment that my sins had brought down upon me was still lighter than what I deserved. I told God that, if He thought it good to use this punishment to make me better, then it would be alright to make my whole leg rotten.

Three days after I confessed my sin and decided to follow God, preaching His Gospel, my foot miraculously became whole again. The Lord chastizes those whom He loves. Through chastisement, I learned to obey, to seek first God's Kingdom and His righteousness, and to do His will on earth as it is done in Heaven.

I remember a dream I had when I was a new believer. I was walking on a very narrow road, only wide enough to put down one foot at a time. A little way in front of me there was no place at all to put my foot, but beyond this point the way gradually widened until a bright broad road appeared. The Lord knows I am weak and often proud, so He used the dream to show me that I could walk a narrow road, and He gives me an assurance of victory.

After I stumbled in weakness and stood up again, I recalled past events, and this dream seemed to be a warning. "Your enemy the devil prowls around like a roaring lion looking for someone to devour" (I Peter 5:8). For a believer, temptations and trials will never cease. Our Lord once became a man and faced many trials. When He faced His death sentence, He willingly drank the bitter cup of the way of the cross because He saw the glory that came afterward. I asked the Lord to show me this eternal glory in the same way and to make me regard all the world's affairs as vanity because of our future glory.

Thanks to God, all the things I have been through have built a sound foundation for any future testing and growth I may encounter. Though I am unreliable, I truly believe that I shall conquer all, relying on my Lord.

5.15 Camel Herdsman's Daughter

Xinjiang [the "New Borderlands"] evokes images rather different from those usually associated with China. It is a province at the far northwest corner of China, a vast area of pasture and wasteland. At its center lies the huge Takla-makan desert. To a westerner, the names and places are reminiscent of the silk road, camel caravans, and perhaps Marco Polo. Its population is composed more of Central Asian tribespeople than of Chinese, and its dominant religion is probably Islam. Like Tibet, it is a part of China added only in the last few centuries of China's several millenia of history. Here we present a story that shows Christianity is also active in Xinjiang. The material herein, drawn from a collection of sources, is presented as one person's story.

Life at Home

I was born in the northern part of Xinjiang in 1955 when the world was changing. I have no memory of my mother. After she graduated from seminary she went to the border regions to preach, but when I was two she passed away. She left behind no token by which I could remember her. The only family I had in that cold desert plateau was my father, a poor camel herdsman. I know now that my father was highly educated and had fled to the desert areas. However, I did not discover this until I was fourteen. The winters there were long and cold. When the cold winds blew, we would retreat into our huts, where before our cow-dung fire I would watch Father sew little colored patches on my blue clothes. I enjoyed this "family" atmosphere immensely. On such occasions I would lean against my father's bent back and chant folks songs of that area: "Tall mountains have no long grass; when the wind blows the rocks protect us."

I did not really think my life was hard — just like a person who eats bitter melon all the time doesn't know that it is bitter — because I could find happiness in our poverty. My father taught me mathematics, language, music, English, and the Bible. When I was still very small, we could converse together in English. I remember when my father was taken by some Red Guards, he said to me, "Put the Bible into some old clothes and hide it under the pile of dried grass." The Red Guards did not understand English. They took away all of Father's books except the Bible. I still have it with me to this day. I learned from my father everything I needed for life, but I especially learned how to walk the way of the cross.

When the Red Guard movement started, our "family" had its second disaster. It was like eating yellow lotus just after eating bitter melon. This time Father was investigated — for five years as it turned out. The times of sitting before the fire watching Father patch clothes were gone and would not return; only in my memory could I obtain the warmth of my father's presence.

Each time I went to see Father, I had to ride for sixteen hours on the train. Gradually I heard from the guards about the enormous crimes that my father had committed against the Party and the people. An engineer at the Yumen oil fields, my father had gone to America to study and was one of China's first chemical engineers trained abroad. But he had left his comfortable life and position and gone to a desolate place to preach the gospel. His study abroad in America then became a "permanent and unresolvable historical question." Because of this, Father became "an American imperialist running dog and spy." Even harder for a person to understand was that they said his object in going to the distant border region was to reject his position as an engineer. At that time it was 1947, just before liberation, so was he or was he not to be charged with subverting the Communist Party? Father sat in the investigation saying nothing at all. For a whole month he said not a word. The guards said to me, "Your father wants to go to see God with a head of granite [a phrase about stubborn believers attributed to Mao]. You should make some money for him to use in his paradise."

However, Father rose even higher in my opinion through all this. Once during a visit, when the guard stepped out to find a light for his cigarette, Father whispered to me, "In time of trouble you must learn to rely on the Lord Jesus." This was to me a profound revelation. Although I had been brought up in a Christian home, before this time there was only myself in my daily prayers, never a Lord. In suffering and hopelessness, I told everything to my Heavenly Father and I complained to Jesus, asking why all this trouble came piling up on our family. But I had never leaned on God nor used His strength to fight on all fronts. That year I was fifteen years old. That one small grain of sand was tossed up to the mountain top by a great wave, where it reflected the light of the sun. Perhaps this was really the Creator's idea after all.

Salvation

Only when I was forced to live alone in my "home," which was a mess no matter how you looked at it, did I come to know the Lord. I remember one cold night when neither stars nor moon were out and a fierce wind was blowing. I woke suddenly from a terrible nightmare. The fire had gone out, and it seemed like the darkness penetrated the room through the door. I cried out into the darkness, "What kind of world is this? Do we live only in order to suffer?" I jumped off the bed and went to open the door to let the cold air take my life away, because I had not a particle of hope left in this world. I was just about to open the door when a voice stopped me — "In suffering rely on the Lord." I became weak all over and felt like a leaf that had fallen from the tree. Before my father's feet I was a worthless daughter, and before the face of God such an insignificant life I led! Trembling all over, I fell to the floor and cried out, "Merciful God, if You want to take me, then let the cruel wind open the door. If You want me to stay on the earth, then stay with me; do not leave me." Then I received an infinite peace. It seemed as if something came down around me and took my frail body inside it. The cold and the noise of the wind had no effect on me. I prayed for a long while and knew clearly the will of God.

As I lit a new fire, the firelight was at the same time the fire of a new life. From that time on I was no longer an orphan.

Whenever afterwards I felt weak or fearful, I found strength in prayer. Years later, many fellow students heard the stories of a fifteen year old girl who lived alone for three years in the mountains. They were all amazed. But I told them, "If you want to get supernatural strength, then you must have faith in the Creator." The love of God is obtained when you give yourself. You need only to rely on the strength of the Lord, to thoroughly break up your ego and offer it completely to God. Then you will be able to conquer all and to fear and love God. There are many roads in a person's life that lead to vanity, pleasure, fame, and fortune. My father traveled those roads but then turned to go through the narrow gate. I was born within that gate and I have never chosen anything outside of it.

Sharing

I had never been to school. All of my knowledge and culture came from my father. When other intellectual youths were sent down to the countryside to work in a production team, I was also placed among them. This was a lucky break for me; I could enjoy society again, and gradually I became accustomed to the collective life. I also tried to spread the gospel to others for the first time. In our fields there was a girl like myself who studied English with me. Once in the fields I was talking enthusiastically. In my excitement I told her about Jesus; she responded with deep silence. Just then the foreman came over and called her away. All afternoon I was extremely agitated; I didn't know what to do to make things right. I was afraid she would tell the leaders of this. If she did, everything would be lost, and I would end up just like my father. That afternoon I felt that everyone was avoiding me. Even the security guards seemed to look at me with scorn. Did God leave me? I started to waver.

That evening the situation became clear. The family of the girl had sent a telegram saying that her mother was very sick. She had already started back home that afternoon. All my fears were self-created. When I understood everything, I was so ashamed. No matter what I did, it seemed I was not up to it; no matter what hardships I had gone through, I was still such a weakling. That night I ran out to a quiet wood nearby and earnestly prayed for God to smash my ego. There is only one way to God's presence and that is the way of total self-giving or self-sacrifice. This is what God revealed to me that night.

After that I prayed unceasingly for that girl, asking the Holy

Spirit to work in her. After twenty days she returned to the fields and immediately sought me out. She wanted me to go on where I had left off and had many questions to ask. I did not know what to say, so I just told her what had happened to me, and to my great surprise, with tears streaming down her face she accepted Christ as her Savior. This was a momentous choice and a fearful one, since, if she told others, she might lose everything. Not long after she became a Christian she was reassigned to work in a munitions factory. She evangelized among her friends and relatives continually. Even to this day, she has never had a printed Bible and still uses the one that I handcopied by the light of an oil lamp.

Up to this time, I had thought that the way to happiness was complete reliance on and trust in God. I knew only about giving myself. I had not had the burden of sharing the gospel. This experience made me see the power that comes from God, and the indescribable happiness that comes from that power. We cannot understand the mysteries of God; we can only receive His ability and the strength that He gives us. Jesus is the Shepherd who takes good care of the sheep. He is not just another sheep. When you have the burden to begin sowing the seed, the Lord will have already prepared everything.

Challenges at University

In 1975 the leaders of the student recruitment office of the Xinjiang Autonomous Region Department of Higher Education went to the countryside on an inspection tour. They heard that I had learned English through self-study and decided to invite me to attend university. That a person from a "counter-revolutionary" family was going to university aroused a lot of discussion. I was certain this was God's will; He wanted to send me to a new place, to test whether I had become a useful vessel. I held on to my unconquerable faith and waited.

So I entered school gates as a student for the first time in my life, and those were university gates! It seemed very strange, but, in a topsy-turvy age in which there were plenty of people who got into university without being able to write an essay and who still became heroes, why shouldn't have I been sent to university when someone recognized my abilities? God let me come that far; it was certainly His will. Even before I was accepted, I resolved to live to the glory of God. Except for taking care that the university would not know that I was a Christian, I would be a mirror on earth for the Lord, a material vessel reflecting the Lord's holiness. I tried to adopt the character of a Christian in all things and to limit my own ego.

Quickly I became one of the "three-goods" students in the English department [good thought, good study, good manual labor]. They praised my good conduct but did not know its source. Because my English pronunciation was very correct, I was asked to record the study materials, and I became the pride of the English department. This bothered me greatly. I received everything from God and from His Word, but I kept it secret. Even when I read my Bible I kept it hidden in my textbooks. Then about this time, something happened.

In those years the "worker, peasant, and soldier" university students were all recommended by local Party committees; I was the only one from neither the Party nor the Youth League. The Workers' Propaganda Team leaders had pity on me because they thought that "all good conduct arises in education by the Party." So they urged me to join the Communist Youth League in order to make the whole class "a sheet of red." How could a Spirit-led Christian join an atheistic organization? Therefore, I refused the Youth League cadre's invitation, using as an excuse, "I am really not doing very well, and my qualifications are not sufficient." The result was that they started a "help" class. One of the "three-goods" students needed help because she had shown some confusion about the League. Should I enter the League still hiding who I was? No, a Christian should not bring shame on the name of the Lord. If everyone praised my good conduct, why shouldn't that praise be given to the Lord and my secret be disclosed? The Holy Spirit gave me strength, so at a "help" meeting called to "investigate the roots, cast aside hindrances, and join the organization," I plainly stated my reason — "I am a Christian." This little phrase startled the whole meeting and caused the leader to become furious.

I couldn't believe what happened next! Suddenly the meeting turned into an occasion to "eradicate feudal superstition." And here was a living negative example to give all the workers assembled there a lesson in thought struggle! The school leadership would certainly want me to show the masses the root of my "faith." I had never expected that they would try to deal with it this quickly. In the din of the meeting I closed my eyes to pray: "Heavenly Father, from the time I was small You have protected me. If this is ordained by You to test my heart, give me grace and allow me to stand up in my weakness."

When I opened my tear-filled eyes, the entire hall was as still as a mouse. Facing the whole school of more than 200 students and teachers, I poured out my sin and told of my own insignificance before the cross. I told them of Christ's suffering for the world and that Christians could not harm society — they could only lead others to do good and to know eternal life.

Most of those who sat and listened to this gospel had assumed that Christianity was nothing but a scourge. However, today a real Christian stood in front of them and their verbal attacks hadn't a leg to stand on. In a world that was everywhere filled with struggle, the Christians appeared holy and dignified. In spite of the fact that many thought I was just telling a fine story — and they were not about to accept God as the Lord of the universe — I saw them as a piece of earth, a piece of fertile earth waiting for reclamation.

When I finished what I had to say, the leader of the Workers' Propaganda Team looked as if he had suddenly awakened from a dream. He immediately upbraided me for using the university as a platform from which to spread my "poison," and he wanted everyone to bring out their criticisms. But the people had already felt the goodness of God; they did not use the standard critical words because they could not make heads or tails out of the situation. Unhappily the leaders dispersed the criticism meeting.

When saving grace comes to light, the first consequence is persecution. In my heart I knew that on the surface this would mean I would lose my chance to attend school. A university intended to nurture the proletariat could not tolerate a Christian. The university was very important to me, but, compared to God, it was not worth speaking about. The grace of God demands that we put aside ourselves. I can give up many things, but I cannot give up God. When I expressed my personal desire to shoulder the cross and follow the Lord, the crowds gathered on the road of darkness all glimpsed the light of His saving atonement.

At once I became the school's "person in the news." Wherever I went people pointed at me behind my back. Nevertheless, more were sympathetic than were ridiculing, and more were inquiring than were criticizing. Moreover, many students came to me privately to talk about questions of salvation. I knew that God had prepared this ground for this day of sowing the seed. My fellow students would, in the future, go to every part of these border regions to teach or to translate. God's way was very important for them, and through them the gospel could be spread widely. This was God's plan. But I would have to leave the university. Who would complete the next stage of the work? In this I had no power and had to rely completely on God to arrange it.

Several times there were meetings to decide whether I should be expelled, but without result. The school definitely wanted to keep me; the Workers' Propaganda Team thought I was a "reactionary" and had to be expelled. Finally they reached a compromise; expulsion from the school would depend on the investigation by the school. But when assignments came after graduation, I would have to be assigned to a rural village.

When this news was given to me, I leaped for joy. When God sends His grace, it must include a turn for the better. My time as a student is hard to forget, but even harder to forget are my times of sharing the gospel when I was a student. At that time I often used this prayer: "Oh Lord, when You do Your holy work of revival, I ask that I may have a part." I did not want merely to be at the university; I wanted the gospel to be spread widely from there. Quickly I gathered around me a small group of seekers after the truth. This group soon grew to include more than thirty people. We divided into two small groups and used holidays and Sundays to assemble in parts or in the countryside. We carried a flag that said "Political Study."

Right up to our graduation we were never discovered by school authorities. The brothers and sisters grew in spiritual discipline, and by the time they graduated their faith had matured and they could stand alone as Christians.

At graduation we were all assigned to different places. From Altai to Karakorum, every city received the tread of our feet.

According to the administration's decision, I was sent to a country school to teach English. I often requested leave time to go and visit my friends scattered in every place. My road was not as difficult as that of my father, who spread the gospel in the countryside thirty years before, but it was still full of suffering. Each time I rode out into the unbounded plateaus, great joy welled up in my heart. It seemed that I could see the Lord working in every field. The seeds broadcast and planted in the earth are fostering life and are a portent of the future.

5.16 School Teacher's Son

As with the previous testimony, the incidents in this second story from Xinjiang are true, although they are in fact drawn from more than one source.

When I stand at the door of my home and look at the Tianshan mountains, I feel like an ant at the foot of a great wall looking up. When the mountain looks down from its awesome presence to where I stand — a mere speck of dust — it makes me feel very insignificant. I often stand silently looking at the Tianshan, at the white clouds unmoving around its peaks. I also reflect often on the testimony of Sister Gan Huiping.

This land of Xinjiang is so great that you can ride a train for a couple of days without seeing a house. Nevertheless, many many Christians know the story of Sister Gan. They know she suffered for the Lord, and they know her testimony about persecution at the university. My father and Gan Huiping's parents were part of the same borderlands evangelistic team thirty-five years ago, but under pressure from the campaign against counter-revolutionaries [1955-56], each went his own way. Although I had never met them, their testimonies were shared and known within the body of Christ. For a very long time, I had had a desire to go see Sister Gan. Sitting on the bus for the five-day return trip, my heart was overflowing. In my mind she was no weak girl but a fearless heroine; she stood before me as a firm example. How different from this endless and jolting road that seemed to wander without any boundaries were the attacks that our parents and our generation received, but in the end that road led to sweetness. I opened the window to look at the great wastes of the Gobi desert, and it seemed to me that at the extreme end of that twisting road I saw a small boy standing there, like a dream of myself 18 years ago.

To me, my parents had always seemed like sheep; there was always some good-for-nothing person ordering them around. Whenever I saw this kind of thing, a great anger would rise in my young heart. At such times, I would heave a gentle sigh for them and love them all the more. At night we would cover all the windows with cloth and kneel on the ground to pray. Once I heard my mother say, "Oh Lord, forgive those who fight with us, for they do not know what they are doing." When I heard this I couldn't understand it. Why not ask God to punish those wicked people? I stole a glance at my mother; she was blinking her eyes to hold back her tears.

Lying on my bed, I asked my mother, "You cry, but they curse you. Why don't you ask God to punish those rotten eggs?"

"My dear child," my mother answered, "it makes your mother happy to speak to God that way. God wishes us to love our enemies; how can we ask Him to punish them? Go to sleep. You are still young. Gradually you will understand these things." I certainly did not understand why I should love those terrible persons. Caught between hate and love, I began to think back.

I knew that my parents were both good people. I was not sure how they had come to receive such unfair treatment, nor could I fathom why people became hateful so suddenly. I often wanted to stand in front of people and say, "Daddy and Mummy are good people; they really are!" But I was too small, just ten years old.

One June morning, my mother woke me early and shoved a piece of paper in my hand. "If Father and I do not come back today, go to the address on this paper. You can stay with them until I come to get you." From my mother's manner I knew that something serious was about to happen, but I never imagined that this was the last day of my childhood that I would eat breakfast with my parents.

They were taken away and were struggled against on a platform erected at a crossroads. On their chests were hung great iron plates. On them were written the words "Counterrevolutionary Christians" and their names with big red X's scratched over them. They couldn't stand because the metal plates were too heavy, and the fine metal wire cut into their necks. There were four persons who grabbed their hair and pushed their heads down low. My father's eyes were facing the ground. I saw him close his eyes; his legs never stopped trembling. I did not dare to come close but remained at a street corner some distance way. I copied my father and closed my eyes, but I didn't know what I should say to God. I couldn't even cry. I could only close my eyes and try to shut my ears against the cries that filled the sky.

Suddenly my ear was given a painful pull. A large hand grabbed my ear and pulled me out of my corner. I opened my eyes and saw a worker from my father's school. With a stern air, he roughly questioned me, "Little Qiang, what are your parents always talking to you about? What are they always doing at home?"

"Mama says that I should be a good boy and not learn bad things. I shouldn't curse anyone, hit anyone, or hate anyone."

Without waiting for me to finish, he put his palms over my two ears and lifted me right off the ground, yelling "Son of a bitch!" at me. Uncle Wang had never been like this before. Every time he had come to visit us he had always said that I had done good work for the principal. I did not understand what had made him suddenly so awful. I cried out because of the pain in my ears. On the platform, my mother couldn't help looking at me. Then her head was pressed even lower. Father never lifted his head. Then I knew that no one could help me, so I reached in my pocket and held tightly to the scrap of paper with the address on it.

Then everyone called me a son of a bitch, even those who were my good friends in ordinary times. Several times people surrounded me to give me a little "training." They usually used the method called "the old lady's short candle," which consisted of twisting my ears until they were red.

My parents were separated to be investigated, and I went to look up the address my mother had given me. But then I thought, whose house could make an exception? So I clenched my teeth and returned "home." On that day I grew up. I learned to pray. I learned to cook meals. I learned how to sell "household goods." From woks and dishes to tables and chairs, if it could be sold, I tried to sell it. Every once in a while someone dropped through the hole in our gate an envelope containing ten or twenty yuan. I used this money to pay my school fees. Only many years later did I find out this money came from a fellow Christian. Each time I received the money, I prayed fervently, thanking God for His care over me. I can't remember what I said at those times, but I dare say it was pleasing to God.

When I was fourteen, my parents returned home. They had aged tremendously. When I saw the frames of Father's glasses patched with a rubber strip, I was reminded of his trembling legs during the struggle session. They had suffered a lot, but they said no, it was all right. So I also said nothing; it was all in the past, and then there were good things to be said.

The problems of my parents were never clearly resolved, nor was there ever specific evidence produced. It was said that they had at one time served the Kuomintang nationalists and were spreading superstition, so they lost their city residency and were sent to a wild border district. There they would receive supervision, and reform from the minority peoples. Father did not allow me to go. They were going to continue preaching the gospel, and he feared they might be arrested again. Then there would be no one to look after me. Moreover, there were no schools in the border region, so he wanted me to stay in the city and study. Fortunately they would still receive fifty yuan each month as salary. Four years earlier I had already developed the skills to lead an independent life, so after they left I resumed my "upright life" and went to school.

In those days the teachers were all undergoing "reform through labor," and the ones standing before the class were members of the Workers' Propaganda Teams. What we studied were the "Three Old

Essays" [Three essays of Mao Zedong: "Serve the People,"
"Remember Bethune," and "The Old Man who Moved a Mountain"].
While I studied I also went everywhere I could to lodge complaints
about my parents' case. At all the government offices they knew me
and gave me a nickname: "Little complainer." When news of my
nickname got back to my school, my fellow students made fun of
me all the more. In the entire school I was the only one whose family
background was that of "religious workers." Moreover, the offices
that I had appealed to about my parents sent the documents of my
inquiries back to the school, and this made my three years there the
worst of my whole life. The main courses that I took in these three
years were faith and despair. The lessons I learned from these courses
were very important for my later life.

When I graduated I had two choices: to go with my fellow
graduates to a rural production team or to go to my parents in the
rural border district. I chose the first, even though I knew my life
could be very bitter. Yet it contained one possibility — that I might
one day be called back to the city. But my desires were not approved.
Knowing that I had gone to complain, the authorities decided my
thought was questionable, and they thought I should go to join my
parents in the border district for reform. All day I reasoned and
argued with them; at night I prayed. In the end, I was given permission
to join a rural production team, except that this team was made up
of petty criminals and idlers. However, I was so pleased I danced
a little jig; I knew God had His hand in this.

The village to which twelve of us "bad" children were assigned
was ringed by mountains. There were seventy households in the
village, all of the Uygur nationality, and they discriminated terribly
against us. The leader worked us so hard we could hardly breathe.
In this time my burden became very heavy. I felt a strong urge to
preach the gospel to these "old Uyg's." I asked God to give me an
opportunity and to prepare my heart. In the end he gave me an
opportunity.

The region where we were was in a basin which received no rain
in the summer. The parched land relied entirely on irrigation from
the melting snows on the mountains. As the days became drier and

the air hotter, the snow on the mountains melted all the faster. The streams swelled until floods threatened. We heard that our village flooded frequently and that each year a lot of effort was required to prevent flooding. Because the working conditions were so terrible, no one wanted to be sent to work on flood control. So our group of bad youth who were "receiving further education from the poor and lower-middle peasants" received this opportunity for "further education."

The river bed that was supposed to prevent floods lay at the foot of the mountains. In non-flood seasons it was merely a muddy stream. Our job was to build a dike at a place some distance from the bend in the river. The work site was far away from everyone else. When we got there, we were delighted because there was no one else there to discipline us. This soon led to discouragement for, as usual, the work assignment given to us "bad youth" was the heaviest. When we looked around there wasn't even a single blade of grass to be seen. When they brought our supper, everyone's eyes filled with tears. We sipped a little of the soup made with muddy water, but we could hardly put our teeth together because of the sand. After one mouthful we scattered the rest on the ground, and everyone went to bed hungry that night. The next day, when we knitted our eyebrows looking at dumpling soup made out of muddy, steamed dough, I prayed aloud before everyone, "Lord, you are my protector. I pray that after I eat this bowl of muddy water, you will keep me from harm and illness and give me strength. Amen!"

My prayer echoed lightly along the river bank. I had never thought I would do something like this. I had not prepared for it. My prayer was short and precise. I knew clearly that this was no ordinary prayer but that God was showing Himself through me. So after I prayed, I ate the bowl of dumpling soup without the slightest discomfort. The others were shocked. It was the first time they had seen someone pray aloud with their own eyes. Besides surprising them, it also showed to those unbelievers that God protected me. When I put down the bowl and chopsticks, they gradually became quiet. They felt that I had played some kind of trick and that I would have stomach pain in the afternoon. I did not urge them to eat; I knew they were waiting to see what would happen to me.

Not eating is one's own business, but everyone still had to work. If a young person doesn't eat for a day and a night he will become dizzy and see spots even without working. The others were all staggering about, but I was the only one who made good progress. At night when I had prayed and lifted my bowl up to eat, Liu Tianshun picked up his bowl and stood in front of me. "Please pray for us too," he said. "We are so hungry we can hardly stand."

Very carefully I replied, "Praying is no use, because you do not believe. God does not answer those who do not believe in Him."

When they heard this they were all disturbed. They stood up around me. "We believe; we really do! You were not injured when you ate. We know that there is a God here in this world. Please pray for us."

I firmly refused to pray for them, because that was something they had to do themselves. Only then would God listen. Finally it was decided that I should lead them to pray. I would say a sentence; they would repeat it.

This was a prayer that I will never forget. With a loud voice and lifted hands I prayed, "Loving Heavenly Father, this group of helpless, hopeless, and suffering people call on Your name. We beg You to send Your power into our lives. Let us eat this muddy soup and not be harmed or made ill from it, but rather increase in strength and health. Release these oppressed ones to walk on the Heavenly Way. Amen!"

Twelve starving voices echoed out along the banks of the muddy river. I could not stop my heart from pounding and for a long time kept my eyes closed in silent prayer. Behind me eleven hungry mouths gobbled down the dumpling soup, the muddy steamed dumpling soup. When it was finished they all let out a shout. Well not a shout, but a song of praise! A song full of life and strength. In those years, all over China there were people who dared to say out under the blue firmament, "I am a Christian." God brought light in the midst of despair. Those who received it received God's great love. We experienced the proof of it; the yellow, muddy soup gave us not a moment of discomfort, and God gave this group of hopeless people a new lease on life.

In summertime in Xinjiang, when the sun is high in the sky, the temperature reaches thirty to forty degrees Celcius. At night it often cools down to below ten degrees. We would put on padded jackets and go out under the twinkling stars, lying lazily on the ground. In a low voice, I would start a song, ... "Have you any troubles? Real troubles? Jesus had more troubles than you. Because He followed the path of the whole world and shouldered all their suffering. Pray to Him. He will wash you in His blood shed at Gethsemane." My fellow students would whisper the words after me, gathering around to learn the song. It seemed to me I heard the voice of a child off in the distance; the happiest person on this earth is the one who is spreading the gospel for the first time.

Giving thanks at meals became our custom. Everyone knew that only God could purify the muddy food. No one dared to try even one meal without praying. In addition there was the singing. But I was not satisfied. I felt my joy at spreading the gospel should not be limited to these two points. I wanted my fields to grow faster. As I saw it, a person's greatest weakness is himself. When we lose hope in difficulties, we ask God for help. When God gets us through our trouble, we forget His love. I was very anxious that God's plan would continually be shown in our experience, surpassing all our expectations.

In the meantime a new labor assignment came — to find stones for building the dike (since we were people with no real skills). To keep us from idleness, they ruled that we had to collect four cubic meters of stones every day. Once a week they would come to inspect, and they would only issue work points when the work was completed.

A person's life has many intersections. You cross one road after another, but you never exhaust your suffering. The twelve of us set out for the knolls on which no grass would grow and we scattered to look for appropriate sized rocks. But very quickly all the good-sized rocks in that area were discovered, and we had to go further afield. The sun heated the sand until it felt like we were walking on a frying pan. When we had to return carrying several dozen kilograms of rocks over several miles with bowed heads and staggering steps, our whole bodies felt dried out like dried bones. If we fell on the sand we could hardly get up again.

On the first day we gathered just a bit under one cubic meter, and for the whole week we could find just four cubic meters. A week of utter exhaustion and we only managed to complete one day's assignment. According to the rules, if we did not complete our work assignment, we would have to return our grain ration. We would have to give up six days of grain rations. At a meeting of the whole village, they ridiculed us as worthless scoundrels. "Hey, even the village idiot can get his work done, but these young people can't. How is that our intellectual youth don't have enough brains to find stones! We minority people can do our work; we are men, but it is hard to tell if these are men!"

Of all the flood-prevention work sites, only ours had failed to get enough rocks. This was clear to everyone. The Party secretary knew it too and knew why, but he wanted to teach a lesson to these rotten-egg Red Guards. We went back to the work site. We felt like a bunch of deflated footballs, and we all laid down in the muck. We did no work. Working or not, we still didn't eat, so we might as well lay here in the water and starve comfortably.

I was sorry and resentful at the same time. I thought of the effort I had spent to get assigned to a rural production team; it did not seem to matter how I struggled, it was all a dead end. The ones on the production team with me were, after all, petty thieves and loafers; no one wanted to give them a second look. The Uygurs didn't even want to regard us as persons. For a couple of hundred miles around there were no buses; it was useless even to think about running off. There was nothing but a dead-end road ahead of me. Thinking of this, I suddenly cried aloud. My cry made my buddies get up from the water; we had encountered the same thing and had the same sorrow.

Tears rolled down the chestnut-brown cheeks of the seventeen year-old youths and fell on their shoulders, on the bloody cuts from piling up the stones, and on their blistered hands. Liu Tianshun said painfully, with one word for each breath, "Mama, do...you...know...what...your...son...has...done...wrong?"

These words fell like a knife upon our hearts. In the depths of depression, staring across the pile of stones, I raised my face to heaven and said in a tearful voice, "Oh God, save us."

When people are in pain, they call for their fathers and mothers, as if they always know what is right, even though parents are not actually like that. Liu Tianshun's parents were both Communist cadres [officials] and had done outstanding work in the war, but at the beginning of the Cultural Revolution both were labeled as "alienated people" [that is, they committed suicide]. That is probably why Liu would often sit alone, lost in thought, or let out an anguished sigh late at night. Society had treated his parents unjustly and left him with neither parents nor home, igniting a rebellious anger in his heart. He began to take other people's money and became especially good at swindling honest and anxious-to-please rural people. When those pitiful old people, some of them childish women who had lost all their money, were standing begging on the streets, he would stand in the crowd looking at the result of his work. "Spring brings happiness to the villages," he would often remark at such heartbreaking scenes.

He called himself a "contemporary gadfly" [referring to a novel about an 18th century Italian revolutionary who acted as an irritant for the sake of justice]. But he did not oppose the government; rather he assisted the government in dispensing "justice." This justice meant allowing every element in society to experience a blow, allowing even the "secure" ones to face hardships. He wanted to use his actions to strengthen the theory of "class struggle." If his strength was sufficient, he wanted to make society cry out in productive indignation against him.

He was a lonely fellow who created sorrow continually. Society did not treat him fairly; he did not treat others fairly. But when the prison doors finally opened to him, he had his fill of the taste of iron bars.

When he told us of these things he didn't have the slightest regrets. He hoped that when he grew older he would have even greater opportunities for giving vent to his feelings.

"I do not fear sitting in prison, because there are both good and bad persons in prison. When it gets to the point where I can no longer carry out revenge, then I will sit in prison simply to die."

This was the path of life that he had sketched for himself. This youth who feared nothing in heaven or on earth, who had seen the flowers of three springs go by from a jail cell, who, when he thought, thought of revenge — an alienated rebel of our generation — this youth now cried aloud for his dead mother.

No one understood us. Those in power hated us as they hated all who criticized them. The masses hated us because they hated youths who destroyed the social order. As far as history would be concerned, we were criminals who could not hold up our heads. We should be thrown out, thrown out to the wilderness where we could suffer and die of starvation. At the age when we should be studying, we were cast into waves of politics that smashed down on our heads and knocked us over. Who would ease the pain in our young hearts or say a word of comfort to us? The world was closed to us. What future could there be for a group of people who did not even have enough to eat? Rocks! Find rocks and we would get food. But where in these sandy hills in the wilderness were there rocks?

Before every despairing person God lays down some kind of hope. I could not see any hope; what does a kid who was separated from mother and home at a young age, who only uses his mouth like a long, thin thread to pray to God, understand about faith and trust? Lying before me was a road without hope. At my side were my companions, in total disarray, scattered on grass clumps or sleeping in the mud. It was as if I were dumped on a battlefield full of corpses, and my despair became even deeper. I thought of writing a letter to my mother to give vent to my bitterness, but to whom could my suffering mama pour out her troubles? I felt that I would soon die of hunger; what should I do for these last few days? I could remember what I had done and how I had served my heavenly Father. So, I thought, I should now use prayer to finish off my time on this earth.

In hunger and suffering I closed my eyes to pray: "My loving Heavenly Father, I pray to You in the midst of despair; draw near to me now. In this world there is nothing left that would make me reluctant to leave; I only ask that You comfort me in the time that I have left here. Bring me back to my father and mother in the wilderness."

What does one say about the life of a teenager? It is bearing shame and indignity, hunger and hardship, and interwoven love and hate. My past experiences tore at my insides, and I began to blame God. "God, what sin have we committed to receive this kind of punishment? My father and mother had no sooner begun to spread the gospel than they began to be persecuted. In my whole life in this world there has not been a day that I recall with pleasure. None of the good opportunities have ever come my way: going to university, living in the city; I even gave up hope of living with my parents. I just ask that I'll be able to find stones and carry on living. I hope that you will provide an opportunity I can make use of. I have been putting all I have into life and rushing around, only to come to this impasse. In my years I've learned two things: one is how to pray, and the other is how to cope with secret tears. Oh God! Please come to my help!"

After praying I was so hungry and tired that I fell asleep. Suddenly I saw someone lying down on the grass, resting his head on a stone about the size of the stones we'd been looking for (to my great surprise). I said, "We've looked all over this sand dune; how come we didn't find this stone?" "Have you looked in the river?" he replied. The light dawned! We had carefully searched each bank....

At this moment I woke from my dreams. I was surprised to find that, although normally upon awakening I couldn't clearly remember a dream, on this occasion it was crystal clear. It seemed there was a Bible story about someone who had gone to sleep resting his head against a stone. I pulled out my handcopied Bible and looked it up; it turned out to be the story in Genesis 28:11 of Jacob going to sleep resting against a stone. I read right through to 29:3 where it says, "When all the flocks were gathered round, the shepherds would roll the stone away from the well's mouth and water the sheep. Then they would return the stone to its place over the mouth of the well." At this, my heart stopped; had the Bible story and the dream not been identical so far? I felt rather nervous.

Dreams are usually caused by an exhausting experience or by having a lot of things happen that one needs to think about; they have no reliable value. So why did I get this dream at this time? God must have been trying to tell me something in the dream or in the Bible; were the stones that we needed underneath the turbid waters of the river? I had no way of finding out except to wake up my mates and get us all into the river to look, but I was still afraid the dream was a result of my brain being overtired rather than an expression of God's glory. I felt I could do nothing but pray: "... if this is truly Your sign, then please let me find a stone in the river." I got up from the sandy ground and went out of the tent. It was nighttime, so dark you could not see your hand in front of your face. Sky and earth were indistinguishable. We knew the nearest public highway was hundreds of miles away, so the only hope for anyone lay in the river. I wanted this to be a revelation from God, so I prayed silently. I knew the direction, so I ran off to the river bank. I ran over the dunes, crunching through the surface of the sand, which had dried like sweat on a shirt collar.

Eventually, my feet touched the chilly waters of the river and I waded in up to waist-level. Suddenly one of my feet hit hard against a stone. I did not ponder it, but simply lifted it up and carried it to the edge. Although I could not see it clearly, I knew that this stone was just the size we were looking for. At that moment, when stretching out my left foot toward the bank, I once more unexpectedly touched a stone.

"What more can I say?" I wanted to rebuke myself aloud. "Do you still lack faith in God?" I put the stone back into the water, and I slapped myself across the face. The burning on the righthand side of my face made me feel a bit better, and I was thinking of doing it again when from my heart came some sincere words of praise for God, after which I rushed back to the tent.

"Hey! Wake up! I've got great news!" My words woke up all my friends sleeping around the tent. Liu Tianshun lifted his head and regarded me blearily. From his wavering, sleepy eyes ran moist tracks of travel-weary tears, like two earthworms snaking their way down his face. Then he gave me a brilliant smile, and I knew he had misunderstood. Formerly we had a "good friendship rule": whoever is feeling depressed in the night and cannot sleep has the right to wake the others up to talk, sing, or shout out loud. This type of friendship was one Liu Tianshun had brought with him from prison — he said it's always like that there. This time he thought I'd gone a bit crazy, that riverwater had soaked my head to uselessness, so that I seemed a bit drunk.

"God has arranged...for us to...find...stones we need..." I panted. The sentence galvanized everyone like a jolt of electricity. They all sat around and examined me closely. I told them of the recent events. Before I had even finished, Liu Tianshun leapt up and rushed out of the tent like a bull after a red rag. The rest of us rushed after him to the river side.

"It's about here at this bend that the stones are most numerous," Liu Tianshun shouted from the water. On the bank, I laid out some firewood to help them estimate their number. Very soon, we had found enough stones to cover seven square metres, so I said, "Who gave us these stones? These stones mean food to us — life!"

"It's God who gave them," they replied together.

"So shouldn't we thank Him and praise Him?" Liu Tianshun came out of the water and said, "What is there to discuss? Lead us in prayer!"

We lifted our hands above our heads and prayed in a respectful way. Over ten voices reached up to the heavens. I felt as though my hands reached up to touch the hem of the Heavenly Father's robe. When we'd all said "Amen," I heard Liu Tianshun and several other boys stealthily blowing their noses.

"Let's all lift our hands again," said Liu Tianshun energetically. "I want to pray too!"

Before this we had prayed a few times, and every time I had led the prayers. After hearing his request, we were moved, so we lifted our hands again..."Our heavenly commander, there is no one on earth who could beat You!" Liu passionately said. "Napoleon was a person who was ever-victorious, but he couldn't get reinforcements at Waterloo and was defeated. At the Waterloos in our life, You, oh Lord, stretch out a helping hand to us...We are the dregs of humanity,

persons for whom love and friendship are enemies. How can we claim
the salvation of the Creator? If You will come to the rescue of our
society's foundlings, we ask You to preserve us forever."

I think that the virtue which God most enjoys is to hear
someone of his own free will open his mouth and pray to Him for
the first time, like a baby saying "Daddy" for the first time. I certainly
know that every time we bring our requests to His throne, with fear
and trembling, He makes us wait for a long time, allowing us all to
reflect on what life would be like without our Saviour's proximity.

"Oh! Little complainer!" Liu said. "I've always felt that I wasn't
really a Christian! I seem to remember a time when you were reading
the Bible to us; it said one had to be baptized into Christ. What's
all this, then?"

This was a new question for me because I'd never seen a
Christian baptism. I could not even remember clearly how I had been
baptized. I think Mum once said that I was very small at the time.
I carefully considered what the Bible said about baptism before
saying, "It could well be that baptism is the most important, most
significant action one performs on earth." My education was slight,
and I could not think of the right words as I tried to explain the
importance of baptism.

"So you must think about it carefully! After receiving baptism
you cannot go around picking arguments with each other or playing
around with women!"

Even though I explained it to them so severely, they were
increasingly keen that I should baptise them. I didn't know whether
or not I was senior enough to baptise people, but it was clear that
God had arranged for me to do this so I pulled Liu to the middle
of the river, put my right hand on the top of his head and raised
my left hand to heaven, saying, "In the power of Jesus' name I baptise
you, Liu Tianshun. Since you share in Jesus' death, you share in His
resurrection to become a sincere and faithful Christian. You will no
longer be a pickpocket." I did not quite know how to say the sentence
about being a pickpocket; I was afraid of hurting his proud heart;
I had thought to go through it all with him first but had not had
the opportunity. It was the kind of thing he needed to talk through

with God personally, anyway. I pulled him from the water, and he said happily that he had swallowed two mouthfuls of water because he wanted to talk to God and forgot that he was in the water.

The others were now immersed in the same way. A group of society's misfits had come home at last to the arms of their Heavenly Father. Society was of the opinion that there was no way to remodel these people and thus banished them to the wilderness, but these youths did reform under the great love of our Heavenly Father. The desire of my parents to see the Gospel instilled in my heart was being realized at this very moment as God revealed His glory in this time of human stress.

We were very excited to be able to share around a handcopied version of the Bible after we had returned to the tent. After we had gradually calmed down, Liu brought up the point, "Today we have all been made anew, we ought to work out how we can repay God."

This was another new idea; before this I was always asking God to give me things without ever considering how I could repay the Heavenly Father. Tianshun's words pierced my heart like a needle. While we were all thinking, Mai Jianguo fell to the ground like a block of wood. Everyone gathered around, but could only see that his lips were pale and that he was paralysed from head to toe. "He has passed out from lack of nourishment! Quickly get him something to eat!" said Tianshun to everyone.

His words were as infectious as a plague; suddenly every person felt the rumbling of their empty bellies as an undeniable force. The food wouldn't be coming soon, either. The next day they would have to work until the afternoon before someone would come to measure the rock pile, and only then could we get food. Tianshun knew that there wasn't a grain of rice, so he was just joking. Everyone was busy getting water to revive Jianguo. I knew that while everyone else was so frantic this was a time to pray. Some people might say, "You've got a person dying but you're standing there praying." That is exactly right; this is a time when you have to pray. It is in prayer that God's words enter your heart.

For the second time I went into the tent, and this time I announced, "God has told me there are fish in the river."

Mai Jianguo had already come around; his weak and weary gaze was like that of a sick chicken, but he carefully watched me. Liu Tianshun sighed and said, "Yesterday I went fishing and there was not a single fish in the river then, and that's truly no lie!"

"It's impossible for God to lie, though." I was very angry, shouting at him and scolding him; I could not condone the fact that someone who had just been baptised could doubt God's truthfulness. I angrily tore off my trousers and tied up the bottoms of the legs, then cut many little holes with a knife so the fish could swim in more easily. Then, with this "fishing net," I stood up and went out of the tent — with everyone following. Jianguo came along too.

Tianshun ran up from the back asking to be forgiven, saying, "I was unthinking." I did not pay any attention to him. In fact I had long since forgiven him; anyway, we were all children!

The blackness before the dawn was darker than at midnight; all things patiently awaited the moment of dawn. We only had one item of fishing equipment, and that was waiting on the bank. Tianshun held it in the river from there, dragging the trousers back and forth in water. The tension mounted still further; the water sounded as though it was running in my heart. Everyone held his breath. A minute seemed to last a year.

My heart almost exploded, and I kept wanting to go into the river in place of Tianshun. The east had already put forth a red line of breaking day. Tianshun's black shadow moved back and forth on the waist-high water. The moment I walked toward him, I heard the sound of water coming from a well — a sound both familiar and unfamiliar — and then Tianshun excitedly said, "Look .."

I peered in the feeble light and made out something pale in the early morning glow, twisting and turning in his hand. Fish! I rushed to those on the banks and shouted, "Hurry up and get some firewood!"

A few minutes later, a fire was going on the bank. We pierced the fishes' mouths with willow twigs and cooked them. Another minute had not passed before Jianguo, moving the fish to one side of his mouth, said, "It's very tasty!" I could not wait until two fish were cooked before eating them up! "This is the first time in my life that I've eaten grilled fish, and it tastes marvellous!" Jianguo ate and spoke at the same time; the oil which oozed from the corners of his mouth reflected the flickering flames. I looked at this child of an Uygur cadre, totally happy inside. He was the first member of a minority that I had known to receive God's grace and become a Christian. Although in many people's eyes he seemed to have been changed into a Han Chinese, in various ways he was just an old Uygur, still!

I fervently hope he will turn into an active force for the Gospel and bring forth a lot of fruit among the Uygur peoples.

As the sun inched its way over the horizon, we started to pray. Standing in the early morning breeze I announced in a clear voice, "Now starting is the first Sunday worship of the Borderlands Gospel Fellowship.."

Tracks of tears started from each eye and ran into the corners of my mouth, salty and wet. I knew this was how my parents had cried, a prayer which I had cried without being able to put a name to it, a prayer for the past and for the future.

Yesterday and today have merged into one road of suffering. How tomorrow will be, we cannot know, but we will be prepared for anything, right up to being imprisoned on behalf of Jesus' name — or just living on this patch of earth where we can all join together and give thanks to God.